BRAHMS
biographical, documentary and analytical studies

Brahms

biographical, documentary and analytical studies

EDITED BY
ROBERT PASCALL

CAMBRIDGE UNIVERSITY PRESS

CAMBRIDGE

LONDON   NEW YORK   NEW ROCHELLE

MELBOURNE   SYDNEY

CAMBRIDGE UNIVERSITY PRESS
Cambridge, New York, Melbourne, Madrid, Cape Town, Singapore, São Paulo, Delhi

Cambridge University Press
The Edinburgh Building, Cambridge CB2 8RU, UK

Published in the United States of America by Cambridge University Press, New York

www.cambridge.org
Information on this title: www.cambridge.org/9780521245227

First published 1983
This digitally printed version 2008

A catalogue record for this publication is available from the British Library

Library of Congress Catalogue Card Number: 82–12882

ISBN 978-0-521-24522-7 hardback
ISBN 978-0-521-08836-7 paperback

Contents

Preface

Brahms needs no *Festschrift* in 1983, but we need to write one! A creative life such as his and its artistic products, by being there, require of us continual exploration. A piece contains all its possible meanings. And an important ultimate class of its manifestations is its life in the minds of men. We will never fix the piece in a description, but by dint of renewed adventures of the understanding we may explore ever further into its world, and open ourselves to its mode of being there.

The three areas of focus in this book are given by its subtitle. Some of the essays herein have one of these areas of focus as primary: Michael Musgrave's is a biographical study, my own a documentary one, and James Webster's, David Osmond-Smith's, Jonathan Dunsby's and Arnold Whittall's are analytical studies. The other essays show how the areas of focus may usefully be blended. George Bozarth's blends documentary and analytical treatments, Siegfried Kross's blends biographical and analytical treatments. In writing on *influence* such blending of areas becomes a necessity, as may be seen in the essays of Virginia Hancock and Imogen Fellinger.

The world of the piece combines genesis and structure. The network of relationships between musical differentiations within a piece forms its artistic statement. This statement is at once understandable yet original, stylistically classifiable yet of radiant and irreducible specificity, and conditioned by its past yet the result of an imaginatively creative act (hence unpredictable before its appearance). The enabling support for this opposition-set is found in *intertextuality*: the piece also has relationships to music outside the piece. Categorizing and controlling these relationships is an important task for music criticism; but those relationships fixed into the piece at the time of its making must be primarily those to the stylistic environment of its genesis.

Any note within a piece supersedes its own present by means of its relationships within and without the piece. From its role in a given structure (the piece) which exists mostly outside its own duration, the note draws significance into its substance. Such drawing and such significance also form the mode of the relationship of any part of a piece, or the piece as a whole, to the stylistic environment of its genesis. And an original creative act must not be thought as a separation from conditions, rather as a transformative occurrence on conditions, living through them as an extension of them. The human productive mind must have its rich starting-point, which Copland calls its 'usable past'; and the musical piece is itself a transformation of its musical past as matter.

Ways of making this matter tractable to analysis are to be found in stylistic concepts, which classify. But the stylistic environment of genesis is not solely comprised of generalities; past individual pieces can be too important to lose their identity in a composer's concepts, though they contribute to and are partially brought under concepts. Important routes into genetic intertextuality for us are by study of: learnt skills, influence-theory, notions of expressivity, genre-theory, and the special status of the string of the composer's own works. All of which routes are used in this book.

A special type of intertextuality is the relationship between a piece and its remote successors, and our view of Brahms's influence on subsequent composers has surely undergone radical revision in recent years. The importance Brahms had for the evolution of Schoenberg's musical styles and techniques, especially in the area of thematic material and its treatment, now makes it clear that Brahms does not only represent a stylistic culmination, in the grand sweep of musical history, but, in a very powerful sense, also a beginning.

Warm thanks are due to Rosemary Dooley and Penny Souster for their hard labours and decisive influence on the book. And grateful acknowledgement is made to the Gesellschaft der Musikfreunde in Vienna for permission to publish the Plates which appear on pages 62, 64 and 86–7.

Robert Pascall
Nottingham, May 1982

MICHAEL MUSGRAVE

The cultural world of Brahms

It is a consequence of the writing of history that the attempt
to chart large movements of ideas tends to distort the real
individuality of those who contribute to them. The aesthetic
issues which frequently turned the discussion of later
nineteenth-century music into verbal warfare led writers,
increasingly so with the passage of time, to ascribe indi-
viduals to positions, rather than to see the field as the
product of their achievements. Of the many distortions which
resulted, few can have been as misleading as that which
interpreted Brahms's interest in the past, and his avoidance
of public statement on the present, as evidence of conser-
vatism and insularity. Yet, whilst we now appreciate the
scope of his historical studies in music, and their relevance,
the extent of his broader culture is still not adequately
grasped. Brahms's life, chiefly spent in one of the great
cultural centres of Europe, was rich in artistic and intellectual content, though, as Hanslick comments, Brahms preferred to hide his learning. Hanslick makes a point of comparison with Liszt, whom he accuses of throwing off essays
with references to famed writers of whom he had scarcely
read a chapter.[1] Despite its malicious tone, Hanslick's
remark does however point to an important truth: namely,
that Brahms's cultural interests were wide and deep, and as
important for our understanding of his artistic nature as the
more vaunted preoccupations of Liszt or Wagner. Whilst
such a broad topic must inevitably raise more questions than
it can begin to answer, some fresh consideration of Brahms's
interest in other arts and his relationship to the world of
ideas generally is certainly timely. It may well be approached
through consideration of his friendships outside professional
music and of characteristics of his vast library, which, in
turn, clarify some central topics of obvious interest – especi-

1 E. Hanslick *Am Ende des Jahrhunderts* (Berlin 1899) 394-5.

1

ally his contacts with visual art and drama, and his relationships with Wagner and Hanslick.

Although Brahms began with fewer advantages of background than any comparable musical contemporary, he early developed a thirst for learning, which remained with him all his life, and he quickly sought out the wider world of ideas of which music was but a part; important stimulus was provided by his cultured teacher Marxsen, which naturally increased when he moved into the Schumann circle at Düsseldorf. Throughout his earlier years his presents were as often works of literature as of music. No better indication of his appetite exists than the contents of the notebook whose title reveals his youthful hero: *Young Kreisler's Treasure Chest.*[2] This includes no fewer than 645 quotations, from the Greeks right up to the latest aphorism of his friend Joachim. His horizons expanded steadily during the Hamburg period, though the move to Vienna, where he began to settle from autumn 1862, offered much more scope. As a prominent young composer, he was soon absorbed into a tightly-knit society in which musical talent opened many doors. Hence, in addition to such established musical figures as Josef Hellmesberger, Herbeck, Gänsbacher and Hanslick, he began in the mid-1860s an intimate friendship with Theodor Billroth (1829–94), widely regarded as the founder of modern abdominal surgery, who is still as revered in Vienna for his work as is Brahms for music. Indeed, Brahms came to number several medical men as friends; from the early 1870s he enjoyed a long acquaintance with the prominent physiologist Theodor Engelmann (1843–1909), professor of medicine at Utrecht University from 1873, as well as the pioneering ophthalmologist Frans Donders (1818–89), who worked in the same city.

Brahms's growing reputation brought him ever broader contacts. His strong literary interests helped, from 1867, to cement a relationship with the noted philologist Gustav Wendt (1827–1912), Lyceumsdirektor at Karlsruhe from 1873, who was important for his work in German literature and the translation of Greek drama, a volume of which he dedicated to Brahms. Brahms had already become acquainted

2 *Des Jungen Kreislers Schatzkästlein* ed. C Krebs (Berlin 1909). Brahms styled himself 'Johannes Kreisler Jnr' after E.T.A. Hoffmann's literary hero, described in *Kater Murr*. Although the weight of the collection rests on classical and romantic poets, it draws on a total of 119 varied sources. Brahms also made a subsequent collection, not published, but discussed by Karl Geiringer in *Zeitschrift für Musik* 100 (May 1933) 443–6.

with the Swiss writer and pastor J.V. Widmann of Bern
(1842–1911) before 1865, and strengthened a friendship
which became very valuable to him from 1874; Widmann, an
acknowledged translator and librettist, was one of Brahms's
favourite travelling companions, and the composer availed
himself of his considerable library at every opportunity. From
about this time, Brahms also restored an earlier contact with
Michael Bernays (1834–97), who became professor of
German literature at the University of Munich in 1873 and
was prominent in Brahms's circle there. But the literary contacts were not only academics; Brahms knew some of his
poets as well. He enjoyed long relationships with the German
poets Klaus Groth (1819–99) and Paul Heyse (1830–1914,
winner of the Nobel Prize for Literature in 1910), and with
the Swiss novelist Gottfried Keller (1819–90); he even went to
some length to meet the ageing Georg Friedrich Daumer
(1800–75). The early seventies also witnessed Brahms's
attempt to consolidate his acquaintance with a painter for
whom he had profound admiration, Anselm Feuerbach, whom
he had come to know through the circle of Pauline Viardot in
Baden-Baden in 1867; Feuerbach had been appointed to
a professorship at the Wiener Kunstakademie in 1873. However, temperamental differences prevented the relationship
from deepening, and the planned portrait of Brahms, which
would surely have been finer than any we have, was never
completed. Specht[3] offers the view that Brahms gave all the
affection he would have liked to lavish on Feuerbach to Julius
Allgeyer (1828–1900), long a friend of his as of Feuerbach,
whom Brahms encouraged to write what has become the
standard biography of the artist.

   In addition to the more prominent relationships, Brahms had
many other important contacts in fields other than music:
figures such as the art historian Wilhelm Lübke (1826–93), the
historian and political writer Heinrich Treitschke (1834–96),
the sculptor Adolf Hildebrandt (1847–1921) and the play-
wright Ivan Turgenev (1818–83), as well as many figures in
Viennese life. The same breadth of interest and mental sensitivity which created such a bond with leading musicologists
(Nottebohm, Chrysander, Ph. Spitta, C. F. Pohl, Jahn and
Mandyczewski) underpinned other relationships, and
Brahms's love of incisive discussion on all manner of subjects
is well attested. However, the scope of his knowledge only

3 R. Specht *Johannes Brahms* tr. E Blom (London 1930) 306.

comes into real perspective when the contents of his remarkable library are considered.

Although some volumes disappeared after his death, the current listing still numbers about 850 titles as against about 2,000 volumes of music or studies of music.[4] As evidence of a great artist's mental life, it deserves a study by itself. Surveyed generally, two features attract attention: its scope and its unexpected emphases. Brahms's library is not merely a collection of books reflecting special enthusiasms, but a body of writings on many subjects which reflect the need to be thoroughly acquainted with the world of ideas, artistic and otherwise, present as well as past. The same scholarly care and desire for a balanced view which led him to correct and annotate many of these volumes, informs the library as a whole. The scepticism of which Brahms is often accused – the extent to which, as Gal recalls, he 'sat on the Seat of the Scornful'[5] – was an integral part of the personality which assembled these books; and the man in whose life reading played such a major part must inevitably have found difficulty in harmonizing with the simpler views of less well-informed friends. Yet, if comprehensive, Brahms's library does provide surprises, since it reveals emphases which do not immediately relate to his musical output. The 'absolutist' who has been accused of a preference for mediocre texts and an insensitivity to their setting reveals a remarkably catholic taste; the artist who essayed in every major genre save opera is revealed as deeply absorbed in drama. Before turning to these issues, however, some further general observations are appropriate.

Apart from the major holdings in literature and a fair number of books of a general educational nature, including many language tutors, Brahms's chief preoccupation emerges as the study of history, though not merely in connection with cultural factors. In addition to broad histories of civilization, such as Müller's *General History of Mankind*, Brahms naturally took a special interest in German history, possessing such sizeable works as Sybel's seven-volume *Foundation of the German Empire* and Hausser's four-volume *German History*.

4 K. Hofmann *Die Bibliothek von Johannes Brahms* (Hamburg 1974). This publication reproduces Alfred Orel's listing of Brahms's music library, originally published in the *Simrock Jahrbuch III*, and includes full references to all books in alphabetical order. For briefer discussions of the library in English see: K. Geiringer 'Brahms as reader and collector' *The Musical Quarterly* 19 (1933) 158–68; K. and I. Geiringer 'The Brahms Library in the "Gesellschaft der Musikfreunde" in Wien' *Notes* 30 (September 1973) 7–14.
5 H. Gal *Johannes Brahms: His Work and Personality* tr. J. Stein (London 1963) 86.

His particular admiration of Bismarck's role in the great events of the time is reflected in collections of his speeches and letters, while evidence of a broader interest in political matters emerges from Treitschke's *Historical and Political Essays*. These major studies define fields of concern which are filled by a variety of other texts from, for example, a modern version of the ancient history by Herodotus up to such a study as Haufen's *Law of Causality in Sociology*. However, Brahms's interest in the present extended beyond political and social theory into the world of scientific advance and innovation. His contact with pioneers in medical science kept him abreast of the latest activity, whilst such everyday innovations as the introduction of electric lighting and the Edison phonograph evoked an enthusiastic response. There is something apt, if altogether unexpected, that such a man as Brahms should find his photograph reproduced in a school text-book, where his face appears as an example of the 'Caucasian Type'.[6]

Cultural factors combined with a love of the outdoors to stimulate his great enthusiasm for travel, especially in Switzerland and Italy, and his library includes a considerable number of travel guides. He found the trips to Italy especially rewarding because of the opportunities they provided to experience at first hand the works of art with which he had partially acquainted himself through reading such books as: Burckhardt's *Culture of Renaissance*, Lübke's *History of Architecture*, Hermann Grimm's study of Michaelangelo and, latterly, Wölfflin's *Renaissance and Baroque*. Widmann emphasizes the extent to which Brahms could be visibly moved by the experience, noting, for example, his response to Parmegiano's *Betrothal of St Catherine* at Parma.[7] But he was apparently no slave to his programme, generally wandering briskly and pausing spontaneously at what took his eye. In Vienna itself he was able to take advantage of one of the greatest collections of sixteenth- to eighteenth-century painting in Europe, housed since 1891 in Kunsthistorisches Museum on the Ringstrasse.

One of the clearest indicators of Brahms's mental outlook is found in the small though significant section of religious texts. Brahms was not a conventional believer and resisted dogmas; Widmann tactfully describes him as of 'liberal Protestant

6 Baenitz/Kopka *Lehrbuch der Geographie* (Bielefeld/Leipzig 1884) 86. See Hofmann *Bibliothek* 8.
7 *Johannes Brahms in Erinnerungen von Josef Viktor Widmann* ed. W. Reich (Basel 1947) (hereafter *Widmann*) 89.

feelings' (*Widmann* 105) and his reaction to being taken for a Christian composer is well known from his exchange with Rheinthaler on the meaning of the texts of the Requiem. All the same, he was deeply absorbed in the ideas from which formal religious thought derived. The centre of this interest was the Lutheran Bible, of which he possessed two copies, one of 1833 and one a collector's item of 1545, as well as three New Testaments, one in Italian and one a seventeenth-century edition bound with the Marot/Beze Psalms. The newer of the Bibles is marked extensively and confirms the intimate knowledge which enabled him to select texts which ideally suited his purpose and the noting of certain passages used in the Requiem and the *Vier ernste Gesänge* is but a small part of the whole. Other early editions of Luther's writings, such as *Of Good Works* and *Colloquia*, confirm the degree of his interest, whilst Widmann recalls an involvement with contemporary religious issues, in his response to the activities of the Swiss Theological Reform Movement (21). Again, however, his outlook was broad, and he also possessed a well-marked copy of the Koran.

The wisdom of ancient writings seems to have exerted much more influence on Brahms than any system of philosophy. Although the character of his musical language has often prompted the epithet 'philosophical', the representation here is meagre and accountable largely to external factors. He seems to have obtained his own copy of Schopenhauer's *Parerga und Paralipomena*, which he annotated fully, but his copy of *The Two Fundamental Problems of Ethics* was given by Tausig in the effort to win Brahms over to Schopenhauer's philosophy, and the biography by Noiré came from the author. In fact his only interest attached to Schopenhauer's musical sayings, of which he possessed a valued sheet.[8] His later, personal contact with Nietzsche (who came, like Mathilde Wesendonck, on the rebound from Wagner) stimulated no interest in his writings. Brahms was very averse to theorizing and also took scant interest in the theories of music which came his way – for example, those of A. B. Marx and Riemann – generally responding to the discussion of philosophical matters with Beethoven's chastening words: 'perhaps the reverse may be true'.[9]

8 K. and I. Geiringer 'The Brahms Library' 13.
9 See D. S. Thatcher 'Nietzsche and Brahms: a forgotten relationship' *Music and Letters* 54/3 (July 1973) 261-80, for a general discussion of his philosophical interests.

Brahms clearly preferred to draw his 'philosophy' from literature, of which the Bible was indeed a prime example, and it is on this foundation that the weight of the library rests. Fully three-quarters of his books are of German literature, comprising poetry, novels, dramas, as well as works of criticism, such as Vischer's *Faust* and Brandes's study of nineteenth-century literature, which he prized highly. They show how unrepresentative is the picture of his tastes given by the texts he set. Thus, in addition to the works of his preferred minor poets and the many folk poems which he drew from such sources as Herder, Arnim-Brentano Erk-Böhme, Kretzschmer-Zuccalmaglio and Arnold, we find a very representative collection of the major Classical and Romantic poets, including several editions of the works of Goethe, Lessing and Schiller, which extend the enthusiasms of the *Treasure Chest*. His copy of the Schiller-Goethe letters seems particularly well used, and we know of his special enthusiasm for the writings of the Grimm brothers, especially those of Jacob. Notable also is the number of poems by little-known writers of his time and earlier, as well as the number of translations of foreign poems, reflecting his interest in such sources. Brahms only read in translation, though he made strenuous efforts to master foreign languages. One gains the impression of a reader always seeking something new within the rather strict bounds he set himself for the marrying of text and music.

Most striking, however, is the interest in drama. Its basis is formed by the dramas of Goethe, Schiller and Shakespeare (in the translations of Schlegel and Tieck) and includes many other significant works, such as F. M. Klinger's *Sturm und Drang* and A. W. Schlegel's *Lachrymus*. Ancient dramas and comedies are represented by works of Sophocles and Plautus. Yet Brahms was equally interested in significant contemporary expression, possessing, for example, Ibsen's *The Wild Duck* and *The Woman from the Sea*; though none are listed, he would also have known the works of his friend Turgenev. However, this interest is certainly balanced by that in comedy. He was particularly devoted to the folk plays of the sixteenth-century Spanish writer Calderón, especially in the eighteenth-century versions of Gozzi, and found special delight in the satirical comedies of the modern Viennese writer Johann Nestroy (1801-62), which he collected; he was particularly proud of a manuscript copy of Nestroy's travesty of Hebbel's tragedy *Judith*, which was obtained with considerable difficulty through Billroth and still contained the censor's deletions. These acquisitions reflect his intense interest in the theatre. He could be very powerfully moved by drama, and Widmann considered him to possess 'extraordinary dramatic instinct' so that he took 'keen pleasure' in analysing any dramatic scheme (Widmann 29). Billroth notes, among other interests, a detailed knowledge of Shakespeare, whom he could quote freely,[10] and comments that he would never decline an invitation to the Burgtheater, confirming Widmann's observation of him as an 'indefatigable theatre-goer', 'who would never miss a first performance of anything significant' (Widmann 28, 77).

Viewed overall, Brahms's books clearly reflect Widmann's assessment of his literary interests in general: '[he was] decidedly conservative in his taste . . . [but this] did not prevent him from at least getting to know all that was written. He read modern literature in the hope of finding it good and great' (77). This theme may be pursued further through some consideration of his interest in visual art, seemingly his strongest preoccupation outside literature and drama, which throws valuable light on his outlook, as well as showing how he was seen by earlier commentators. In addition to the classical art of the High Renaissance and other epochs, Brahms took a keen interest in the work of two contemporaries, though of quite different inclinations, Feuerbach and Max Klinger: one realized traditional values in modern terms, whilst the other rejected them in favour of new approaches. Anselm Feuerbach (nephew of the philosopher Ludwig Feuerbach) was a major representative of the movement known as Romantic Classicism, in contrast to the Realism of such figures as Von Menzel and the Leibl Group. After early imitation of Courbet and Delacroix, he became influenced by ancient Greek and Roman art and the Italian High Renaissance painters, developing his own style into 'idealized figure compositions of a lyrical, elegiac nature'. He is regarded as one of the greatest of the 'German Romans', who aimed at a melancholy gravity based on 'uniformly dark tones of muted violets and dull, greyish greens', which stood in total contrast to the brightness of the Nazarene painters or to Hans von Makart.[11] His subjects were chiefly tragic figures of Greek mythology or Italian literature, the most significant being the

10 C.A.T. Billroth Johannes Brahms and Theodor Billroth: Letters from a Musical Friendship tr. and ed. H. Barkan (Oklahoma 1957) 148.
11 The New Encyclopaedia Britannica (Chicago 1974). Micropaedia IV 117.

two versions of *Iphigenia* (1862, 1871), *The Judgement of Paris* (1870) and various compositions on the Medea theme.

Feuerbach's style appealed greatly to Brahms who, according to Specht, was also drawn to the same qualities in his very appearance (Specht 303). Brahms frequently commended Feuerbach's art to friends and did all he could to encourage the awkward painter, though his warnings of the shallow nature of Viennese criticism – notably with regard to the exhibiting of *The Battle of the Amazons* – were not heeded, with sad consequences for this picture represented a decisive failure for Feuerbach. Although Brahms spoke little of details, the nature of the attraction can be deduced from his choral work *Nänie*, which he composed to Feuerbach's memory and whose personal significance emerges from Brahms's letter to the painter's stepmother.[12] This gravely beautiful setting of Schiller's poem on Thetis's lament for Achilles reflects the qualities of formal perfection and emotional restraint so strong in Feuerbach's work. A comment to Heuberger indicates how easily Brahms could transform a visual experience into musical terms,[13] although he did not always find the process as simple. Specht makes much of the affinities, seeing Feuerbach's work as 'a transposition of one and the same artistic phenomenon' as that of Brahms (Specht 170) and claiming, with every justification, that the various maxims on artistic values recorded in Feuerbach's *Legacy*[14] would have been warmly acknowledged by Brahms. Whilst this is certainly true of the classical *Nänie*, it seems, however, too limiting a characterization in most other cases. If parallels in aural and visual colouring are always clear, the general complexity and ambiguity of much of Brahms's musical language suggests that Specht emphasized the broader relationships in order better to project Brahms as a custodian of established values, and to sharpen the contrast with the successors with whom Specht was increasingly involved, especially Mahler.

The limitation of Specht's view becomes clearer if Brahms's relationship with the sculptor, painter and engraver Max Klinger (1857–1920) is considered. Unlike that of Feuerbach,

---

12 Max Kalbeck *Johannes Brahms* III (Berlin ²1913) (hereafter Kalbeck III) 295.
13 R. Heuberger *Erinnerungen an Johannes Brahms* ed. K. Hofmann (Tutzing ²1976) 21. Brahms suggested that Heuberger write 'such an Adagio' in response to one of the Medea paintings, although on another occasion he admitted to not understanding a work (ibid. 38). For a fuller discussion of the artistic relationship see: K. Huschke 'Anselm Feuerbach und Johannes Brahms' *Zeitschrift für Musik* 100 (May 1933) 434–40.
14 *Ein Vermächtnis von A. Feuerbach* ed. H. Feuerbach (Berlin 1912).

Klinger's work points decidedly to the future in both content and technique; his treatment of subjects has been seen as prophetic of the world of Freud and the Surrealist artists, whilst his linear techniques in various forms of drawing and engraving were highly individual, and significant in the development of poster design. Klinger's attitude to the classical values of Feuerbach is immediately clear if comparison is made with his own *Judgement of Paris*, which caused a storm of protest in 1887 because of the naive directness of its expression. But it was in fields other than painting that his greatest advances were made. Earlier attention was attracted by a series of ten pen and ink drawings entitled *The Glove*, which depict the obsessive involvement of a young man with an elusive glove; the glove appears in bizarre contexts related more to dream than to reality, a quality which, in various ways, informs his later works. He was especially receptive to the power of music and is noted for a major sculpture of Beethoven,[15] one of Wagner remaining uncompleted at his death. However, Brahms was his greatest musical love; he dedicated to him the already completed cycle *Amor und Psyche*, and there followed a succession of works inspired by Brahms's music, culminating in the vast cycle of 41 engravings, etchings and lithographs of various sizes produced between 1885 and 1894 which he designated 'Brahms-Phantasie'. The centre of the work is a series inspired by Brahms's setting of Hölderlin's *Schicksalslied*, preceded by evocations of individual songs and introduced by a prelude entitled 'Akkorde', which recurs before the main set. The element of 'fantasy' lies not only in the poetic response to Brahms's texts and music but to the very subjects. The works relating directly to the *Schicksalslied* are themselves preceded by various items which explore the mythical background to Hölderlin's text, some with specific, some with general titles.

Despite initial resistance – Simrock had not consulted Brahms before using Klinger's work on the title pages of new works – Brahms's response to his art became intense. Nor was it merely one of pride at so lavish a tribute to the imaginative potential of his music. Brahms recognized the significance of the fusion of poetry, music and visual art, expressed with such force and musicality, which marks the series as a turning point in the artist's development. Indeed,

15 See P. Vergo *Art in Vienna, 1898–1918* (London 1975) 67. (This source also reproduces Klinger's *Christ on Olympus* ibid. 45.)

the pictures drew from him an unexpectedly warm response. To Clara he wrote in 1894, 'They are not really illustrations in the ordinary sense, but magnificent and wonderful fantasias inspired by my texts. Without assistance . . . you would certainly often miss the sense and connection with the text. How much I should like to look them through with you and show you how profoundly he has grasped the subject and to what heights his imagination and understanding soar'[16] To Klinger himself he particularly stressed the interaction, praising the 'rich, fantastic invention which is at the same time so beautifully serious and allows one to think and imagine further – all this (being) so suitable to open the way for music'. He was even inspired to declare that they showed that 'all art is the same and speaks the same language'.[17]

It is perhaps a consequence of the emotional nature of Klinger's work that Brahms never appears to have commented to him on the nature of the meanings he deduced. They are not easy for the modern viewer, since Klinger's style seems too immediately and effusively romantic for our modern, 'structural' approach to Brahms. The first of the *Phantasie* is a case in point, employing Klinger's frequent image of swelling seas and mythical sea creatures, a style more familiar to the general reader through such a work as Böcklin's *Sea Idyll*.[18] Yet, the basic idea of 'Akkorde' – that of the constant flow between the musical stimulus and the visual image and its associations – is very clear (see Plate 1). Hence, Klinger depicts in the right foreground a pianist on a platform raised above swirling waters, below which sea creatures pluck at a large harp, appropriately embossed with a Neptune-like figure-head, whilst a small ship flees across the sea to an island haven, enclosing a temple, with vast cloud-encircled peaks in the background. Beside the pianist, a female figure motions the communication of the written music to the harp, and thus to the deep, whilst the sea creatures can be seen to return it. The title seems both to symbolize the harmony of natural and made music, and to identify its nature in the basic musical gesture of the title,

16 *Clara Schumann-Johannes Brahms Briefe aus den Jahren 1853-1896* ed. Berthold Litzmann (Leipzig 1927) (hereafter *Schumann-Brahms Briefe*) II 538.
17 J. Brahms *Johannes Brahms an Max Klinger* (Leipzig 1924) 5, 7.
18 Arnold Böcklin (1827-1901) was also admired by Brahms. 'Sea-Idyll' (Meerstille) is reproduced in Vergo, ibid, 65. Klinger's 'Akkorde' is reproduced overleaf. For fuller discussion of the *Brahms-Phantasie'* see M. Lehrs *Max Klingers 'Brahms-Phantasie'* (Leipzig 1895).

Plate 1 'Akkorde' from Max Klinger's *Brahms-Phantasie*. Published Leipzig 1894 by Klinger himself.

which also expresses the passionate mood of the conception. Brahms made his only really specific comment to Klinger in connection with the stimulus of his work to enable one to 'think further', stating 'I often envy you with your pencil for being able to be so precise; I am often glad that I do not need to be' (Klinger 7). Just what Brahms meant by this, and to what extent visual images inspired musical thoughts is a matter of immense interest which would be greatly served by modern reproductions of Klinger's work.

The extent of Brahms's interests in other arts inevitably raises the question of his own aesthetic outlook as a musician, particularly as regards the setting of text, the relation of music and drama, and broader issues concerning music's capacity for expression. Although he left few clues, it is possible to deduce its outlines sufficiently to approach at greater length the two most controversial human relationships of his life, those with Wagner and Hanslick.

Brahms's brief comments on song-setting illuminate his own output by the light they throw on his attitude to text and its treatment. Given his discriminating attitude to literature, it is to be anticipated that he considered it pointless to set texts which he felt complete in themselves, hence his comment to Henschel: 'Schubert's "Suleika" songs are to me the only instances where the power and beauty of Goethe's words have been enhanced by the music. All other of Goethe's poems seem to me so perfect in themselves that no music can improve them.'[19] Although he did set other Goethe texts, the spirit of his remark is clearly reflected in his output as a whole, where the great lyrics of the eighteenth- and nineteenth-century are conspicuously absent. His sensitivity was equally strong to poetic structure and he was strict in his teaching of Jenner, who recalls that 'he would immediately establish whether the musical form and the entire text corresponded. He censured mistakes of this kind especially strongly as defects in artistic understanding and as revealing insufficient penetration of the text'.[20] This approach is clear in his own settings, where the through-composition of strophic poems is rare, most songs achieving a balance through variation of the strophic form. Brahms's own songs only emerged after long consideration, so that the structure of the poem was totally absorbed before the composition took

19 G. Henschel Musings and Memories of a Musician (London 1918) 113.
20 G. Jenner Johannes Brahms als Mensch, Lehrer und Künstler (Marpurg [2]1930) 31 (my translation).

shape. His aversion to less considered methods stimulated a hasty reaction to Henschel: 'there are composers who sit at the piano with the poem before them, putting music to it from A–Z until it is done. They write themselves into a state of enthusiasm which makes them see something finished, something important in every bar' (Henschel 87).

Although Brahms would seem to have had little occasion to speak from first hand about the relation of drama and music, his attitude to the subject was completely consistent. As with the sanctity of his poetic texts, so he held the integrity of a drama to be a prime consideration. His feeling for dramatic schemes led him to become very conscious of the adverse influence of any extraneous element; he even criticized Goethe for weakening the effect of the fine text of *Tasso* through its 'long duets' (Henschel 107). The role of music was equally clear to him. Widmann recalls that

it seemed to him that to compose music for the whole drama was unnecessary, even harmful and inartistic; only the climax, and those parts of the action where words alone cannot suffice, should be set to music. By these means, on the one hand, the librettist gains more space and freedom for the dramatic development of the subject, and, on the other, the composer is enabled to devote himself exclusively to the demands of his art, which can best be fulfilled when he has musically complete mastery of the situation (as, for example, in an *ensemble* portraying a joyful climax). Besides, *he* held it to be a great presumption to expect music to accompany a purely dramatic dialogue all through several acts. (*Widmann* 29)

This attitude naturally influenced his own preferences in opera; indeed, although he acknowledged some contemporary German works warmly, notably Goetz's *Taming of the Shrew* (1875), little escaped his censure. Apart from Wagner's creative importance, the line of descent from Weber's *Euryanthe*, including his mentor Schumann's *Genoveva*, was of less interest to him than more distant models, such as the operas of Cherubini, especially *Médée* (1797), and, most notably, those of Méhul. Various commentators stress his affection for Méhul's *Uthal* (1806), Kalbeck even ascribing to its colouristic influence Brahms's omission of violins from the Serenade in A major and first movement of the Requiem. Indeed,when Brahms discovered that Felix Mottl had staged a performance in Karlsruhe in 1891, he commented 'But that is actually my work. Years ago I gave the material to Devrient and Levi . . . . Mottl then found (it all) and produced the work accordingly' (Heuberger 49). In this opera a sharp distinction exists between spoken dramatic dialogue and that which lends itself to orchestral accompaniment and to relation with set numbers.

Uthal is also interesting for its text. The libretto is based on the 'Ossianic' poems of the eighteenth-century Scottish poet James Macpherson, and evokes a primitive world of family rivalry and conflict. Brahms was highly susceptible to the romantic atmosphere of 'Ossian' in his earlier years, having set the 'Gesang aus Fingal' as Op. 17 No. 4 and 'Darthulas Grabesgesang' as Op. 42 No. 3, the former using two horns and harp; and it is not impossible to conceive of a Brahmsian realization of parts of the *Uthal* text. In view of the essentially straightforward role which music performs in the Méhul setting, it seems surprising that Brahms never found a convincing libretto, not even by Widmann, who had successfully provided libretti for Goetz. Whatever his true reasons – and the subject warrants a fresh study in itself – we know something of the subject-matter to which he gave thought, during the period in which Allgeyer and Widmann record his enthusiasms for opera: it is surprising. Contrary to likely expectations, Brahms's preoccupation was not with serious drama, but with comedy, albeit never untinged by other elements. The only classical subject in which he appears to have shown interest, and that but little, was Widmann's *Iphigenie in Delphi*; this author's dramatized fable, *Der geraubte Schleier*, attracted more interest, though Brahms never pursued it. The real focus of his attention lay in the Calderón/Gozzi fables which he read in translation, of which Widmann draws attention to three: *Der Raube*, *Das laute Geheimnis* and *König Hirsch*. Although Brahms gave scant details of his interest in the first two, Allgeyer actually produced a full three-act libretto of *Das laute Geheimnis* for him, although it is no longer available for reference, having been sold in 1930 (Heuberger 172). Widmann notes his particular attraction to *König Hirsch*, in which he admired 'above all, the comic with its continual undercurrent of the serious'. However, Widmann had considerable reservations about providing a 'rational and poetical libretto' for such a 'grotesque and extravagant farce': he found these qualities to be far outweighed by the 'childish trivialities' of the story and the technical problems relating to the various physical transformations involved, fearing a second rate *Magic Flute*, an undertaking quite inappropriate to Brahms (*Widmann* 30).

An examination of the play must support his reservations.

Though it shares the magical and farcical elements of Mozart's work, it seems to lack comparable qualities of seriousness and it is very difficult to imagine Brahms, who was so sensitive to dramatic effect, coming anywhere near making a success of its musical treatment. The story concerns the deception of a King, Deramo, by the misuse of magic in the attempt to change his choice of Queen. The transformations involve that of the King into a Stag and into an Old Man, and that of the Magician, Durandarte, back into his proper state from the guise of a Parrot in which he first appears. The ease with which Brahms could have employed music according to his principles is apparent from musical indications in a later English version[21] with its use of atmospheric and interludal music and of a leading-theme for one of the chief characters. Whilst Brahms's failure to discuss the project seriously with Widmann over twenty years or so may suggest no more than a fanciful interest, it is as well to recall that he is known to have taken part in a Singspiel performance of a play by Turgenev with music by Pauline Viardot, and that some of his shorter songs reveal qualities which would have graced such a genre.[22]

The extent of Brahms's interest in dramatic music places his supposed antipathy towards modern opera, especially Wagner in a somewhat different perspective. Indeed, the traditional view of the Wagner–Brahms relationship must qualify as one of the classic examples of the kind of distortion referred to earlier, though it was already well advanced after Wagner's death, when Brahms despairingly questioned why he himself had been made an 'anti-pope'. (Kalbeck III 409). Yet, if Brahms and Wagner prompt comparison in the broad sense of characterizing different trends, in at least two crucial senses they are not properly to be compared at all: namely, as regards generation and degree of mutual interest. It is easy to forget that Brahms was born fully twenty years after Wagner and began his work with different aesthetic presuppositions. When Cosima Wagner

21 The King Stag, English version with performing notes by Carl Wildman, in E. Bentley The Classic Theatre I (New York 1958) 289–367.
22 Brahms's interests were certainly genuine; even Wagner came to hear of them (C. Wagner Diaries ed. M. Gregor-Dellin and D. Mack, tr. G. Skelton, II (1878–83) (London 1980) 518). He was offered libretti by Geibel and Turgenev (who wrote a romance of banditry especially for him). See Max Kalbeck Johannes Brahms II (Berlin [3]1921) (hereafter Kalbeck II) 165–6, and Sotheby's Catalogue Continental Autograph Letters and Manuscripts (12–13 May 1981) 155, 137. Brahms also set the Songs of Ophelia from Shakespeare's Hamlet for a performance in Prague. See K. Geiringer Fünf Ophelia-Lieder (Vienna [2]1960).

noted of a Brahms Concerto that it had 'not a single melody' and that he hurried to disguise suggestions of earlier composers through resort to 'oblique harmonies and contrived curiosities',[23] she was partly acknowledging features which, as Schoenberg stressed, belonged to later aesthetic norms. The difference of generation also affected the attitude of the composers to each other. Since Brahms did not follow Wagner's principles, Wagner had little cause for constructive interest in him; indeed, the stimulus for most of his later remarks was irritation at Brahms's success in forms which Wagner had declared outworn – as well as at his undeclared claims to the expression of a German spirit through such works as the *German Requiem* and the *Triumphlied*. If it was one thing to overwhelm the younger composer with praise for showing, in the *Handel Variations*, 'what could still be done in the old forms' (Kalbeck II 117), it was quite another to take seriously the stream of works in traditional forms, especially when they gained Brahms equal, or even greater, honours. 'That silly boy'[24] was Wagner's characterization when he discovered that Brahms had also been awarded the Order of Maximilian at the same time as himself. Although odd remarks suggest that Wagner continued to acknowledge Brahms's abilities, he saw him as an anachronism, a fluent craftsman who, as he so often remarked of others, could only 'compose, compose. . . ', and yet who was, by his very skill, damaging in his influence on the middle classes, because he was not a 'poet'.

Brahms's attitude towards Wagner was of a different kind, since he was profoundly interested in his work; Wagner was clearly a favourite topic of conversation throughout his life. Despite the bitter antipathy of Clara and the growing coolness of Joachim, Brahms early acquainted himself with Wagner's ideas. Thus, the *Treasure Chest* seems to show the young composer allying himself with Wagner's attitude in a quotation from *Opera and Drama*: 'the generator of the artwork of the future is none other than the artist of the present, who anticipates the life of the future and longs to be contained in it. Whoever cherishes the longing within himself already lives in a better life; but only One can do this: the Artist.'[25] Although Brahms admitted to a dislike for the *Faust*

23 C. Wagner *Diaries* 362. (Wagner took even greater offence at the award of a
    Doctorate by the University of Breslau.)
24 C. Wagner *Diaries* I (1869–1877) (London 1978) 716.
25 R. Wagner *Oper und Drama* (Leipzig 1852) 212, tr. W. Ashton Ellis (London 1893)
    376.

Overture in 1855, his interest increased steadily, so that, when Wagner came to Vienna in 1863 to perform parts of *The Mastersingers*, he offered his services through Cornelius in the copying of parts. This was a significant gesture in view of the embarassment he had suffered through the debacle of his *Manifesto* three years earlier. Something of the objectivity with which he entered into the Wagner camp emerges from his comment to Joachim: 'I shall probably be called a Wagnerian, but it will of course be chiefly owing to the spirit of contradiction that cannot but be excited in a sensible man by the frivolous way in which the musicians here talk against him.'[26] Although, in the circumstances, it is hardly surprising that Brahms should have been seen to maintain a low profile, his later remarks to Heuberger indicate that he became quite well acquainted with Wagner and exchanged ideas with him. It is especially interesting to note his observation of Wagner's advice to younger composers that they should work along other lines than his. Brahms did just that, and, in contrast to Wagner's later attacks on him, retained his outlook until the end of his life, saying that 'neither Schumann, nor Wagner, nor I have learnt what is right . . . Schumann took one way, Wagner another, and I yet another' (Heuberger 50, 94).

Brahms's knowledge of Wagner was based on the study of both scores and performances and his claim to be 'the best of all Wagnerians' was firmly grounded indeed. Although his library does not include all the works – lacking, surprisingly, *The Mastersingers*, as well as the Ring-Dramas save *Rheingold* – the extent of his knowledge of the former is confirmed in various remarks; such evidence as his corrections of trombone parts in Wagner's presentation copy of *Rheingold* (in the Gesellschaft der Musikfreunde) suggests that his comments on the cycle were also based on intimate knowledge. He was, for example, sufficiently well informed on the background to Wagner's works to suggest a model for Beckmesser's lute, in Cornelius's song 'Ihr Freunde, wenn ich gestorben bin' Op 5 (Heuberger 43). Nor was Wagner immune from Brahms's passion for collecting: he possessed autograph sheets of passages from *Rheingold* and the concert ending of the *Tristan* Prelude, as well as the first edition of Wagner's Sonata for Piano in B flat major (1832). Brahms's failure to attend Bayreuth is certainly no indication of a lack of interest.

26 *Johannes Brahms Briefwechsel V: Johannes Brahms in Briefwechsel mit Joseph Joachim* ed. Andreas Moser (Berlin 1908) 326.

We have his words to Henschel that he 'repeatedly heard
Rheingold and Walküre at Munich' (Henschel 109), and it
seems likely that his failure to attend when invited by the
singer in 1876 was not due to his stated reason – the price of
the seats – but to the fear of controversy, which he freely
acknowledged by 1882 in connection with *Parsifal.*[27]

As in other spheres, Brahms's wide knowledge led him to
speak with authority about the other man's work, though
never publicly. His remarks appear considerably more
balanced than might be deduced from earlier commentators
and unusually so for the volatile atmosphere in which these
issues were discussed. He was both generous in praise and
pointed in criticism. Whilst he was not alone in duly acknowledging the vast scope of Wagner's achievement – his lofty
aims and immense energy in the creation of a specifically
German theatre at Bayreuth – he was surely exceptionally
sensitive to Wagner's achievements as a musician and,
especially, man of the theatre. Indeed, in parentheses, it is
fascinating to note the seeming resistance of Brahms's circle
to the acknowledgement of this fact: hence, Kalbeck felt
obliged to interpret Brahms's remarks on *Tristan* in order to
remove any suggestion that he might have admired the work as
a whole, or even that he might have been envious of it. All that
Brahms said was that, in contrast to *Götterdämmerung*, which
'interests and fascinates one, and yet, properly speaking, is
not always pleasant . . . with the *Tristan* score it is different.
If I look at it in the morning, I am cross for the rest of the day'
(Henschel 111), a remark which merely suggests a fundamental difference of sympathy towards the two works.

Brahms recognized in Wagner the attempt to redefine the
relation of music and drama and freely acknowledged his
achievement in many remarks, especially noting to Heuberger
'the amazing clarity of his thoughts' (Heuberger 180). Indeed,
it was this point which stimulated him to his most frequent
criticism of Wagner: the adverse influence of his vast
conceptions. He frequently sought to distinguish between the
Wagner *he* understood and the 'misunderstood' Wagner
idolized by the younger generation (102). Cosima Wagner
roundly condemned Brahms for an equivocal attitude in telling
a student that he regarded Wagner as dangerous, only to
amend his meaning to: difficult for young people, on dis-

27 *Johannes Brahms Briefwechsel I: Johannes Brahms in Briefwechsel mit Heinrich
und Elisabet von Herzogenberg* ed. Max Kalbeck (Berlin [4]1921) 183.

covering that the student was a Wagnerian.[28] Yet this was Brahms's consistent attitude. He considered Wagner's work perforce to expose dangers, and became increasingly inclined to see him as a conservative, stressing his relation to Mozart, Brahms's own symbol for the lost age of musical purity: 'Wagner is really much closer to Mozart than many people imagine' (Heuberger 68). No post-Wagner operas that he heard in Vienna escaped Brahms's censure, though in making a partial exception of Humperdinck's *Hansel and Gretel* (68), he was anticipating later judgement. In fact, the only other contemporary opera he really acknowledged was Bizet's *Carmen*, which embodied the Mozartian virtues within Brahms's operatic frame of reference.

However, admiration and interest could not lead Brahms to commitment. Wagner's aesthetic outlook was indeed far removed from his own and he could only ever appreciate his work partially. Familiarity with Brahms's output and attitude predicts the many areas of his reservation. Of central significance is the question of text. His own preferences may well have helped to commend *The Mastersingers*, of which he remarked 'could I fail to respond to its gaiety and greatness?' (Kalbeck III 409). Yet, the subject-matter and expression of the *Ring* were something different. In conversation with Henschel he criticized Wagner's 'stilted, bombastic language' which, though it made a resonant impression, did not communicate real meaning to him, although he did not explain his reservations further. Brahms was equally perplexed as to the larger meaning of the Tetralogy, asking more than once what becomes of the Ring and what Wagner means by it (Henschel 107). His reaction was partly due to the wide literary background from which he approached the work. He had possessed Karl Simrock's *Das Niebelunglied* of 1839 from 1855 and was well acquainted with Fr. Hebbel's *Die Niebelungen-Trilogie* (1862), in which the heathen and Christian orders clash. Hence the suggestion to Henschel 'perhaps the Cross . . . Hebbel has dared it in his Niebelunge. . . that might at least be an idea – thus to indicate the termination of the reign of the Gods'. Brahms was not at ease with the mythical world of the *Ring* and considered that even the 'finest moments', such as Siegfried's withdrawal of the sword, 'would be *really* powerful and carry one away, if it all concerned – let us say, young Bonaparte, or some other hero who stands nearer to our sensibilities, has a closer claim

28 C. Wagner *Diaries* I 734.

to our affection' (Henschel 106–7). It is worth noting that in Brahms's only vaguely operatic undertaking, *Rinaldo* Op. 50, Goethe portrays his hero in an intensely human predicament.

Consistent with the nature of much of his subject-matter, Wagner's sense of time-scale and of the fusion of formal elements was unacceptable to Brahms. These composers had totally different concepts of time, Wagner gaining the effect of ever greater concentration through length, Brahms striving for this effect through brevity. It is hardly surprising that Brahms should have recommended taking a theatre box in order to be able to move around or take a drink. His description of *Walküre* was of 'a taxing pleasure', though he enjoyed recalling to Heuberger, with an amusing example, that 'even (true Wagnerians) sleep' (Heuberger 43, 160). Brahms's enjoyment was restricted to the passages of greatest dramatic impact or musical self-sufficiency and he was wont to comment to the effect 'Yes, there are many fine things, but . . .' Even *The Mastersingers* prompted reservations about the 'spinning-out of the strongly defined pieces', of which he often tired (39). Yet the distinction was not merely between the more defined events and their treatments, but concerned the nature of Wagner's sound-world. Wagner's expansion of usable sound to encroach on what Brahms would have joined Clara Schumann in regarding as noise, excluded him from much participation; and any suggestion of the harsher Lisztian sonorities, which he loathed, was castigated. Hence, he dismissed Siegfried's *Funeral March* in *Götterdämmerung* as Lisztian rather than Beethovenian, partly for its use of cor anglais and bass clarinet, obviously feeling that Wagner's great climax required music of a different stamp (16). It seems not unlikely that he would have accorded with Billroth's comment[29] on the physical aspects of singing the bigger Wagner roles, illustrated by Clara with her assertion that Joachim's wife had 'ruined her high notes' in this way (*Schumann-Brahms Briefe* II 546).

Brahms's reactions to all these features naturally determined his preferred works. Subject and form gave *The Mastersingers* pre-eminence among the music-dramas, although he actually regarded *The Flying Dutchman* as the finest work and knew it well enough to quote text in a letter to Billroth (*Letters* 195); the self-identity of formal elements may well have combined with its obvious thematic unity to commend it. Of the *Ring* he acknowledged a definite preference for

29 C.A.T. Billroth *Wer ist musikalisch?* ed. E. Hanslick (Vienna 1896) 195.

Die Walküre and *Götterdämmerung*, disliking *Das Rheingold* and *Siegfried*. He was very guarded about *Tristan*; although 'warmly acknowledging the many musical beauties of the work', he is recorded as having had 'a particular dislike' for it (111), and he may well have agreed with Elisabet von Herzogenberg's very 'proper' observation of its 'rejection of the fresher, more innocent conception of sensuality for a sultry, oppressive atmosphere of supreme desire which arouses a kind of evil conscience in the listener – a feeling that his presence amounts to an impropriety'.[30]

Yet, Brahms's attitude to Wagner was never without equivocation. His basic view was probably that expressed to Clara in 1870: 'I am not enthusiastic . . . about Wagner in general, but I listen as attentively as possible, that is, for as long as I can stand it. I confess that it provokes one to discussion. . .' (*Schumann–Brahms Briefe* I 617). But the enthusiasm could vary. To what extent the seeming growth of interest in later years reflected a changing aesthetic position, or simply a desire to defend the reputation of an admired artist who could no longer do it for himself, it is impossible to say. Although he claimed elsewhere in this passage that Wagner would not have prevented him from writing an opera 'with the greatest pleasure', it seems unlikely that this was the case, at least from this time on. Quite apart from the problems of libretti, *Rinaldo* speaks convincingly of his limitations in thinking dramatically in music, and one cannot imagine him having achieved within his declared operatic framework, the creative synthesis of past with present that is so characteristic of his instrumental works.

It is abundantly clear from the scope of Brahms's outlook that he can only be characterized as an 'absolutist' – even very generally – with considerable qualification. For whatever reasons he eschewed dramatic and programmatic music in his own output, he was keenly interested in the issues involved; indeed, quite apart from such works as *Rinaldo* and the *Alto Rhapsody*, his 'absolute' music can suggest a programmatic background. We know that Brahms considered writing incidental music for a production of *Faust* at the Burgtheater and, though he did not confirm this as the subject of the overture he entitled *Tragic* (Kalbeck III 258), it is difficult to believe that such an atmospheric passage as the introduction to the finale of the First Symphony evolved without some extra-musical

30 *Johannes Brahms Briefwechsel II: Johannes Brahms in Briefwechsel mit Heinrich und Elisabet von Herzogenberg* ed. Max Kalbeck (Berlin [4]1921) 78.

stimulus: it could so easily be an operatic prelude in the tradition of Weber. Such considerations lead to the subject of Brahms's relationship with the figure with whom Wagner was perhaps more in conflict than with any other: Brahms's lifelong friend, the Viennese critic Eduard Hanslick (1825–1904). Hanslick's early book, Vom Musikalisch-Schönen[31] did much to encourage the polarization of attitudes through which Brahms and Wagner became opposing symbols.

Brahms's first reaction to Hanslick's book is often quoted; to Clara he remarked in 1856 'I have tried to read, but found such a number of stupid things at first glance through it, that I gave up' (Schumann–Brahms Briefe I 168). Less quoted is his response to Hanslick's presentation of the second edition in 1863, when their friendship began fully: 'I must give you the greatest thanks for your book, Musikalisch-Schönen, to which I owe enjoyable hours, clarification, indeed, real assurance. Every page invites one to build further on what you have said . . .'[32] Although naturally couched in different terms, these remarks suggest a considerable change of attitude over the intervening seven years, of which the Manifesto of 1860 was also reflective, and if we may still rightly doubt Brahms's interest in such a book (his copy seems hardly read), it is likely that the only passage which he marked – the key phrase on page 38 'Tonend bewegte Formen sind einzig und allein Inhalt und Gegenstand der Musik' (tr. 'the essence of music is sound and motion' (48)) – reflected approval. However, Brahms must have taken exception to the broader thesis of which this is a part, expressed, for example, in the assertion that 'the beautiful tends to disappear in proportion as the expression of some specific emotion is aimed at' (tr. 40). Indeed, it seems likely that the whole tenor of Hanslick's argument was a primary factor in accounting for the 'such very different points of view' which he admitted to Clara in later years (Schumann–Brahms Briefe II 596).

These differences resulted in turn from more fundamental differences in musical perception. Despite Hanslick's justified reputation as an educator and observer of the musical scene, his horizons were profoundly limited in comparison with those of his friend. It was inevitable that there would be tensions between the composer who, quite apart from his individuality, was intent on bringing to the Viennese the music of

31 Leipzig 1854. On the Beautiful in Music tr. G Cohen, ed. with Introduction, M. Weitz (Indianapolis 1957).
32 E. Hanslick Am Ende des Jahrhunderts 388.

Gabrieli, Schütz and J. S. Bach and the critic who could admit that, for him, music really began with Mozart and culminated in Beethoven, Schumann and Brahms himself.[33] Indeed, it is clear that Hanslick never came to terms with Brahms's more challenging works. His first responses were lukewarm and, whilst the traditional outlines of the *Handel Variations* impressed him, he could only comment of the fine op. 26 Piano Quartet that its themes were 'dry and flat' and reminiscent of Schumann's last period. The famous review of the First Symphony actually reflects more respect than understanding and he was denied full appreciation of the Third and Fourth Symphonies, his reaction to the former prompting Brahms to admit feeling 'in the very good company of Richard Wagner' in not being understood (Heuberger 132). An indication of the nature of the problem emerges from Billroth's correspondence with Brahms, where Billroth notes that Hanslick could never really approach the First Symphony because of his inability to respond to the spirit of 'Faust, Bach or Beethoven', noting specifically of the *Parzengesang* that he would 'probably get a shock in the first two bars [since] only from the third bar does one feel oneself . . . secure in the D minor' (*Letters* 122). Brahms knew exactly what he was doing when he dedicated to the witty and urbane critic so vividly described by Graf, the Waltzes Op 39.

What then was the real basis of this friendship, and what its effect on the musical life of Vienna? Brahms greatly admired Hanslick both as a professional and as a man and would probably have echoed Billroth's recognition of his capacity to 'limit objectives and competently expand within [them]' (*Letters* 213). Hanslick's acceptance of his limitations appealed to Brahms and there is no record of animosity between them, Brahms referring to him after Billroth's death as 'my oldest and most intimate friend'. His lavish praise was not only given in public, as Heuberger recalls on the occasion of Hanslick's seventieth birthday (Heuberger 85), but he wrote likewise to Clara: 'I cannot help it, but I know few men for whom I feel as hearty an attachment as I do for him. To be as simple, good, benevolent, honourable, serious and modest and everything else as I know him to be, I regard as something very beautiful and rare' (*Schumann–Brahms Briefe* II 596).

Just what effect this relationship had on the great issues of the day is a matter for conjecture. Despite his admiration for

33 E. Hanslick *Aus meinem Leben* (Berlin 1894) II 307.

Brahms, Karl Goldmark was of the view that the liaison had been very dangerous in consolidating conservative attitudes and considered that Hanslick wielded a much stronger sword with Brahms as ally than without.[34] Yet, equally, Brahms obviously saw the erosion of what he considered traditional values keenly and may have believed, on balance, that Hanslick's outlook was beneficial, even if he disputed his way of expressing it. To what extent Brahms should have felt obliged to undermine a friendship is open to debate; historians would naturally wish him to have done so. Thus Geiringer observes that 'the fact must not be overlooked that . . . Brahms never did anything to hinder the malicious attacks which the journalists of his circle . . . continued to direct against Wagner.'[35] But composers do not act for the benefit of historians, and it can be as well reasoned that he was right to hold back, given that he realized only too well how his views were too subtle for the partisan times and how he would merely spark off more controversy. Brahms cannot have been unaware of the reasons for Hanslick's pointed interest in him when he came to Vienna. As Graf puts it 'he laid hold of the heavy timber of Brahms's music to save himself from the flood of Wagner's, the waves of which were rising every day'.[36] For his part, Brahms certainly appreciated critical support in this period, and by the time he was firmly established, a friendship had been formed which clearly took precedence over other considerations.

Absorbing as the varied aspects of Brahms's cultural world appear in themselves, they fall into a different perspective when placed in relation to the life of later nineteenth-century Vienna. Although Brahms died just before the explosion of thought in the arts and sciences which has so powerfully affected our century, his latter years were spent in proximity to a creative environment of ever-increasing momentum. To what extent his own interests in scientific matters and in such an artist as Klinger were reflected elsewhere is an important subject for further research; it is not yet impossible that valuable information remains to surface in this connection. But whatever remains to be added to our picture, it can never be of real value if it is interpreted in the traditional terms of polarity. It is abundantly clear that Brahms had no interest

34 K. Goldmark Erinnerungen aus meinem Leben (Vienna 1922) 122.
35 K. Geiringer 'Wagner and Brahms, with unpublished letters' The Musical Quarterly 22/2 (1936) 178–189.
36 M. Graf Composer and Critic (London 1947) 248.

whatever in the unqualified use of such terms as 'progressive', 'conservative' or 'original'. Although he certainly existed within a bourgeois social context, abhorring the lifestyle of Wagner and warming to the nationalistic attitudes of Bismarck and Treitschke, his mental world, embattled as it may have been, was disposed towards other concerns. He was inclined to let the future, like the press, take care of itself, whilst directing his own attention towards such basic issues as those of musical organization and the relation of music to words, drama and other stimuli. When Brahms referred to the young Schenker as 'nowadays the only one that writes about music',[37] he was pointing to a much deeper preoccupation. He was profoundly averse to any pretentiousness or looseness of thought in aesthetic matters and suspected the 'New Germans' in this regard. Contrary to the traditional view, he was always willing to acknowledge success within his code of values, even though the expression involved should differ from his own. Thus, whilst he could quite genuinely regard the symphonies of Bruckner as inflated, he could equally acknowledge the 'scherzo' of Mahler's Second Symphony as a piece 'of genius' (Specht 239). Much of his deep absorption in the past reflected the belief that aesthetic principles had become clouded in the all-embracing romantic world in which he lived. It seems ironical that Brahms, who gave every indication of anticipating a full span of years, should have died just before the emergence of a younger Viennese generation who, though in different terms, would reassert the principles he so cherished: it must surely give cause to reflect on just how the ageing master might have responded to such figures as Arnold Schoenberg, Karl Kraus, Ludwig Wittgenstein. . .

37 M. Mann 'Schenker's contribution to music theory' *The Music Review* 10/1 (1949) 8.

VIRGINIA L. HANCOCK

The growth of Brahms's interest in early choral music, and its effect on his own choral compositions

After Brahms's death in 1897, the contents of his large personal library eventually came, essentially intact, to the Archive of the Gesellschaft der Musikfreunde in Vienna.[1] The history of his lifelong interest in Renaissance and Baroque music may be traced in that library. The earliest evidence comes from 1848 (the year when the fifteen-year-old Brahms included a Bach fugue in his first piano recital): he wrote his name and that date in an old copy of David Kellner's 1743 treatise *Treulicher Unterricht im General-Bass*, which also had a copy of Mattheson's *Die Kunst, das Clavier zu spielen* bound in at the back. This is just the first of a number of eighteenth-century books of instruction in musical practice which are to be found in his collection.

Brahms also made many manuscript copies of early music. The first surviving copies are taken from a collection entitled *Musica Sacra*, newly published by Schlesinger of Berlin (c. 1852): the four pieces copied are Durante's double-choir 'Misericordias Domini', Lotti's 'Vere languores nostros', Corsi's 'Adoramus te, Christe', and the Crucifixus from Palestrina's *Missa Papae Marcelli*.[2] After Brahms had made these copies, he used the remaining space at the bottom of a page to write down two Hungarian melodies (one of these is the tune he used for the Piano Variations Op. 21 No. 2), which he dated 17 January 1853.

In April 1853, Brahms left Hamburg with Eduard Reményi on the concert tour which resulted in his friendships with

1 See Eusebius Mandyczewski 'Die Bibliothek Brahms' *Musikbuch aus Oesterreich* 1 (1904) 7–17; K. and I. Geiringer 'The Brahms Library in the "Gesellschaft der Musikfreunde," Wien' *Notes* 30 (September 1973) 7–14; and Virginia L. Hancock 'Brahms and his library of early music: the effects of his study of Renaissance and Baroque music on his choral writing (Diss. U. of Oregon 1977) (hereafter Hancock 'Library').

2 Virginia L. Hancock 'Sources of Brahms's manuscript copies of early music in the Archive of the Gesellschaft der Musikfreunde in Wien *Fontes Artis Musicae* 24 (1977) (hereafter Hancock, 'Sources') 113–21.

Joseph Joachim and Robert and Clara Schumann, and which thus changed his life decisively. His new friends shared and encouraged his enthusiasm for early music. Schumann had studied and performed some of the rediscovered works which were being circulated in manuscript and published copies, and his library in Düsseldorf contained a considerable collection.[3] After Schumann's breakdown and hospitalization in 1854, Brahms spent much time in this library, organizing it and then studying and copying material. Among the copies he made at this time are: two of the Responsoria by Ingegneri, which throughout the nineteenth century were attributed to Palestrina; nine sacred continuo Lieder from about 1700, taken from the examples in Winterfeld's *Der evangelische Kirchengesang* (1847); German folk songs from Becker's *Lieder und Weisen vergangener Jahrhunderte* (1849–50); and examples of German chorale tunes, with their histories, copied from Winterfeld and from Tucher's *Schatz des evangelischen Kirchengesangs* (1848). Brahms was also able to add some printed works of early music to his own library at this time: Schumann's copy of Becker and Billroth's *Sammlung von Chorälen aus dem XVI. und XVII. Jahrhundert* (1831) is there; and a very important addition was Clara Schumann's Christmas gift to him in 1855, the first volume of the Bach *Werke*, in which she wrote, 'Meinem geliebten Freunde Johannes Brahms als Anfang'.

By early 1855 Brahms was studying counterpoint and writing 'all possible sorts of canons',[4] and early in 1856 he and Joachim agreed to exchange counterpoint exercises, using as a textbook Marpurg's *Handbuch bei dem Generalbasse und der Composition* (1755–8). Joachim was never as diligent in this study as Brahms, but he evaluated the large amount of material that Brahms sent him, and cheerfully paid the fines they had agreed on when he failed to produce his own exercises in return.[5] Brahms's library contains two copies of Marpurg's book; the one he used in this project is heavily annotated with underlining, NBs, and cross-references, especially in sections dealing with the various kinds of seventh chords, with the preparation and resolution of dissonance, and with the notation of figured bass.

3 For a partial list, see Wolfgang Boetticher *Robert Schumann: Einführung in Persönlichkeit und Werk* (Berlin 1941) 229, 296.

4 *Clara Schumann–Johannes Brahms: Briefe aus den Jahren 1853–1896*; ed. Berthold Litzmann (Leipzig 1927) (hereafter *Schumann–Brahms Briefe*) I 73.

5 *Johannes Brahms Briefwechsel V: Johannes Brahms im Briefwechsel mit Joseph Joachim* ed. Andreas Moser (Berlin ³1921) (hereafter *Briefwechsel* V) 123–7, and occasionally thereafter to 305.

Although Brahms later destroyed most of his counterpoint exercises, we can see some of the immediate results of the project in his earliest surviving choral works, published years later. For example, the *Geistliches Lied* Op. 30 was the subject of a discussion between him and Joachim in June 1856. Brahms doubted the success of the organ interludes, but was pleased with the Amen. Joachim liked the work on the whole, but complained of the harshness of the dissonance in the Amen which results from the motion of the tenor part, 'beautiful in and for itself', against the soprano and alto; he felt that Brahms was so used to thinking polyphonically that he tended to disregard the clashes that resulted from the motions of individual lines.[6] On the other hand, Joachim felt that the Benedictus canon, which Brahms had written on 25 February 1856 and had described to Clara Schumann as 'recht hübsch (*Schumann–Brahms Briefe* I 178), possessed a 'noble solemnity' that was enhanced by its strictness. Brahms and Joachim had their most detailed discussion of Brahms's canonic mass in June 1856,[7]

Ex. 1   Brahms, Benedictus

6 *Briefwechsel* V 142–8. It is clear that Brahms enjoyed dissonance of certain kinds for its own sake, both in his own and in other composers' works. He once told Florence May that he particularly loved the suspensions in Bach's music, and wanted them played so 'as to give the fullest possible effect to the dissonance'. See May *The Life of Johannes Brahms* (London 1905) I 17. Georg Henschel is quoted as saying that Brahms once told him, 'I love dissonances very much, but on heavy beats, and then lightly and gently resolved!' See Max Kalbeck *Johannes Brahms* III (Berlin [2]1912–13) 85.

7 *Briefwechsel* V 141, 151–3. For a summary of the later history of the *Missa canonica*, see Siegfried Kross *Die Chorwerke von Johannes Brahms* (Berlin-Halensee [2]1963) 514–24. Until recently, the Mass was thought to be lost (except for the Benedictus); but in autumn 1981 it was acquired by the Gesellschaft der Musikfreunde, where it will receive its first public performance in May 1983.

and in the same month Brahms finished his manuscript copy of the complete *Missa Papae Marcelli* of Palestrina.

The counterpoint project was broken off abruptly by Schumann's death in July 1856, and although Brahms and Joachim discussed its revival intermittently up to 1861, they never again pursued it systematically. Brahms did continue with his own study of early music, however, and, after he returned to Hamburg, he worked in the city library, collected materials from second-hand bookshops, and renewed his friendships with people who shared his interests and allowed him to use their private libraries. One of these, Theodor Avé Lallement, had earlier offered to let Brahms rummage in his attic and keep any music of which he found duplicates (*Schumann–Brahms Briefe* I 156), and in 1858 he gave Brahms a copy of Winterfeld's three-volume *Johannes Gabrieli und sein Zeitalter*

(1834), an important and useful addition to his growing library.

Brahms soon found a practical use for some of the early choral music he had been studying and collecting when he took the post of court-musician at Detmold, beginning in the autumn of 1857. His duties there were to teach the piano, perform solo piano and chamber music, and conduct a small choral society. During his first season he worked on Rovetta's 'Salve Regina' (which he had copied from an 1813 issue of the *Allgemeine musikalische Zeitung*), an unidentified piece by Praetorius (possibly 'Maria zart'), Handel's *Messiah*, and works by Mozart and Schumann. He also reported to Joachim that they were making 'experiments with folk songs' (*Briefwechsel* V 191). Presumably these experiments were his early choral arrangements of German folk songs, most of which he took from the two-volume collection published by Kretzschmer and Zuccalmaglio in 1838 and 1840, *Deutsche Volkslieder mit ihren Original-Weisen*. In 1854 Brahms had copied some material from this source in Schumann's library, and in 1856 his Hamburg friend Karl Grädener had given him his own copy. The collection remained his favourite source of folk-song material throughout his life, in spite of the attacks of more scholarly investigators,[8] and his copy is filled with his own markings – notations of sources and variants, references to other collections, and corrections. One particularly interesting annotation, in view of Brahms's habits as a composer, appears in the song 'Ulrich' (Vol. II, No. 15). Brahms noticed that the real rhythm is not $\frac{3}{4}$ throughout, as it is printed, but rather is two bars of $\frac{2}{4}$ followed by two of $\frac{3}{2}$. He wrote in a new time signature after the first two bars, and showed where the beats actually fall in relation to the text-structure. This is only one of a number of examples of his marking rhythmic patterns in his early music collection that do not conform with either original or editorial bar-lines. Similar annotations are found in the Bach *Werke*, in Brahms's manuscript copies of Isaac's 'Innsbruck' and Hassler's 'Mein G'müth ist mir verwirret', in a volume of works of Eccard and Stobaeus, and in a manuscript copy of Forster's *Ein Ausbund schöner Teutscher Liedlein* that had been given to Brahms. The majority of these markings identify hemiola figures, which are, of course, found abundantly in Brahms's own music; and a few other examples are similar to

8 See Brahms's correspondence on the subject with Spitta, Deiters and others, cited in Imogen Fellinger 'Grundzüge Brahmsscher Musikauffassung' in *Beiträge zur Geschichte der Musikanschauung im 19. Jahrhundert* ed. Walter Salmen (Regensburg 1965) 114–16. Also Walter Wiora *Die rheinisch-bergischen Melodien bei Zuccalmaglio und Brahms* (Bad Godesberg 1953).

the way he himself disregarded bar-lines in innumerable situations in his own compositions, writing with a freedom and flexibility that has been compared by many writers to the practices of early music. (See Hancock 'Library' 290–304, for several examples).

At the time he was composing the Detmold folk-song settings – straightforward chordal presentations of the melodies, which are invariably in the top voice – Brahms told Joachim that he had very little practical knowledge of how to write for choirs. When he wanted to write vocal counterpoint he composed canons on sacred texts, much like most other composers, who since the time of Bach had relegated contrapuntal construction to formal fugues in sacred music. As he became more experienced, he learned the effectiveness of incorporating ideas from his counterpoint studies into even the lightest of secular choral works, giving them a texture typical of much early music.

In his second autumn season with the Detmold choir, 1858, Brahms worked on two Bach cantatas – first No. 4, 'Christ lag in Todesbanden', and then No. 21, 'Ich hatte viel Bekümmernis'. He had subscribed to the Bach *Werke*, beginning in 1856, and for the rest of his life the arrival of each volume was an event of great importance to him. His copies show the evidence of the careful study he gave them.[9] He also subscribed to the complete works of Handel, but did not devote the same attention to them that he did to Bach's music. In Hamburg, where he spent the major part of each year, he began to work with the *Frauenchor*, composing for them and also arranging music by other composers for women's voices, including a substantial amount of early music.[10] The 1859 season was his last in Detmold, but he continued to work with the women in Hamburg, and wrote new music not only for them but for mixed voices and men's voices.

Much of Brahms's choral music from the years 1857 to 1862 shows the effects of his increasing practical knowledge of the medium, as well as those of his continuing study of Bach, of German chorale-settings and Renaissance Tenorlieder, and of Italian church music. Some of the connections with early music seem quite obvious: for example, Brahms's friend Julius Otto Grimm pointed out a resemblance between Cantata No. 4

9 See Hancock 'Library' 155–9 for a description of the annotations in these volumes. Brahms made some analytical notes in the fugues of Cantata No. 21, perhaps in connection with his work on it at Detmold.
10 Walter Hübbe *Brahms in Hamburg* (Hamburg 1902) 66; Sophie Drinker *Brahms and his Women's Choruses* (Merion, Pa. 1952) 103–4.

and Brahms's 'Begräbnisgesang' Op. 13;[11] and the Marienlie-
der Op. 22 are clearly influenced by German Renaissance
practice.[12] Even such apparently simple and romantic pieces
as the Lieder und Romanzen Op. 44 show a much more natural
use of contrapuntal techniques to enrich the part-writing and
overall vocal interest than is apparent in Brahms's earlier
secular choral music. The effortless handling of six parts in
the Gesänge Op. 42 may be in part the result of his careful
study of the works given as examples in the third volume of
Winterfeld's Gabrieli, and certainly the two motets Op. 29
reflect Brahms's interest in the cantatas of Bach, and perhaps
in other works by his German forebears.[13]

One of the reasons Brahms remained in Hamburg until 1862
was that he hoped to be chosen as director of the Philharmonic
concerts. He was severely disappointed when he learned, in
the middle of his first visit to Vienna for the 1862/3 winter
season, that Julius Stockhausen had been selected instead.
However, he had had a successful season in Vienna and had
enjoyed the city's many attractions, including its two major
music libraries, the Hofbibliothek (now the Nationalbibliothek)
and the Archive of the Gesellschaft der Musikfreunde. Therefore, when he was offered the position of director of the
Wiener Singakademie for the following season, he returned to
Vienna with enthusiasm and with a new impetus for learning
and composing choral music.
    With the Singakademie, Brahms repeated a few Renais-
sance and Baroque works – Bach's Cantata No. 21, Rovetta's
'Salve Regina', and Isaac's 'Innsbruck, ich muss dich lassen' –
that he had already enjoyed working on with his other choirs.
He also performed three sections of Bach's Christmas Ora-
torio, though unfortunately the quality of the concert compared unfavourably with a St John Passion done at nearly the
same time by the Singverein, a much more able and better-
financed chorus. After a major concert failure Clara Schu-

11. Johannes Brahms Briefwechsel IV: Johannes Brahms im Briefwechsel mit J. O.
    Grimm ed. Richard Barth (Berlin [2]1912) 83.
12 See Hancock 'Library' 206–7. Brahms was attracted by traditional Marian verse,
    as the poems he chose to set and the markings in his folk-song collections show. He
    was particularly fond of Eccard's 'Übers Gebirg Maria geht', which he probably
    knew from Winterfeld's Der evangelische Kirchengesang, and which he also
    owned in a copy made for him by Clara Schumann. He arranged it for the Frauen-
    chor and also performed it in his first choral concert with the Singverein in Vienna
    (1872).
13 See Kross 120–36; and Hancock 'Library' 211–6.

mann accused him of trying to change Viennese musical taste too abruptly;[14] this concert included the Rovetta piece, Schütz's 'Saul, Saul, was verfolgst du mich?', a twelve-voice Benedictus by Gabrieli,[15] an Easter motet by Eccard, and sections from Bach's Cantata No. 8, 'Liebster Gott, wann werd' ich sterben?', along with two more up-to-date, but still very sober, works by Beethoven and Mendelssohn. Brahms was much more successful with his last concert of the season, made up entirely of his own music, and was invited to continue as director of the Singakademie; but he declined the offer.

Presumably it was his work with the Singakademie that prompted Brahms to write the seven folk-song settings made soon after arriving in Vienna, and published with seven earlier ones in 1864.[16] These later settings show a much closer connection with the techniques of the sixteenth-century German polyphonic Lied than do his earlier ones. By this time he had made manuscript copies of Lieder by Lassus, Scandellus, and Praetorius; and he also had at some unknown time acquired a large manuscript collection of Tenorlieder, from which he had copied pieces by Zirler, Stoltzer, Greitter, and Senfl (Hancock, 'Sources' 119–20). Soon after its publication in 1862, Avé Lallement had given Brahms a copy of Meister's *Das katholische deutsche Kirchenlied in seinen Singweisen*, which contained a large appendix of polyphonic settings that Brahms annotated copiously; and in the Vienna Hofbibliothek he found a copy of Corner's *Gross' Catolisch Gesangbuch* of 1631, from which he copied several of the sacred folk songs that he set for the Singakademie.[17] The Corner and Meister collections also provided him with the text and tune for the motet 'O Heiland,

---

14 *Schumann–Brahms Briefe* I 437. See also Kalbeck, *Johannes Brahms* II ([2]1908) 99–105, for an account of all Brahms's concerts with the Singakademie.

15 The Schütz and Gabrieli pieces are both in Winterfeld's *Gabrieli* III, and Brahms's copy still contains some of his performance markings. The parts prepared for this performance survived until recently in the archives of the Singakademie, but unfortunately most of them have now been destroyed. I shall offer a description and discussion of this material in my forthcoming article, 'Brahms's performance copies of early choral music in the Archiv of the Gesellschaft der Musikfreunde in Wien and at the Wiener Singakademie'.

16 Chronology of composition of the folk-song settings is based on Werner Morik *Johannes Brahms und sein Verhältnis zum deutschen Volkslied* (Diss. Göttingen 1953; rpt. Tutzing 1965), with revisions made on the basis of the contents of the Hamburg Stimmenhefte by Siegfried Kross, 'Zur Frage der Brahmsschen Volkslied-bearbeitungen' *Die Musikforschung* 11 (1958) 15–21.

17 Hancock 'Library' 33–5, 222–9. The forthcoming article by George Bozarth, 'Johannes Brahms and David Gregor Corner's *Gross' Catolisch Gesangbuch* of 1631', is to contain a catalogue of the traditional texts and tunes copied by Brahms from this source, together with an analysis of Brahms's sketches of some of the folk-song settings.

reiss die Himmel auf' Op. 74 No. 2, a set of chorale variations which is in itself a compendium of the various early music techniques that Brahms had been studying (Hancock, 'Library' 216–22).

After the first year in Vienna, Brahms for some time turned his attention as a choral composer mainly to the composition of large-scale works with orchestra. Of these, the much-studied Requiem can easily be shown to contain the largest number of musical ideas inspired or at least suggested by knowledge of Renaissance and Baroque choral music; and, of course, the long history of the work's composition covers the period of Brahms's most concentrated study of early music. He can in no way, however, be accused of copying directly any musical material from pieces he knew; rather, by the time the work was complete, he had so thoroughly incorporated early music practices into his own style that numerous *fully assimilated* examples of their use may be found throughout the Requiem, as indeed in all his compositions from this time on.[18]

There is less evidence of a direct relationship between Brahms's choral compositions and the additions he made to his library of early music for the two middle decades of his career (about 1865 to 1885) than there is for either the earlier or later periods. After he arrived in Vienna, his library projects included some exercises in transcription of lute and organ tablatures, partial transcriptions of pieces by Schütz and Calvisius from partbooks, and the copying of sections of a ceremonial Serenata of 1662 by Cesti. In 1869 he was given a beautifully copied transcription of all five volumes of Georg Forster's *Ein Ausbund schöner Teutscher Liedlein* in appreciation of a performance of the Requiem in Karlsruhe; he studied them with the same care that he devoted to much of his library of early music (Hancock, 'Library' 114–7). His main acquisitions of new editions of early music at this time were the accumulating volumes of the Bach and Handel *Werke*, and still more collections of German folk songs. Some of the Bach volumes from these years contain annotations that point out unusual text illustrations, rhythmic complications, and contrapuntal features. One of Brahms's rare verbal notes was elicited by a passage in Cantata No. 91, where the bass recita-

18 Brahms's freedom from a too-heavy reliance on historical models, in spite of his preoccupation with early music, is agreed on by most writers about his choral music. The matter was first discussed in detail by Philipp Spitta in his article 'Johannes Brahms', in *Zur Musik* (Berlin 1892) 387–427.

tive containing the text 'durch dieses Jammerthal zu führen' has a remarkably chromatic setting with two striking parallel fifths. Brahms marked the fifths and wrote 'wie schön' in the margin; he also included this passage in the collection of counterpoint examples he kept for many years under the title 'Octaven u. Quinten u. A.'.[19]

During the three seasons, 1872–5, that he was director of the Musikverein (the performing organizations of the Gesellschaft der Musikfreunde), Brahms successfully introduced a number of Bach and Handel works to the Viennese audience, returned to some of the old a cappella favourites from his earlier choir directorships, and chose a few small early works he had not performed before, including parallel settings of the chorale 'Es ist genug' by J. R. Ahle and Bach. But he did not make the mistake of filling entire programmes with music that was perceived as archaic or morbid, as he had during his time with the Singakademie. On balance, his performances were well received, but Brahms still found the necessary administrative and social tasks of a conducting position irksome, and relinquished the post after three seasons. Much of the performance material for these concerts may still be found in the Archive of the Gesellschaft der Musikfreunde.

Very little of the choral music of Brahms's middle and late years can be said to have been written for any specific singing group. Rather, he was able to compose for his own reasons, whatever they may have been (and he was, as is well known, extremely reticent about such reasons). We are fortunate that he continued to write choral works, many of them a cappella, even after he stopped conducting his own choirs and therefore no longer needed such music for his own particular use.

The two collections of secular choral songs from Brahms's middle years, Opp. 62 and 93a, contain a number of settings of traditional texts of a folk-like character.[20] The apparently simple nature of these works disguises a wealth of contrapuntal detail which makes them as interesting to sing as any of his music where the parts are more obviously independent. In the settings of more subjective and emotional poetry, Brahms used practices even more clearly derived from early

19 The collection was published in facsimile by Universal-Edition of Vienna (1933) with a commentary by Heinrich Schenker. It has recently been reprinted, transcribed, translated and discussed by Paul Mast in 'Brahms's study, Octaven u. Quinten u. A., with Schenker's commentary translated' Music Forum 5 (1980) 1–196.
20 Opp. 62 No. 6 and 62 No. 7, 'Es geht ein Wehen' and 'Vergangen ist mir Glück und

music, such as the strict canonic passages in expressive works like 'Waldesnacht' and 'All' meine Herzgedanken'. Why he should have chosen to do so is unknown; perhaps by this time he had so completely integrated such practices into his personal style that he no longer needed to have specific reasons of tradition or text for using them. In some cases the old techniques are used for more contemporary romantic expression: for example, in 'O süsser Mai', the anticipatory imitation and hemiola cross-rhythms used as the poet turns away from the beauties of nature seem to exemplify the confusion and contrariness of his mind. The sacred texts of the motet 'Warum ist das Licht gegeben?' Op. 74 No. 1, considered by most writers on Brahms to be his greatest a cappella work, did not prompt him to any sort of hackneyed employment of traditional compositional methods. The motet may contain practices of an earlier era in many of its details, but in sum it belongs entirely to the late nineteenth century.[21]

The most important addition to Brahms's library of early music during the later years of his life was the complete edition of the works of Heinrich Schütz, edited by Philipp Spitta and issued beginning in 1885. By 1888, when Brahms composed most of the five secular Gesänge Op. 104 and the Fest- und Gedenksprüche Op. 109, seven volumes had been published; and in 1889, the year of Brahms's last choral works, the Op. 110 motets, the Geistliche Chormusik of 1648 appeared. Brahms had been attracted to the music of Schütz before this time: in fact, as early as 1858, when Clara Schumann offered to copy early music for him that she encountered on her travels, he had requested her to look especially for works by Eccard and Schütz (Schumann-Brahms Briefe I 221, 224). But until the appearance of the complete works, only a small amount of Schütz's music was available in published editions, and we cannot demonstrate that Brahms knew much of it: he did own Winterfeld's Gabrieli, which contains three complete pieces (SWV 269, 335, 415) and a number of fragments illustrating particular points; Brahms's friend Franz Wüllner published a performing edition of three of the Psalmen Davids

Heil', were actually composed years earlier in Hamburg; the conscious archaism of the latter is not, therefore, a product of the 1870s. Dates of composition for Brahms's choral music are given by Kross in Chorwerke.

21 The 'Warum' motet has been much discussed. See, for example, Spitta in Zur Musik, Kross Chorwerke 367–74 and Hancock 'Library' 246–51. In this work Brahms integrated his early Benedictus canon into the larger structure with perfect ease and appropriateness.

(SWV 24, 25, 35) in 1878 and sent him a copy;[22] a copy, made by someone unknown, of 'Wer will uns scheiden' (SWV 330) is in Brahms's library; and he himself made a partial score from partbooks of the first piece in *Symphoniae Sacrae* III, 'Der Herr ist mein Hirt' (SWV 398). It is also possible, of course, that Brahms may have known some of the few other works that were in circulation, including the six-part 'Selig sind die Toten' (SWV 391), which had been published at least twice earlier in the nineteenth century.[23]

Not only do Brahms's volumes of the complete works of Schütz contain many of his markings, but he copied out a number of fragments from the Italian madrigals, the Passions and the *Psalmen Davids*. The features which attracted his attention include: the kinds of disguised parallel motion he was collecting for 'Octaven u. Quinten' (one passage also appears there); clever uses of imitation and diminution; some examples of text illustration; and striking, unexpected, or particularly expressive chromaticism and dissonance, especially use of the diminished fourth interval (or the augmented fifth) and of cross-relations (Hancock, 'Library' 60–6, 167–70).

Ex. 2   Passage from Schütz's *Matthäus Passion* copied by Brahms

Most of Brahms's own choral music of these late years shows no obvious resemblance to the music of Schütz – not that we would expect it to – although he may have been stimulated by the appearance of the polychoral *Psalmen Davids* to the composition of a cappella works for many-voiced mixed chorus.[24] Only the a cappella double-choir medium of the

22 *Johannes Brahms Briefwechsel XV: Johannes Brahms im Briefwechsel mit Franz Wüllner* ed. Ernst Wolff (Berlin 1922) (hereafter *Briefwechsel XV*) 91.

23 On the question of Brahms's possible knowledge of Schütz settings of texts that he chose for the Requiem, see Michael Musgrave 'Historical influences in the growth of Brahms's Requiem' *Music and Letters* 53 (1972) 3–17; and Hancock 'Library' 233–5.

24 Brahms was eagerly awaiting publication of the polychoral *Symphoniae Sacrae* III of 1650, perhaps because 'Saul' (SWV 415), which he had performed in 1863 with the Singakademie, comes from this set, as does 'Der Herr ist mein Hirt' (SWV 398), which he had transcribed from partbooks. His letter to Philipp Spitta in 1888, expressing his enthusiasm for the volumes which had appeared so far, and asking

last motets was actually new to his own music at this time.[25] In other ways, these late works seem, even more than the 'Warum' motet, to represent a synthesis of all that Brahms had learned over the years about choral composition and about early music.

Of the Op. 104 Gesänge, 'Im Herbst', a song linked with Brahms's other settings of Romantic nature poems, was written earlier than the others, and contains fewer features directly related to early music. However, it uses rhythmic figures which can be interpreted as hemiola, and contains considerable unobtrusive text-painting, illustrating entire phrases rather than individual words. Even in 'Verlorene Jugend', the most folk-like of this group, Brahms employed canon and a pattern of overlapping hemiolas. The six voices of the remaining three songs are handled with great freedom, as in earlier Brahms works for this combination. They are employed more freely than is evident in the Schütz works published by this time, but perhaps have some resemblance to the works in Winterfeld's Gabrieli that Brahms had copied out so many years before, and to other large-scale works he had performed.[26] In these three songs, the culmination of Brahms's long career of writing great secular choral music, he used old techniques of part-writing, imitation, and text illustration in combination with the resources of nineteenth-century harmony and motivic concentration to produce entirely satisfying results for both performers and listeners.

Of the last six motets only 'Ach, arme Welt' Op. 110 No. 2 is for four voices rather than eight. It seems unlikely that the resemblance of the first few notes of its melody to the whole-tone scale of the chorale 'Es ist genug' can be accidental.[27]

when the 'grossen Kirchenconzerte' would be published, marks the renewal of their correspondence, which had lapsed since 1879. See Johannes Brahms Briefwechsel XVI: Johannes Brahms im Briefwechsel mit Philipp Spitta und Otto Dessoff ed. Carl Krebs (Berlin 1920) 88.

25 Brahms owned and had studied an edition published in 1853 of Bach's motets, four of which are for double choir. There is no record of when he acquired this volume, or of his ever performing any of the motets. See Hancock 'Library' 159–61.

26 In the manuscript copies Brahms made from Winterfeld's Gabrieli, he seemed to exhibit a specific concern with the arrangement of the many voices; see Hancock 'Library' 39–42 and 175–83, for descriptions of these copies, and of Winterfeld's work and Brahms's markings in it. The large works Brahms prepared for performance include, in addition to those already mentioned, Eccard's 'Der Christen Triumphlied auf's Osterfest'; Stobaeus's 'Auf's Osterfest' (both prepared for the Singakademie, but only the first performed), and Palestrina's 'Haec dies' (six voices, prepared for the Singverein but not performed).

27 Kross Chorwerke 462. See also Hancock 'Library' 254–9, for a discussion of possible relationships of Brahms's tune and its harmonization to those of Bach and Ahle.

40   Virginia L. Hancock

The cadential hemiola is used here almost as a matter of course, as it is in many of Brahms's other works. The other two Op. 110 motets do resemble in a number of respects some of the music of Schütz which Brahms had been studying at about the time they were composed. In particular, the free and unpredictable use of dissonance, unconventional voice-leading, and the juxtaposition of passages of complex writing with moments of extreme simplicity, are similar to aspects of early Baroque practice which Brahms marked in his Schütz volumes (Hancock, 'Library' 262–8).

Although on the surface they seem much more straight-forward in construction and expression than the two double-choir Op. 110 motets, the *Fest- und Gedenksprüche* Op. 109 also reveal on closer examination some of this Schütz-like quality, especially in their rhythmic subtleties and the details of text-painting. They show once more how fluently and naturally Brahms incorporated all types of practices from early music into his compositions. Cadential hemiolas provide solemnity and stability, and the many contrapuntal combinations and uses of imitation give a complex and fascinating texture to what could have been mere monuments of grandeur. Brahms himself did not value these pieces as highly as the Op. 110 motets (*Briefwechsel XV* 164; *Schumann–Brahms Briefe* II 407), but perhaps his opinion was related more to the rather sententious nature of their texts than to any weakness in their musical construction. The way in which their surface splendour is supported by a wealth of beautifully written detail illustrates, as well as any of his music, not just the debt Brahms owed to the past, but the way in which he was able to make old ideas productive in his own work. The final Amen of the *Fest- und Gedenksprüche*, with its strictly constructed series of canonic entries piling up dissonance over an immovable bass pedal, provides a final glorious example of this relationship, and brings us in memory back to the early years of Brahms's creative career and the beginning of his continuing love for and involvement with Renaissance and Baroque music.

IMOGEN FELLINGER

Brahms's view of Mozart

Besides the Fifth Symphony and Violin Concerto of Beethoven, Brahms considered one of the 'most powerful experiences' of his youth to be his acquaintance with Mozart's *Don Giovanni.*[1] The more obvious influence on Brahms of Beethoven and Schubert has led to a comparative neglect of the importance of Mozart in this regard. Mozart's relevance for Brahms is not as evident as that of Beethoven, and often can only be traced indirectly. Hans Engel's argument, however, that Brahms was 'no declared Mozartian, though not only an admirer, but also a connoisseur of Mozart's art',[2] seems to summarize the facts far too sketchily and superficially. Remarks by Brahms in letters or in memoirs by friends and contemporaries, as well as other authentic documents, make it obvious that throughout his life he applied himself consciously and extensively to Mozart and his music.

I

The young Brahms first came into contact with the tradition of the Classical period through his teacher Eduard Marxsen, who at the beginning of the 1830s had studied in Vienna music theory with Ignaz von Seyfried (a piano pupil of Mozart and composition pupil of Albrechtsberger, who himself was a pupil of Mozart) and piano with Carl Maria von Bocklet (who stood in close relation to Beethoven and Schubert). Through Marxsen, whose compositional technique was grounded in the Classical age, an immediate tradition from Mozart and Beethoven to Brahms was established. Exactly how Marxsen passed on this heritage of the Classical period to his pupil is rather obscure, as is the extent to which he laid any particular ground work for Brahms's first conceptions of Mozart's music;

1 *Johannes Brahms Briefwechsel V: Johannes Brahms im Briefwechsel mit Joseph Joachim* ed. Andreas Moser (Berlin ³1921) (hereafter *Briefwechsel V*) 92.
2 H. Engel 'Die Meister liebten Mozart' in *Mozart-Jahrbuch* (1955) 173.

nor is it known which Mozart piano works Brahms had in his early Hamburg repertory. We do know, however, that at the age of ten he played, apart from the Quintet Op. 16 by Beethoven, one of Mozart's piano quartets[3] with colleagues of his father. In performing dance music, in order to earn money for his family, he used to play not only marches by Schubert but also sonatas for four hands by Mozart with the Hamburg musician Christian Miller (Kalbeck I 48). In spring 1848 he saw a performance of Mozart's *Figaro* in Hamburg which deeply impressed him.[4] Perhaps because of that performance he included in the programme of his first solo concert as a pianist in Hamburg on 21 September 1848, in addition to a fugue by J. S. Bach and the works of contemporary virtuosi according to the taste of the time, an aria and duet from *Figaro* (Kalbeck I 44). In the second concert on 14 April 1849 he presented, among other compositions, Beethoven's 'Waldstein' Sonata but Mozart only in a virtuoso arrangement entitled *Phantasie über Motive aus 'Don Juan'* by Thalberg.[5] In his Hamburg years he was already putting parts from earlier music into score, among them Mozart's Piano Concerto in D minor KV 466, which he later used for his own performances (Kalbeck I 255). In this connection Brahms's letter of 22 February 1855 to Joachim is of some interest; he wrote that in his early years (about 1848) he was 'chaotically enthusiastic' about music (*Briefwechsel* V 92), that is to say, that he did not yet have firm views on the compositions he heard in that time, including those by Mozart and Beethoven.

The confrontation with the historical reality of his time, mainly a fear that he would not be able to fulfil the expectations set up for him with the publication of Schumann's enthusiastic article 'Neue Bahnen' (New paths) at the end of October 1853,[6] and a growing consciousness that the musical instruction he had received from Marxsen was not profound and comprehensive enough for him to become a composer in his own individual way,[7] caused him to take stock of his situation and to develop that special sense of responsibility towards his own work so characteristic for him during his later life. Consequently he suppressed compositions which Schumann had considered worthy of publication by Breitkopf & Härtel,

3   Max Kalbeck *Johannes Brahms* I (Berlin [3]1912) (hereafter Kalbeck I) 240.
4   Kalbeck I 46 and F. May *The Life of Johannes Brahms* (London 1905) I 80–1.
5   A. von Ehrmann *Johannes Brahms: Weg, Werk und Welt* (Leipzig 1933) 19–20.
6   *Neue Zeitschrift für Musik* 39 (28 October 1853).
7   I. Fellinger 'Brahms und die Musik vergangener Epochen' in *Die Ausbreitung des Historismus über die Musik* ed. W. Wiora (Regensburg 1969) 150–1.

among them 'sonatas for violin and piano' and 'quartets for
string instruments',[8] which he later destroyed. It is indeed
remarkable that Brahms published compositions belonging
to these two genres only in the course of the 1870s, after
having studied Classical models thoroughly and having fully
developed his own personal style. Only through these profound studies during the second half of the 1850s, mainly
through his own strength, and impulse, did Brahms acquire
the comprehensive compositional ability, which enabled him to
become the master he was.

II

Brahms's assiduous studies of the art of music and its past are
to be considered as essential and decisive for his development
as a composer and for his outlook on music. He applied himself extensively to Mozart and his music, radically deepening
and expanding his knowledge of that composer. His great
enthusiasm, rooted in the early years, continued, but was
now accompanied by an increasing awareness of the distinction and value of Mozart's work in comparison with that of
other composers and theorists of the eighteenth century,
among them Kirnberger. Thus he wrote to Clara Schumann (5
March 1856): 'I revel in Mozart's sonatas! Then I shut the
Kirnberger furiously and throw it away' (Schumann–Brahms
Briefe I 181). This lively enthusiasm for Mozart's compositions was followed by a view of the unsurpassable perfection
in his works: the more Brahms prosecuted his studies, the
greater became his respect for the achievements of this
master.

In the 1850s and early 1860s Brahms collected, mainly for
study-purposes, scores of Mozart's works, both in manuscript, of which the most valuable was the autograph score
of the Symphony in G minor KV 550,[9] and in many original
editions. His collection was augmented by presents from
friends, for example in 1856 the score of Don Giovanni from
Ferdinand David (Schumann–Brahms Briefe I 168), and in
1860 the scores of the Entführung aus dem Serail and
Idomeneo from Joachim (Briefwechsel V 272, Schumann–
Brahms Briefe I 346). The numerous early Mozart editions in
Brahms's library (now in the Archive of the Gesellschaft der

8 Clara Schumann–Johannes Brahms: Briefe aus den Jahren 1853–1896 ed. Berthold
  Litzmann (Leipzig 1927) (hereafter Schumann–Brahms Briefe) I 1–3.
9 Brahms was given this autograph in 1864 by Anna, Landgräfin von Hessen, as
  thanks for his dedication of the two versions of his Opus 34, and an autograph of
  the version for two pianos.

44   Imogen Fellinger

Musikfreunde, Vienna), often contain insertions in his own
hand and bear witness to the extent of his collection and
study.

In his theoretical studies, concerned mainly with questions
of counterpoint, Brahms included some consideration of compositions by Mozart. This is most apparent in his autograph
study 'Octaven u.[nd] Quinten u.[nd] A.[nderes]', consisting
of approximately 140 examples of consecutive octaves and
fifths and similar progressions, taken from compositions of
masters from the sixteenth to the nineteenth centuries. About
a tenth of these examples is taken from Mozart's works –
from his operas, such as Così fan tutte, Idomeneo, Don
Giovanni and Die Zauberflöte, from the 'Jupiter' Symphony,
two Piano Sonatas KV 283 and 310, the Sonata for Violin and
Piano KV 526 and 'Lied der Trennung' KV 519.[10] Brahms
seeks to differentiate the nature of various types of such
progressions. His marginalia show a categorization mainly
according to aesthetic criteria, for example regarding bar 61
of the Sestetto from the second Act of Don Giovanni he
wrote 'NB/Schöne 5' (NB/Beautiful 5ths).

Besides these theoretical studies Brahms was concerned
with the performance of compositions by Mozart, mainly with
the piano concertos, some of which he played in concerts in
the second half of the 1850s. These concerts clearly show a
fundamental change in programme planning compared with
the concerts of the early Hamburg years, especially in presenting piano concertos by Mozart and Beethoven. On the occasion of the Festival commemorating the centenary of
Mozart's birth, which took place in Hamburg on 26 January
1856, Brahms contributed the D minor Concerto KV 466, one
of his favourites since his youth, provided with his own
cadenzas (Kalbeck I 255). Unlike the current fashion he
tended to compose cadenzas more in the style of the concerto
concerned and to keep the modulations in them more in
accord with the movements to which they belonged.[11] Nevertheless, Hamburg taste of that time took them as being rather
'modern' (Kalbeck I 255).

Some piano concertos by Mozart, principally those in G
major KV 453 and A major KV 488, he studied and per-

10 J. Brahms Oktaven und Quinten u.A. ed. from the Nachlass with comments by
   H. Schenker (Vienna 1933); P. Mast 'Brahms's study, Octaven u. Quinten u.A., with
   Schenker's commentary translated' Music Forum 5 (1980) 1–196.
11 cf. P. Badura-Skoda 'Eine ungedruckte Brahms-Kadenz zu Mozarts D-Moll-
   Konzert KV 466' Österreichische Musikzeitschrift 35 (1980) 153–6.

formed with the Princess Friederike of Lippe-Detmold in autumn 1857 and 1858 at the Court of Detmold, acting himself as conductor (*Briefwechsel* V 192, *Schumann-Brahms Briefe* I 239). He recommended to Clara Schumann that she include one or the other of Mozart's piano concertos, which were new to her, in her programmes, mainly the C minor Concerto KV 491. Following Brahms's advice, she played first the G and A major concertos in order to become acquainted with them, at the Court in Detmold at the beginning of February 1861 and then the C minor Concerto with Brahms's cadenza in the same year in concerts on 22 November in Hannover and on 12 December in Leipzig (*Schumann-Brahms Briefe* I 350-1, 353, 383-4, 387). Brahms apparently intended to revive these concertos. To Clara Schumann he wrote (7 February 1861): '. . . one can have no greater pleasure than when these concertos are brought to life' (*Schumann-Brahms Briefe* I 355). This and similar remarks hint at the fact that in the 1850s and early 1860s Mozart's piano concertos were not part of the living Classic-Romantic tradition.

Very little is known about Brahms's performing practice in Mozart's piano works. What Florence May recorded of Brahms's performance of Mozart's Piano Sonata in F major KV 533 seems characteristic however; one of her lessons with Brahms was partly devoted to this piece. In Brahms's opinion Mozart's music had to be played with expression, according to the musical context, which becomes obvious from the notation. Florence May writes: 'He taught me that the music of this great master should not be performed with mere grace and lightness, but that these effects should be contrasted with the expression of sustained feeling and with the use of the deep legato touch . . . "Now," he said, "with expression", and he repeated the first few bars of the subject, giving to each note its place as an essential portion of a fine melody' (May I 17-18).

Just as Brahms in the mid-1850s had initiated the public revival of unknown or little-known works by Mozart mainly through the performance of some of the piano concertos, so, as Artistic Director of the Gesellschaft der Musikfreunde in Vienna from 1872 to 1875, he set about performing some very little-known or completely unknown vocal works, representing novelties for the Vienna of the time. Thus he performed in the first concert on 10 November 1872 the Concerto Aria 'Ch'io mi scordi di te?' KV 505 for soprano with piano obbligato and orchestra, composed in December

1786.[12] On 8 December of the same year Brahms conducted the first performance from the manuscript of Mozart's *Offertorium de Venerabili Sacramento 'Venite populi'* for double four-part chorus and organ, two violins ad libitum (KV 248a = 260), composed in Salzburg in 1776, which he had discovered in Vienna in Köchel's private collection of Mozart's autograph manuscripts. Before the concert, which was performed with his own organ accompaniment, arranged from the figured bass, Brahms had sent this composition (without his organ arrangement) to the publisher J. P. Gotthard in Vienna.[13] Score and parts were published anonymously in February 1873. As in several other cases Brahms wanted this edition published without his name appearing as editor or arranger; this was because he did not consider such a task to be an achievement in any real artistic sense. He simply intended to bring this hitherto unpublished composition by Mozart to the notice of a broader public. The preface of this edition, dated 'Wien d. 18. Nov. 1872' and signed by 'Ludwig Ritter von Köchel' as the owner of the autograph, reads that the edition follows Mozart's manuscript, consisting of two parts, one containing the score of the voice parts and the organ part (under the heading: 'Offertorium de Venerabili (bei Aussetzung des hochw. Gutes) a 2 Chori, di Wolfgango Amadeo Mozart m.p. Salisburgo 1776') the other, in two sheets, the score of the two violin parts (entitled: 'Die Violini ad libitum zu diesen[!] Offertorium Venite Populi etc.'). In the interest of performance some expression marks are supplied, which are included in parentheses, for example the '(f)' at the beginning of the composition (score, page 3). On 25 January 1874 Brahms conducted the cantata 'Davidde penitente' for two sopranos, tenor, choir and orchestra KV 469,[14] composed by Mozart in 1785, which Friedrich Rochlitz in 1807 took as an example of the 'greatness

12 Solo: Frau Wilt, Piano: Julius Epstein, cf. review in *Allgemeine Musikalische Zeitung* VII (1872) col. 773 by F.[ranz] P.[yllemann]. No material is extant from this performance in the Archive of the Gesellschaft der Musikfreunde, Vienna according to information kindly given by Dr Otto Biba.

13 O.E. Deutsch. 'The First Editions of Brahms' *The Music Review* 1 (1940) 270, was mistaken in assuming that Brahms published his organ arrangement. The printed organ voice (Pl. No. J.P.G 379) shows only the figured bass. The present location of Brahms's manuscript of the organ accompaniment, arranged from the figured bass, announced in 'Leo Liepmannssohn. Katalog 232: Zum 7. Mai 1933', p. 5, no. 16, entitled 'Mozart, Offertorium: Venite populi'. from the estate of Samuel de Lange, who played the organ at the first performance, is unknown.

14 Solists: Frau Bettelheim, Frau Wilt, Herr Walter, cf. review in *Allgemeine musikalische Zeitung* IX (1874) col. 93 by F.[ranz] G.[ehring], carried over from *Deutsche Zeitung*. No performance material which could be ascribed to Brahms is extant in the Archive of the Gesellschaft der Musikfreunde, Vienna.

and sublimity of thought' in Mozart's music.[15] An aria from this work was repeated in the concert of 28 February 1875.[16]

III

Besides all this practical activity, Brahms paid particular attention to the sources of Mozart's compositions, not only having close relationship with but also playing an active part in the Mozart research of his time. His own copy of Köchel's *Verzeichniss* (1862) (received from Joachim in 1863 as a Christmas present) (*Briefwechsel* V 19), now in the Archive of the Gesellschaft der Musikfreunde, shows various corrections and additions in his own hand made on the basis of his own extensive knowledge of Mozart's works. These were taken into consideration in Graf Waldersee's second edition (1905) and/or in Einstein's third edition (1937). On the one hand Brahms inserted names of composers for works wrongly ascribed to Mozart by Köchel, for example regarding KV 227 he noted in the margin: 'NB/John Bird.', meaning of course William Byrd, or as regards KV 235: 'NB/Ph. Em. Bach'.[17] In addition he corrected orthographical errors, altering at KV 359 'Silimène' to 'Celimène', following the manuscript (corrected in Köchel 3rd edn), and supplied names of poets, such as '*Gabriele v. Baumberg*' to KV 520, giving the source 'x Wiener Musenalmanach x für 1786.' at the bottom of the page (supplied in Köchel 2nd edn). KV 54 he identified with KV 547, 3 (noted in Köchel 2nd edn). It is not known whether Brahms noted these corrections and emendations for his own purposes alone, whether he passed them on to Köchel, from whose estate they came perhaps to Waldersee, or whether Brahms had sent them directly to the latter. He knew Köchel's own supplements, published in the New Series of the *Allgemeine musikalische Zeitung* (II 1864 col. 493-9, signed L. R. von Köchel) under the title 'Nachträge und Berichtigungen zu v. Köchel's Verzeichniss der Werke Mozart's' (Supplements and corrections to Köchel's Catalogue of Mozart's Works), which he had put into his own copy of

15 *Allgemeine musikalische Zeitung* IX (1806/7) col. 471.
16 R. von Perger and R. Hirschfeld *Geschichte der k.k. Gesellschaft der Musikfreunde in Wien* (Vienna 1912) 305. There is no title given of the Aria in the programme. But by its printed text 'Bei der Stürme brausendem Schmettern' it can be recognized as No. 8: 'Fa l'oscuro ombre funeste' according to the programme. Of this Aria no performance material in connection with Brahms is preserved in the Archive of the Gesellschaft der Musikfreunde, Vienna (information received from Dr Biba.)
17 cf. 2nd edn: 'Anh. V, n. 284b. William Bird', 3rd edn: 'Anh. 109 XII William Byrd (1543-1623)' and 2nd edn: 'Anh. V, n. 284e. Ph. Em. Bach'.

Köchel (between pages 172 and 173). It is quite astonishing and of great interest to observe the detail and erudition of Brahms's musicological work on Mozart.

Brahms approved, in principle, of the collected editions of the works of great masters which began to appear mainly from the 1870s and was appointed as a member of their boards several times. However, he often criticized the practice of such undertakings as not being based on an established plan. In December 1878 he wrote to Clara Schumann: 'Apart from Bach and Handel I do not like any of the collected editions, and regarding Härtel one can observe too much and too often that many interfere, that there is no firm plan or idea. Regarding Chopin for example, the width of print changes for no apparent reason, and complicated things are always printed narrow and simple wide. As regards Mozart, there are still worse things' (Schumann-Brahms Briefe II 162–3). But he mentions no details. He also wrote to Ernst Rudorff on 1 November 1877, that he was 'not particularly enthusiastic about the Editions [of] Handel and Mozart'.[18]

Brahms's profound knowledge of and interest in the manuscripts of Mozart enabled him to participate in the Collected Edition of Mozart's Works as adviser and editor. Ernst Rudorff, editing the 'Concertos for One Wind Instrument with Orchestra' (Series XII), wrote to Brahms on 18 December 1880 for his opinion regarding a corrupt passage in the score of the Rondo of the Second Flute Concerto (KV 314), enclosing a page with his corrections (Briefwechsel III 178–80). To Rudorff's question as to whether this was the right version, Brahms answered after having consulted the manuscript parts extant in the Musikverein in Vienna, that the passage concerned was 'corrected everywhere' except the Flute and Violino I. Brahms regarded it as important to present this passage 'in an altered version in the edition, and freely altered at that', but he stood firm 'not to alter the imitation' (Briefwechsel III 180–1). It is of interest for Brahms's view of Mozart's style, that he wanted the structure of the imitation to be kept and to find the best solution within it, and not, like Rudorff, to alter the structure fundamentally.

In 1876 Brahms undertook the rather difficult task of editing Mozart's Requiem. George Henschel describes the extreme care Brahms dedicated to the edition of this work: 'Then we went together through the full score of Mozart's Requiem, which he had undertaken to prepare for a new edition of that

18 Johannes Brahms Briefwechsel III: Johannes Brahms im Briefwechsel mit . . . Ernst Rudorff ed. Wilhelm Altmann (Berlin ²1912) (hereafter Briefwechsel III) 172.

master's works. I admired the great trouble he had taken in the revision of the score. Every note of Süssmayer's[!] was most carefully distinguished from Mozart's own.'[19] And, to friend Joachim, Brahms wrote (Vienna, 24 May 1876): 'I have just completed a difficult editing job. The Requiem of Mozart. I did not cease looking alternately at the two manuscripts'. The engraver's exemplar of this edition, sent by Brahms to the publisher Breitkopf & Härtel, mentioned in his letter of 22 May 1876 to that firm, is most probably lost. Only Brahms's printed edition, which appeared in May 1877 and his Revisionsbericht (critical report), published only in 1886 are extant.[20]

On the evidence of the two sources of Mozart's Requiem, Mozart's fragmentary manuscript and Süssmayr's completion, Brahms published the composition as a whole, marking in the score the parts by Mozart and Süssmayr with the letters 'M.' and 'S.' respectively. In his Revisionsbericht he gave an account of the basis of his procedures and intentions. He argues that he 'had to present the Requiem in just this way', that he 'could only by an exact presentation of the two manuscripts, in which the work survived, give a true and reliable picture of how Mozart left his work, and how immediately after his death his pupil completed it'. He continues: 'Mozart's manuscript contains the first movement completely and the score draft of movements 2–9, showing also insertions by one or two other hands that have tried to complete the score.' (At first Joseph Eybler had been asked by Constanze Mozart to try to finish the work.) Brahms's Revisionsbericht, formulated in a concise and exact way, makes evident that his edition is based on careful and detailed studies. Brahms set store by rather precise indications as to which parts were contributed by Mozart and which by Süssmayr. Thus, regarding page 57, bar 1 of the edition: 'The four voice-parts and the unfigured bass are by Mozart; the parts for the two violins, the viola and the

19 George Henschel Personal Recollections of Johannes Brahms (Boston 1907) 34.
20 W.A. Mozart's Werke. Kritisch durchgesehene Gesammtausgabe. Serie 24, No. 1: Requiem von W.A. Mozart. Köch. Verz. No. 626. And Mozart's Werke. Revisionsbericht. 'Allgemeine Bemerkungen. Es redigirten: . . . Serie XXIV, Nr. 1 J. Brahms'. These kinds of editorial sources were preserved since publication in the Archives of Breitkopf & Härtel, Leipzig. Nearly the whole collection was destroyed by bombing during World War II, and the greatest probability is that Brahms's engraver's exemplar of Mozart's Requiem KV 626 for Series XXIV, 1 was destroyed as well. There is now nothing to be found either in the Archives of VEB Breitkopf & Härtel, Leipzig, or in the Staatsarchiv Leipzig, to which these kinds of sources were transferred many years ago, nor is there anything to be found in the Archive of Breitkopf & Härtel, Wiesbaden. From information kindly given by Mr Franz Xaver Neumann, archivist of VEB Breitkopf & Härtel, Leipzig and Dr Gerd Sievers in Breitkopf & Härtel, Wiesbaden.

figured bass are additions by Süssmayr.' This applies mainly to passages where Brahms found results contrary to Otto Jahn's description of the manuscripts. Regarding the last six bars on page 27 of the edition, of which Jahn wrote that Süssmayr had 'copied [them] incorrectly', Brahms argued: 'The same hand which completed this passage in Mozart's manuscript has also written the viola part on page 24, bars 5–7 for once better than Süssmayr'. Again Brahms was obviously referring here to the handwriting of Joseph Eybler. The figuring is given as it appears in the manuscripts. As regards the dynamic marks also, Brahms followed the manuscripts strictly with the exception of analogous passages. The trombones are set in small type in passages where the indication 'colla parte' is noted in the manuscript. In this respect Brahms followed the advice of Friedrich Chrysander, whom Breitkopf & Härtel had asked about the use of these instruments.[21] Brahms intended thereby to give the users of the edition, especially conductors interested in Mozart's work, a 'true copy of that noteworthy work and of all its mysteries'. Brahms's Revisionsbericht makes clear that he had studied the manuscript descriptions given by Otto Jahn. Brahms knew Jahn's W.A. Mozart (Leipzig 1856–9) as a whole; this can be seen from his copy, preserved in the Archive of the Gesellschaft der Musikfreunde, which bears the note 'Wien, Weihnacht 1862/Zum 2. Male' (Vienna, Christmas 1862/For the second time). This biography exercised an important influence on musicology in general and on Mozart research in particular in the second half of the nineteenth century, and Brahms went through it more than once.[22] His numerous markings in his copy reflect some of his views on Mozart. They show which parts of the picture given by Jahn of this great composer aroused his interest or corresponded with his own conceptions. Artistic procedures of Mozart are described which Brahms had made his own or which formed part of his outlook on music.

Several cruxes in Jahn's biography can be identified, which seem to have been a focus of Brahms's interest. On the one hand he has marked passages in which the importance of Mozart as a great man and character is stressed, for example his 'ethical integrity' (III 139 n. 13), as well as his greatness as composer. Accordingly Brahms has marked with a blue pencil

21 Johannes Brahms Briefwechsel XIV: Johannes Brahms im Briefwechsel mit Breit-kopf und Härtel . . . ed. Wilhelm Altmann (Berlin 1921) 263.
22 cf. Brahms's letter of 27 November 1883 to Rudolf von Beckerath, in K. Stephenson Johannes Brahms und die Familie von Beckerath (Hamburg 1979) 40.

Haydn's famous letter of December 1787 to Roth in Prague, in which he praises Mozart's outstanding importance: 'If I could only impress on the soul of every friend of music, and on high personages in particular, how inimitable are Mozart's works, how profound, how musically intelligent, how extraordinarily sensitive, for this is how I understand them, how I feel them. . .' (III 312).

On the other hand there are comments by Jahn on Mozart's creative process which were marked by Brahms, and chapter 11 in the third part of the biography attracted his special interest. It deals with 'Mozart's individual way of composing', 'Rough sketches of musical thoughts and modifications of the first conception', 'More elaborated sketches', 'Score drafts' etc. (III viii). Brahms was clearly interested in the procedures and working-methods within the creative process of a genius like Mozart, mainly in the fact that even a genius is not able to compose without diligence and labour; the important thing is, however, that the composition becomes successful and that after its completion the arduous labour and care spent on it are not obvious. Thus Brahms marked a paragraph such as the following:

If invention of genius is a gift from bountiful nature, so art is only a possession, which is achieved with trouble and labour; the strength to work with supreme effort without getting tired, and to make work fruitful, is a privilege of genius. One is doing Mozart wrong in diminishing the status of the truest and most careful diligence, to intensify the astonishment of unwise people; the complete beauty of the accomplished work of art is not proof that no labour had been necessary to create it, but rather proof that it is successful (I 598–9).

Concerning remarks on the creative process and methods of composition, Brahms was interested in passages in which Jahn dealt with fundamental artistic concepts, albeit in relation to Mozart:

The important thing, which no true artist lacks, is the strength to keep the first creative impulse alive with its full energy during the whole course of the inner process and assimilation of artistic ideas, from the first conception to the complete maturation and ripening, through all changes, interruptions and interferences with this development; and to keep by that the idea of the whole in each moment of creation as everywhere the fully efficient and authoritative power for all details of the formal conception. (III 432)

Or again, Brahms marked:

. . . no single motif is of importance for itself or is able to enforce itself; but just as the plant sprouts from a germinating seed-corn, so the musical work of art develops from a basic feeling, the strength of which is strong enough to penetrate completely in each moment all details and to bring them together as a whole ... (I 436)

In addition Brahms was interested in Jahn's discussion of Mozart's self-criticism; how Mozart used to be firm with his compositions and not satisfied with the first draft, and how as a rule he destroyed his preliminary work and studies when a composition was completed. Jahn stresses the fact that, though from the 1770s mostly clean copies of Mozart have survived, it would be wrong to think therefore that Mozart had worked without sketches and studies and without ever having altered a work radically (I 598-9).

A further matter of concern for Brahms were Jahn's remarks on Mozart's instrumentation: '. . . it is sufficient here to say that to observe a moderate use of the total instrumental strength . . . is neither an abstract economy, nor a calculated changing and confrontation of different effects, but is always drawn with a clear view and a careful control of plentiful resources' (II 479).

It is of special importance that Brahms was mostly interested in those passages of Jahn's biography in which the author dealt with questions regarding Mozart's creative process and methods of composition, with general artistic procedures as well as with Mozart's self-criticism and instrumentation – matters in which Brahms likewise was of course personally concerned regarding his own work. He seems to have had no interest in Jahn's rather romantic description of Mozart's compositions except one paragraph on the Symphony in E flat major KV 543 (IV 130), one of his favourites, and also some information on corrections in *Idomeneo* (II 567) and on the libretto of the *Entführung aus dem Serail* (IV 79).

IV

Brahms's view of the genres of instrumental music and also of opera was determined (besides Beethoven's) mainly by Mozart's works. This applies on the one hand to the genre of the symphony. Its most ideal model Brahms saw realized in Mozart's Symphony in G minor KV 550. Mozart's unsurpassable mastery in this work he characterized to Heinrich von Herzogenberg in the following manner: 'all is quite natural, and as if it could not be any other way, nowhere a harsh colour, nothing arbitrarily put on it etc.'[23] He took this symphony as an example of the genre in demonstrating to composition pupils the incomparable scope of Mozart's genius and in stressing the fact that it would be best to draft a composition as a whole, leaving all details to elaboration.[24]

In this respect, Mozart's chamber music, too, was of great importance for him. That Mozart's string quartets of the mature years played an important background role in his creative imagination when composing his own quartets, becomes evident from a letter to his publisher Fritz Simrock (24 June 1869): 'Moreover as Mozart has taken extreme care to write six beautiful quartets [KV 387, 421, 428, 458, 464, 465], we will do our utmost to make one or the other passable. You will get them one day. But if I were publisher today I would stop driving . . .'[25] Obviously Brahms was thinking of Mozart's letter of 1 September 1785 to Haydn, in which Mozart called his six string quartets 'il frutto di una lunga, e laboriosa fattica'.

Brahms retained similar Mozartian background associations with regard to other of his chamber works. In his inscription of a copy of the original edition of his Violin Sonata in G major Op. 78 to the designer Heinrich Groeber, he referred to Mozart as well as to Beethoven by writing on it the incipits of the first movements of the Violin Sonatas in G major of both masters (Beethoven, Op. 96), setting above them the words spoken by the Himmelskönigin (Queen of Heaven) from Faust's 'Verklärung' (Transfiguration) in Goethe's Faust: 'Komm, hebe dich zu höhern Sphären!/Wenn er Dich ahnet, folgt er nach' ('Come, rise to higher spheres!/If he senses, he will follow').[26] In this way Brahms indicated that his Sonata was continuing the tradition of Violin Sonatas by Mozart and Beethoven, even choosing the same key as two notable examples.

That Brahms again had Mozartian chamber music in mind when composing his String Quintet in G major Op. 111 becomes obvious from his remark in a letter to Joachim, after having completed the composition (27 November 1890): 'Now I

23 Johannes Brahms Briefwechsel II: Johannes Brahms im Briefwechsel mit Heinrich und Elisabet von Herzogenberg ed. Max Kalbeck (Berlin [4]1921) 127.
24 Max Kalbeck Johannes Brahms IV (Berlin [2]1915) (hereafter Kalbeck IV) 88 n. 1.
25 Johannes Brahms Briefwechsel IX: Johannes Brahms Briefe an P.J. Simrock und Fritz Simrock ed. Max Kalbeck (Berlin 1917) (hereafter Briefwechsel IX) 75. Brahms's letter is obviously an answer to Simrock's letter of 16 March 1869, in Johannes Brahms und Fritz Simrock. Weg einer Freundschaft. Briefe des Verlegers an den Komponisten ed. K. Stephenson (Hamburg 1961) 50.
26 Max Kalbeck Johannes Brahms III (Berlin [2]1913) 383–4 n. 1.

wish heartily that the piece will please you a little, but do not feel embarrassed to say the contrary. In this case I will console myself with the first [= F major Op. 88] and for both with Mozart's!' Mozart's Clarinet Quintet KV 581, which Brahms heard in Meiningen during March 1891 in an unsurpassable performance by the clarinettist Richard Mühlfeld (Kalbeck IV 224) inspired him to compose a work for the same setting, his Clarinet Quintet in B minor Op. 115.

As we have seen, from early days Brahms had a close affinity with Mozart's piano concertos. In his copy of Köchel's Catalogue the following numbers are underlined in blue pencil: 450, 453, 466, 467, 482, 488, probably in order to mark his favourites. The playing of these concertos 'is like scooping from a real Fountain of Youth' he wrote to Clara Schumann. In the same letter he advised her to play the Concerto in C minor KV 491: 'It is the most effective and also at present new to you' (*Schumann–Brahms Briefe* I 355). In his conversations with Richard Heuberger he called this concerto 'a miracle of art and full of genial inspiration!'[27] Besides this concerto, he also preferred the D minor KV 466, which he recommended to Clara Schumann in June 1878: 'The D minor namely is always respectfully accepted by the public.' The 'Coronation' Concerto (KV 537) however he did not consider as 'one of the most beautiful' (Heuberger 93).

Finally Brahms had a special appreciation for Mozart's contributions to the operatic genre. Besides *Don Giovanni* and *Figaro, Idomeneo* played an important role for him. In his discussions with Heuberger he emphasized: 'Look at *Idomeneo*! In general a miracle and full of freshness, because Mozart was at that time quite young and audacious! What beautiful dissonances, what harmony!' (Heuberger 93). As model for a planned opera he thought, apart from Beethoven's *Fidelio*, of Mozart's *Figaro*.[28] He especially admired the way Mozart overcame difficulties of libretto in this opera. 'Mozart has composed it, not as a mere text, but as a complete, well-organized comedy', he explained to Heuberger, praising the genius and technical mastery (Heuberger 12). But in discussing it with Billroth he chiefly stressed the uniqueness of this opera: '. . . each number in Mozart's "Figaro" is for me a miracle; it is simply incomprehensible how anybody was able to create something

27 R. Heuberger *Erinnerungen an Johannes Brahms* ed. K. Hofmann (Tutzing 1971) 93.
28 Max Kalbeck *Johannes Brahms* II (Berlin ³1921) 171.

of such an absolute perfection, never has anything like this been made, and not even by Beethoven'.[29]

V

Thus Brahms's view of the genres of instrumental music and also of opera is not only determined by the example of Beethoven, as is obvious, but to an important degree also by the imagination in Mozart's works. Brahms had no closer relationship to compositions of Beethoven of certain genres, than he did to those of Mozart. He even made clear qualitative distinctions between Mozart's and Beethoven's compositions, as is already evident from his view of Mozart's *Figaro*, quoted above.

In Brahms's opinion Beethoven's early works could not be compared in quality with Mozart's late works. Current opinion of Beethoven's day – according to Brahms – had done Mozart wrong in underestimating his importance in comparison with Beethoven. This was only due to the fact that Beethoven meant for that time something new, something modern. In Brahms's view this opinion of Beethoven had now to be revised. He exchanged views on this topic in conversation with Heuberger on 23 February 1896:

I understand very well, that the new personality of Beethoven, the new outlook, which people found in his works, made him greater, more important in their view. But fifty years later this judgement has to be altered. The attraction of novelty must be differentiated from inner value. I admit, that the Concerto [= C minor Op. 37] of Beethoven is more modern, but not so important! I am able to understand too, that Beethoven's First Symphony did impress people colossally. In fact, it was the new outlook! But the three last symphonies [= KV 543, 550, 551] by Mozart are much more important! Some people are beginning to feel that now. (Heuberger 93)

Brahms shared Heuberger's view, that the best quartets by Mozart are more substantial than Beethoven's chamber music before about Opus 24, and stated: 'Yes, the Rasumovsky Quartets, the later symphonies, this is a new important world. It had already begun with the Second Symphony.'

Hardly less striking is Brahms's observation on the weaker use of dissonances in Beethoven's music, in comparison with Mozart and J. S. Bach. In his discussions with Heuberger he

29 *Billroth und Brahms im Briefwechsel* ed. O. Gottlieb–Billroth (Berlin and Vienna 1935) 315.

pointed out: 'Dissonances, real dissonances, you will find used much less in Beethoven than in Mozart. Just consider "Idomeneo"!' In comparing Beethoven with his predecessors Brahms made the further point that Beethoven's occasional pieces are second-rate, whereas Haydn and Mozart both continued to compose at speed their very best in such works (Heuberger 93–4).

VI

In the light of such consideration, Brahms became more fully aware of his own historical context. He recognized his own situation in the development of music history as late, compared with the Classical epoch. This fact did not suggest that musical development was coming to an end but that he saw in it a never-ending process, as becomes clear from a letter to Clara Schumann (11 October 1857): 'Who can say that something has reached its goal, when such a goal can never be reached. Small-minded people have wanted to set a full-stop after each genius. With Mozart, if we will name the penultimate' (Schumann–Brahms Briefe I 208). In Brahms's opinion however it was no longer possible for composers to create so many compositions of such power as the masters of the Classic period had done. Specifically by contrast with Mozart, it seems, did Brahms become aware of the difficulty of his own situation as a composer in his own time. He expressed such thoughts more than once, for example in his letter to Simrock from 1869, dealing with his future string quartets cited above, or still more distinctly to Simrock in February 1870:

Stop driving your composers, it could be so dangerous, and it does no good in any case. Composing is not like weaving and sewing. Some honourable colleagues (Bach, Mozart, Schubert) have mischievously over-indulged the world. But if we are not able to write as beautifully as they could, then we must surely in addition protect ourselves from trying to write as quickly as they did. It would also be unfair to accuse us of being lazy. There are various things which make writing difficult for us (my contemporaries) and some things which make writing especially difficult for me. (Briefwechsel IX 92)

His intentions required supreme effort and the concentration of all his powers to create works of validity for the future in a new, personal style oriented on different genres of instrumental music from the Classic epoch (including Mozart). Through his art and with his own particular outlook on music, Brahms was trying to achieve an equally elevated level. There was naturally a discontinuity at first between holding classical ideals and the desire to realize compositions of similar rank in a new age and idiom. With such an artistic ambition it is no wonder that Brahms was forced again and again to counter the driving of his publisher Simrock, evidence of little artistic sense and understanding on the part of this publisher. We recall that Brahms completed his first published string quartets Op. 51 only in 1873 and his first published violin sonata Op. 78 in 1878.

This serves to explicate Brahms's remarks regarding the 'quick writing' and 'rapid completion' of his colleagues in thinking of the swift production of contemporary composers such as Joachim Raff. Brahms's *agens* as a composer wishing to reach the 'very best' makes more understandable the hesitation he had in admitting that a work was completed.[30]

Brahms had a special relationship to Mozart's music in practice, as he did also to the ideals that lay behind it. It and they have an undeniably important part in the formation of his artistic outlook.

30 cf. Brahms's letter of October 1884 to Hans von Bülow, in *Hans von Bülow Briefe und Schriften* ed. M. von Bülow (Leipzig 1907) VII 307.

ROBERT PASCALL

Brahms and the definitive text

With two exceptions (the lost early Violin Sonata in A minor, and the Chorale Preludes Op. 122), every work of his own which Brahms wanted published was published during his lifetime and under his supervision. Because of this it has been and is still widely assumed that the musical texts for the great majority of his works are definitively established.[1] The present study is designed as a challenge to that assumption and as a preliminary general mapping of the areas of difficulty. It is perhaps surprising that the issues involved have not been seriously raised before in Brahms scholarship; and the focussing of attention on them at this juncture must certainly be considered timely, in view of the proposals and discussions concerning a possible new *Brahms Complete Edition*.

It is quite clear that for a large number of Brahms's works, including, for instance, the First Symphony, no definitive text exists in a unified state – albeit because of matters of detail, chiefly to do with performance signs. And the primary reason no definitive text exists in a single copy is that during the publication process deterioration and revision of the text could occur concurrently. Deterioration is simply a matter of normal human error in transcription, whether this be by copyist or engraver; copyists' errors are generally both more substantial and more numerous than engravers' errors, but engravers' errors are just as real. Correction of such deterioration was acknowledged by Brahms also to be inefficient, whether this correction was done by himself, friends, or a publisher's house-editor; and, as evidence adduced below surprisingly suggests, corrections required by a proofreader might not necessarily be made to the plates. For Brahms the last resonances of compositional revision were mixed into

---

1 For example, in the newly appeared *Johannes Brahms, Sinfonie Nr. 1, c-Moll, op. 68 Taschen-Partitur* (Goldmann Schott, Mainz 1981) we read on p. 177: 'Der Notentext der 1. Sinfonie von Johannes Brahms bietet der musikalischen Textkritik keine grundsätzlichen Probleme. (There are no fundamental text-critical problems set by the musical text of the 1st Symphony of Johannes Brahms.)'

publication and its aftermath. Such compositional revision
reached a crisis at proof stage, when the piece in a real sense
escaped from his control into the world – escaped in terms of
distribution and use. But he continued to touch up some compositions after their initial publication, and this gives rise to an
interesting set of problems, which will form the focus of the
closing stages of this study.

When Brahms had completed a fair copy of a work, he
customarily tested it by performance and consultation with
close friends. Copies would already be needed, especially if
the work was for substantial forces. He used copyists throughout his life. The first two piano sonatas were copied, and the
copies used for the printing process as engravers' exemplars;
Op. 122 was being prepared for this process by copying at the
time of Brahms's death. He did not always know the copyists
who worked for him. An unpublished letter he wrote to his
friend Dietrich in January 1854 has: 'You probably still re-
member, that on my departure from Düsseldorf I left the C
major Sonata and several songs at the musician's (flute
player) so-and-so of so-and-so street for copying.'[2] The parts of
the First Symphony were copied mostly in Karlsruhe under the
supervision of the work's first conductor, Dessoff; the parts of
the Fourth were copied in Meiningen under von Bülow's supervision. The copy of the Violin Concerto solo part which served
as engraver's exemplar Joachim had copied in Berlin.[3] But
Brahms did have regular copyists, and we know of his
Viennese copyists Hlawacek and William Kupfer. Brahms
replaced the former by the latter in the early 1880s (on
grounds of age and speed),[4] and, as Kalbeck has shown, Kupfer
became a highly valued colleague in Brahms's later years.[5]
Brahms was not in the habit of copying his own music, apart
from presentation copies of shorter pieces and songs, and he
relied much on copyists, especially in the generation of pre-
publication performance part-sets. The copying of scores
seems to have occurred spasmodically. Thus copyists' scores
were used as engravers' exemplars for the Third Symphony
and the Clarinet Quintet, but Brahms's own autograph for the

2 This letter, now in the Pierpont Morgan Library, also contributes to Brahms-
  chronology; from it may be simply deduced that the song 'Mondnacht' (usually
  assigned to 1854) was finished by the beginning of November 1853.
3 See the review by Linda Correll Roesner of the Facsmile of the Autograph of the
  Violin Concerto in Current Musicology 30 (1980) 60-72.
4 As Brahms wrote to Simrock on 7 November 1883; Johannes Brahms Briefwechsel XI: Briefe an Fritz Simrock ed. Max Kalbeck (Berlin 1919) 38.
5 Max Kalbeck Johannes Brahms IV (Berlin ²1915) 549.

C major Piano Trio and the Fourth Symphony. Large works could have a mixture of copy and autograph used as their engravers' exemplars: the First Symphony was printed from copies of movements 1 and 4 and from the autograph of movements 2 and 3; the Second Symphony from a copy of movement 1 and from the autograph of the remaining movements.

Copyists' parts were also used as engravers' exemplars. Indeed they were often clearly preferred to the alternative of engraving the parts from a score exemplar. Brahms was, of course, always at pains to ensure that the parts and score agreed, and on several occasions asked Simrock's house-editor, Robert Keller, to check the two sources against each other. Brahms had a high respect for Robert Keller's ability in matters of this kind, but nevertheless there are often small differences between parts and score which survive in print, concerning such things as placement of dynamics, crescendos, or presence of staccato marks. Surviving manuscript parts which served as engravers' exemplars are very rare and exist only for four chamber works and the solo part of the Violin Concerto.

Plate 1 shows a copyist's page from a 1st violin part of the First Symphony; it contains bars 268–90 of the Finale. Of the prepublication copyists' parts for this work only three first violin parts, four second violin parts and one viola part survive (none of which were used as engravers' exemplars); these have recently come to light in the Gesellschaft der Musikfreunde, and are of especial interest, since they transmit the otherwise lost initial performing version of the slow movement (which underwent substantial revision just before publication).

The particular violin part from which Plate 1 is taken is numbered IX; and is likely to have some accumulated errors. But just because of such a possibility, it is useful to us in demonstrating a number of characteristic mistakes for copyists working under pressure. Firstly there is the omission of a repeated bar. We also find the following: in line 4, bars 2–3 erroneous bowing marks (the three-quaver groups should all be in one bow each), last bar beats 2–4 omission of staccato marks; in line 6 erroneous extensions of bowing marks backwards to include the crotchets; and in line 7, bar 3 the incorrect placing of 'p dim' (which should be at the beginning of the bar), an incorrect rhythm on beat 4 (which should be ♫.) and the omission of a bowing mark over this beat. In addition there is a staccato mark missing in line 4, bar 1, but this was

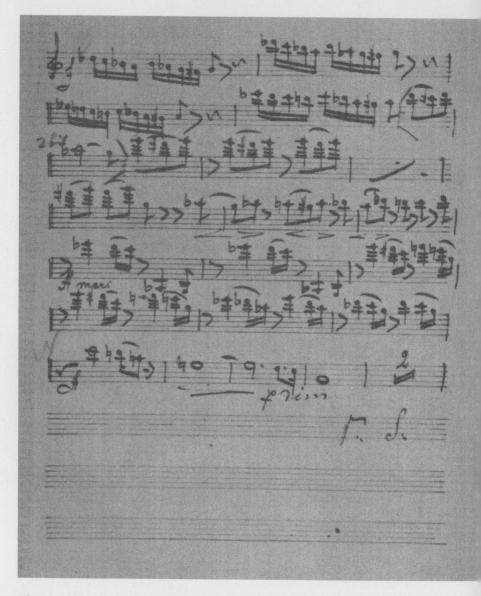

Plate 1 Symphony No. 1 Op. 68, first violin part (No. IX), bars 268–90 of the Finale; manuscript

also missing in the autograph score from which the parts were generated. Not all these errors need be the work of a single copying, for there is clear evidence in this set that parts were copied one from another. What is perhaps surprising to us is that, in a part needed and almost certainly used for performance, the correction is so minimal.

The main engravers and printers of Brahms's music were the firm C. G. Röder of Leipzig. They were leaders in the world of music printing in the latter half of the nineteenth century, and at their height employed some 200 engravers.[6] They produced fine copy, fast; it took them for instance only about six weeks to engrave the score of the Violin Concerto. Most of Brahms's publishers used Röders: Senff, Rieter–Biedermann, Fritzsch, Peters, A. F. Cranz all used them, as did Simrock from 1870 (about the time Simrock was successfully establishing his near monopoly as a Brahms publisher). Breitkopf & Härtel did their own engraving, as did Simrock up until 1870, and Spina (a very minor Brahms publisher) used an engraving firm called Eckel, in Vienna. All this of course becomes important when considering engravers' habits as a criterion for editorial decisions; and this is especially important in cases where no manuscript material survives from before publication.

The autograph of the Andante of the First Symphony (now in the Pierpont Morgan Library, New York) was used as engraver's exemplar, and Plate 2 shows the opening 21 bars of the movement in the Simrock/Röder print which was produced from it. This Plate is reproduced here from Brahms's personal copy of the print (now in the Gesellschaft der Musikfreunde). It proves a highly interesting page from the viewpoint of establishing the existence of uncorrected engravers' errors in Brahms's scores, and we shall discuss it at some length, particularly concentrating on three areas. These three areas, bars 11–13, 17–21 and 4–5, represent three different cruxes for the modern editor.

The dynamic profile in the woodwind bars 11–13 used to read *rf* on the end of 11, *dim* just after the beginning of 12 and *p* at the beginning of 13. It has thus been changed since the autograph, and changed so decisively that this must be Brahms's own proof correction; though it is surely probable he wished the apex of the crescendo *on* the strong beat rather than after it. In the absence of any surviving proof copy, the criteria for the deduction that we are indeed dealing with a

6 William Gamble *Music Engraving and Printing* (London 1923) 85.

64

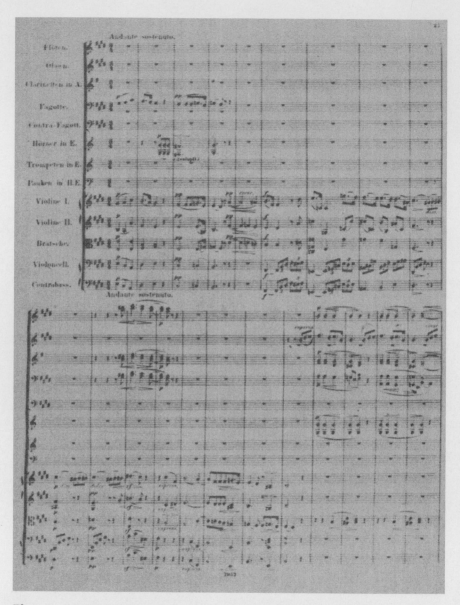

Plate 2   Symphony No. 1, personal copy (*Handexemplar*), page 27

proof correction are: the radicality, consistency and musical sense of the change.

In bars 17–21 of the autograph the crescendo–diminuendo hairpins in the accompanying instruments begin on the second beats of the bars 17 and 19, apex at the subsequent bar-lines, and the diminuendos occur during the first beats of the following bars. This is quite clear and musically significant. Only the flute diminuendo in bar 21 has a slight left shift in its placement on the page, and the horn crescendo in bar 20 is a little short; but the standardizations required are obvious. And there is no possible explanatory justification for the random mess the engraver has made of the performance signs of the whole passage; the flute, bassoon and horn parts in particular seem very far from the exemplar. There is no difficulty in deciding that here we are dealing with engravers' error, and the criteria for our deduction are: the arbitrariness, inconsistency and lack of musical significance of the changes.

This was clearly a difficult page to engrave, for conditions are extremely cramped; yet the making of the actual signs is not nearly as careful as in some other Brahms scores (for instance, the Second Symphony). Examination of the hairpins in the Andante of the First Symphony as a whole, under magnification, reveals that this engraver had real problems in making hairpins. He had special difficulty at the points, and the two lines frequently meet before the end of one of them, or cross, or sometimes they do not meet at all. The apertures and finishings of lines at the open ends are frequently irregular. The apertures of double hairpins are not consistently aligned. There is occasionally a 'ghost-subtention' of one of the lines before the solid initiation, where he made a false start or end. And sometimes the lines are crooked.

It may be argued that changes of the kind shown in bars 17–21 did not matter to engravers; hairpins could expand, contract and shift according to purely graphic/manual criteria within a wide equivalence system. And it has to be argued, at least in this particular case, that the changes did not greatly matter to Brahms, since either he did not notice them, or he did not consider them important enough to warrant revision. (The proof copy of Brahms's piano-duet arrangement of the Second Symphony, to be discussed further below, *does* however show some emendation of crescendos by Brahms.) It is surely clear that, whatever the engraver or Brahms may have thought of such changes as are contained in bars 17–21, these changes certainly matter to modern editors, scholars and performers.

Either our modern editions of Brahms are antiquarian, seeking chiefly what was issued to the world under his name with all its accumulated error, or they should make an attempt to establish a text free from error, representing the conception of the composer in his chosen notations. The modern editor's task seems clear: where an engraver is not simply standardizing (that is, clarifying Brahms's manuscript indications) an editor must prefer Brahms's manuscript reading.

It may further be argued that such changes were not significant to engravers, publishers or Brahms himself because they make little musical difference. Those inclined to take this line should be referred to the opening of the Finale of this symphony. Here in bar 2 the initial '*fp*' is followed by a crescendo, which in the autograph (not used as engraver's exemplar) begins on beat 3, but which in the print has been extended backwards to follow the '*fp*' immediately, at least in some instruments, for there is inconsistency. The two versions here surely show a difference of musical substance; not only are beats 1–3 quiet according to the autograph version, but the crescendo when it does come is in a sense more telling, without being quite so large.

Such printers' distortions are sometimes difficult to uncover, because they may be surrounded by legitimate improvements. And this leads to consideration of the third area of attention on page 1 of the Andante: bars 4–5. In the autograph Brahms began the string crescendo only at the beginning of bar 5, going to the trouble of deleting an overrun of his pen in the second violin part. The print has the crescendo beginning on bar 4, last beat. The modern editor, scholar or performer wonders whether he has to do with a Brahms proof correction or a characteristic engraver's error, and cannot decide on criteria of consistency and musical sense (for both versions fulfil these criteria). It seems very strange that an engraver would ignore the deletion; yet he did. There is no sign of alteration to the printed crescendos; all three are made with two lines only, as are all hairpins on this page, and show no elongation of the point. Further, the viola bowing mark here was added at proof (for it is not in the autograph) and is in consequence slightly squeezed in; it was thus added after the crescendos had been finalized.

Parts and/or arrangements can sometimes assist in making a decision between proof revision and engraver's error in a score. But the use of the score as engraver's exemplar for the parts (as happened in the Andante of the Symphony) can nullify this possible assistance. And differences in layout can often vitiate the assistance; for instance, the autograph (engraver's exemplar) and the print of the piano duet arrangement of the Andante has the last beat of bar 4 well occupied by a large *pp* sign, which forces the crescendo to begin at the earliest just on the bar-line. (In any case the piano cannot make a crescendo during this held chord.)

This lengthy investigation of page 1 of the Andante has surely established uncorrected engraver's error as a reality for this work, and hence a possibility for all others. The inconsistency of performance signs on page 1 of the print of the Third Violin Sonata for instance is further confirmation. Clearly such a complex score as a symphony represents a high risk in this regard, and the amount of error in a song or piano intermezzo, if it exists at all, is usually rather small. Examples so far have not included note error (these are, in any case, usually non-controversial). There were four note-errors in the First Symphony print as a whole, two of which were later spotted by Brahms, and corrected in subsequent issues; the remaining two are incorrect accidentals. Other characteristic engravers' errors are: omission of staccato marks, or their confusion with accents, omission of dynamic marks, and the misplacing of a note on the stave by an interval of a third.

Improvement by correction at proof stage was not necessarily or customarily 100% efficient. Brahms himself seems to have been an erratic proofreader. It was his habit to correct proofs of his music, though not always to include part-proofs, which he then left to the publishing firm. The first issue of the Third Symphony is an appalling example of bad proofreading; this issue was so erroneous that three months following publication, after a major reading by Robert Keller, Simrock issued a correction list running to some 52 corrections of the score and 225 corrections of the parts. Yet the proof copy of the Second Symphony arranged for piano duet shows many corrections by Brahms to phrasing and performance signs, often simply changing phrase or staccato marks from one side of the notes to the other – surely a fastidious sort of correction. And the proof of the Motet, Op. 74 No. 2 shows him changing punctuation in the prefatory text. He used to request proofs 'in exemplarmässigem Zustand' (like the final product) in order to facilitate a piano run-through, and where he found much error he often asked for a second proof, to be read by himself and/or Keller. Improvement by compositional emendation at proof stage is of the highest importance, for Brahms regarded this stage as the culmination of his finalizing process. The proof of Op. 74 No. 2 shows an emendation removing consecutive octaves between alto and tenor; and there are a number of other proof-correction cases involving such removal. For the Violin Concerto he planned a holiday with Joachim to coincide with the proofreading, thinking only then to fix the readings of certain passages. Since the archives of Simrock and Röder were both destroyed in the last war, proof copies of Brahms's music are very rare indeed.[7] But one may of course deduce proof changes by comparing engraver's exemplar and print, and where there is a significant change one is able to discount engraving error. And the proof changes for the Fourth Symphony were recorded in the autograph engraver's exemplar.[8]

The surviving proof copy of Brahms's arrangement for piano duet of his Second Symphony deserves a study to itself, and extensive comment within the general mapping of problems offered here is clearly inappropriate. This copy is important firstly because it contains so many marks; there are 62 pages of notes, and Brahms's own corrections on 54 of those pages. Secondly, it takes a position in what seems, in the present state of knowledge, to be a string of documents rarely preserved: an autograph, a copyist's manuscript which served as engraver's exemplar, the proof, and (of course) the print. Unfortunately the second proof, which we know was pulled, from evidence in correspondence, is lost. And thirdly, there are fifteen places where Brahms has emended this present proof and his emendations have not been taken into the print. One of these, on page 55, involves an alteration of notes – a redistribution of parts between the hands of the primo player, and an alteration of one note value (see Example 1). Some

Ex. 1   Op. 73, arrangement for 4 hands 1 pf., Primo, last movement, bars 258–9 (a) as printed (b) the ignored proof-correction

7 The proof of the Second Symphony in its arrangement for piano duet is in the Gesellschaft der Musikfreunde; that of the Motet Op. 74 No. 2, in a private collection in Nottingham.
8 *Johannes Brahms 4. Symphonie in e-Moll Op. 98 Faksimile* (Eulenburg, Adliswil-Zürich 1974).

others are of lesser importance, involving the repositioning of slurs above or below notes. Either there was a lack of understanding or sympathy for these corrections of Brahms's (perhaps because the work entailed in some of them seemed so great for the gain involved, in what was, after all, an arrangement), or there was a financial constraint of some kind imposed by the publisher. Without the second proof, or some decisive written evidence, we cannot know the full story – for instance, whether Brahms was persuaded to change his mind; but this remains a highly significant matter, which should be a topic for future investigations.

In the Gesellschaft der Musikfreunde there are 39 bound volumes of Brahms's own printed copies of all his published works. They were bound after their reception in the Gesellschaft on Brahms's death, and include the *Sonatensatz* (publ. 1906) and Op. 122. The ordering follows in a broad way that of the subsequent *Complete Edition*. A number of the copies are clean, including 36 opus-numbered works; but many have annotations in pencil or crayon. Alterations of musical substance to the texts are to be found in the following categories: (i) changes of notes; the biggest of these is a ten-bar cut in *Rinaldo* Op. 50, the smallest a one-note change in the First Cello Sonata Op. 38, (ii) changes of scoring, in the Second Serenade and the Fourth Symphony, (iii) changes of time signature, in three works from C to ¢ , in one from ¢ to C, (iv) changes of tempo indications, in six works, (v) expression marks added or altered, also in six works, and (vi) phrasing marks added or revised.

These personal copies (*Handexemplare*) have mostly been considered as providing evidence only of improvement to the text, in accordance with a blanket application of the theory: *die Fassung letzter Hand*.[9] But they were Brahms's personal copies, for private use, and may include marks which do not improve the public version of the text at all. There may be experiment not intended for incorporation into the text; two clear cases of this will be presented below. There may be tampering by others; at least three other hands have marked these volumes (Mandyczewski, who for instance corrected Op. 24 and Op. 35 according to the autograph he had seen; an unknown conductor of the Third Symphony; and an unknown bass singer of Op. 112; there is also a wierd analyst of Op. 103 No. 11 who is looking for four-bar phrases in a piece con-

9 Georg von Dadelsen 'Die "Fassung letzter Hand" in der Musik', *Acta Musicologica* 33 (1961).

structed initially in six- and seven-bar phrases). And they may include emendation so removed from the main creative thrust, that we should be led to the description of a separate version (as, for instance, in the removal of expression marks in his Op. 3 Songs, when they were reissued in 1882); a problem here of course is that it is often difficult to attach a date to the personal copy entries, for Brahms himself did not do so. The personal copy may omit corrections made by Brahms in subsequent editions. Further, these are not the only copies of his music which he marked. The Hofmann Collection in Hamburg has, for instance, a copy of the Third Symphony, first issue, which Brahms gave to Mandyczewski in June 1884. This has correction marks by both Brahms and Mandyczewski, and some of Brahms's are at variance with the text as delivered by the Vienna personal copy. The Hofmann Collection also has a copy of the Song 'Dein blaues Auge' Op. 59 No. 8, with a new vocal part, to suit the voice of Gustav Walter.

Brahms had a more public and decisive way of revising his music after publication, and that was to write to his publisher (or, possibly, printer) directly, and request a revision of the plates. He did this three times for the First Symphony, for instance.[10] And in 1890, fully 20 years after its publication, he altered the Alto Rhapsody in the following terms:

In my Alto Rhapsody I am constantly irritated by a silly slip which still remains. I don't know how it crept in or stuck there, but can it be altered conveniently? At the close, score p. 38 and 39 the alto ought to read:

er-quik - ke sein   Herz,   er - quik - ke   sein

Pauses and *f. dim* 39.1 are missing in the tenor, also ⏤ ⏥ (as in the bass). Before the next *a* the natural sign is quite superfluous and p. 39 second bar the ties in the horns are wrong, thus:

10. 23 November 1877, December 1877 and 19 December 1878. See *Johannes Brahms Briefwechsel X: Briefe an P. J. Simrock und Fritz Simrock* ed. Max Kalbeck (Berlin 1917) 58, 61, 100.

Please alter the voice also in the vocal score. You see, when one cor-
rects a mistake in a Simrock edition – there are 12 more lying next
to it.[11]

Particularly worthy of note from our viewpoint is his delay in
writing, his diffidence in suggesting the alterations, and his
lack of surprise at the other errors he has uncovered.

Plates could, it seems, easily be emended, and that without
announcing a new edition; and they were. Brahms even suggested that few scores should be drawn on the initial print-
run of the Second Symphony to allow more mistakes to surface.
However, Brahms's correspondence with Simrock does not
survive in a complete state, and his correspondence with
Röder (if indeed there was ever very much) hardly survives at
all. He also wrote directly to Robert Keller, but none of this
correspondence is published, and although a few letters have
recently come to light in America, scholars are presently being denied access.* Here we have a clear growth-point for
research: the task is to identify, describe and exemplify the
different states of the text in the edition. Issues from around
1897 off the original plates should play an important part in
this as delivering one version of *die Fassung letzter Hand* to be
considered. Dating later issues is a difficult matter, but can be
done from advertisements, provided these were printed inte-
grally with the note-text (wrappers could of course be printed
separately) and from significant listings of agencies on title
pages.

Of course, some works of Brahms's went through second
editions during his lifetime and were announced as revised by
the composer. The first of these was the A major Serenade Op.
16, first published in 1860 and issued in a revised edition in
1876 on Brahms's initiative. For this second edition it had
undergone a major review of the dynamic profile, carrying
with this also some scoring changes. And in 1888 Simrock
bought up Brahms's works which had been published earlier
by Breitkopf & Härtel (Opp. 1–4, 7–11, 24 and 29–31). Simrock
invited Brahms to emend these compositions, and this he did in
the cases of the piano works; also from this invitation grew the
recomposition of the Piano Trio Op. 8.

In the light of all this public activity, we must reconsider the
marks in the personal copies and establish a different cate-

11. *Johannes Brahms Briefwechsel XII: Briefe an Fritz Simrock* ed. Max Kalbeck
    (Berlin 1919) 30 (a letter to Simrock, postmarked 12 October 1890).

*   While this was true at the time of writing, it is now fortunately no longer the case:
    these letters were acquired in the summer of 1982 by the Library of Congress,
    Washington DC.

gorization, one which can also serve as the basis of an editorial methodology for dealing with them. This will be a sevenfold categorization, in two broad groups; the first three categories are editorially dead, the subsequent four editorially significant, requiring active responses. The seven categories are as follows.

(i) Marks in a hand other than Brahms's. The assigning of marks to this category is usually straightforward, for Brahms had a distinctive hand. But doubt must hang over some phrasing marks, for example some of those in the personal copy of the Second Symphony.

(ii) Marks which are performance indications, increasing visibility or accentuating some feature, but which do not change the musical text of the work. Brahms characteristically used blue crayon to make printed marks more visible to himself on the conducting rostrum. An example is to be found on the last page of the first movement of the Second Symphony (page 28). A large blue double hairpin in the last three-and-a-half bars of the upper system, together with the word 'Horn' also in blue crayon in the right-hand margin alongside, does not correct anything; it serves to mark a general crescendo and diminuendo in strings and woodwind, followed by an entry of the horns at the beginning of the next system, where the horn parts are then bracketed (again in blue crayon). Clearly performing experience can generate marks which are editorially active (for instance, changes of phrasing for a specific performance, fingerings in some piano music), and these marks would then properly belong in other, subsequent, categories.

(iii) Marks which record an experimental reading. (The personal copy becomes a sketch-book.) The last page of the first movement of the Second Symphony again provides an example. Here we see him shifting, in graphite pencil, the offbeat chords on the woodwind in bars 509–12 (inclusive) onto their preceding strong beats. He has annotated the emendation in the left-hand margin 'NB?' The pencil alterations to the music are very light and may have been partially erased. The emendation was never taken into an edition by Brahms. Another example of an experimental reading may be found in the Romanzen aus L. Tiecks Magelone Op. 33, Song No. 3 'Sind es Schmerzen'. On page 21 of the Rieter–Biedermann edition, at the change back to C time, Brahms experimented with a different melodic line for the first four vocal bars. This is again in graphite pencil and has '?NB' noted twice in the right-hand margin; under the upper of these '?NB' notes appears the word 'richtig'. But, apart from a slight suggestion of erasure in bar 1 of the pencilled suggestion, there is no indication which of the two very different versions, printed and pencil, is indeed the right one. However, we know from Brahms's correspondence with the firm of Rieter–Biedermann in 1894–5 that it is the printed version which, after much vacillation, is the true *Fassung letzter Hand.*[12] The editors of the *Complete Edition* unfortunately took the pencil version, which is the text we know today. And this is of course a strong editorial lesson that the personal-copy marks are indeed to be treated in conjunction with available correspondence. A further example which, in my view, should be placed in this category of experiment is the alteration of two minims to staccato crotchets in the first movement of the Violin Concerto; there is strong evidence of attempts at erasure in the personal copy. But this alteration also was taken into the old *Complete Edition.*

(iv) Marks which are corrections of printers' errors, whether or not these were notified by Brahms to the publishers. Some of these are clearly corrections (for instance, where accidentals have been omitted), others – where both versions are musically satisfactory – need reference to pre-publication materials, and yet others – where no pre-publication materials exist (as in the First Cello Sonata Op. 38) – cannot be distinguished from post-publication compositional improvements.

(v) Marks resulting from the impulse of a new projected edition. (The personal copy becomes a manuscript.) The marks in the Piano Trio Op. 8 version 1 show the inception of version 2. The marks in the Second Serenade Op. 16 – the most colourful of all the personal copies – record the major revision of dynamic profile and scoring which Brahms carried out for the second edition; and it probably served as the engravers' exemplar.

(vi) Marks showing compositional improvement which were consolidated by an emendation of the plates at Brahms's instigation, by letter to Simrock, Keller or Röder (or their equivalents in other publishing houses). An example here is the alteration of the tempo mark Brahms made in the coda of the first movement of the First Symphony, from 'Poco Sostenuto' in the first issue, to 'Meno Allegro'. (Brahms thereby brought the coda into a closer relationship with the main body of the movement, rather than keeping a relationship with the slow introduction – which, incidentally, he had not spotted

12 *Johannes Brahms-Briefwechsel XIV: Johannes Brahms im Briefwechsel mit Breitkopf und Härtel, Bartolf Senff, J. Rieter-Biedermann*... ed. Wilhelm Altmann (Berlin 1921) 410, 414, 416.

before publication.) He made this change by letter in December 1878.

(vii) Marks recording private improvements, not consolidated by Brahms in alteration to plates or attempted alteration. The first movement of the Third Violin Sonata provides an example. The printed version and the pencilled emended version are given in Example 2, a and b respectively.

Ex. 2   Op. 108, first movement, bars 48–52 (a) as printed by Simrock
           (b) the alterations to the LH in the personal copy

There is of course a major change of musical substance involved to the second subject of the movement here. Although it may not look a large emendation, five- or six-note spread chords take much longer to play than three-note spread chords; and the rhythmic effect of the passage is much changed. In this work there is no written confirmation in the correspondence consolidating the change, nor does any available subsequent issue prior to the *Complete Edition* carry the emendation.

Clearly here we have an opportunity for editorial discretion to operate. On the one hand there is the edition as published by Brahms, as given by him to the world. On the other there is a private emendation, not an experiment, carrying *die Fassung letzter Hand*. In the light of Brahms's reluctance as a correspondent (though he wrote an enormous number of letters) and in the light of the manner of his revision of the *Alto Rhapsody*, quoted above (which is clearly very significant), we should have no reservations about editions which take Brahms's private emendations into their publications.

The categorization of the personal-copy marks offered here is hard to apply, and the resolution of all marks into one or other of the categories will, I think, not prove possible in the present state of knowledge. But the usefulness of the categorization may be tested on a problematic marking in the Andante of the First Symphony which is shown in Plate 2 – the additional oboe phrasing in bars 17 and following. This cannot be regarded as simply a reinforcement of *espress* because it is more particular; it is therefore not a mark in category ii. This is not a correction of a printer's error (category iv), or the record of a subsequent emendation to the print (category vi), nor was it inspired by a projected new edition (category v). Therefore, if it is in Brahms's hand, it belongs to categories iii or vii, and is an experimental reading or a private emendation.

Although the blue crayon is characteristic of Brahms, the nature of the mark does not initially look Brahmsian. But the uncharacteristic marginal squiggle is in fact the beginning of a highly characteristic Brahms mark, which has been almost wholly cropped in binding; it is the beginning of his favourite 'NB'. And the entry is certainly in Brahms's hand. From the bold writing in blue crayon, which does not of course erase so well as pencil, and the (assumed) absence of a query mark, we are surely right to deduce that this is not an experimental reading. And from the writing also, we can be reasonably certain Brahms did not make the mark on the conductor's rostrum itself, though the mark was probably generated by performance exigencies – perhaps some oboist being too detached with the notes.

Brahms could not really make up his mind about the marking of this most important passage. In the sketch for the movement,[13] legato slurs occur only over the notes in the second half of bars 18 and 20, a marking preserved in the return of the passage in bars 90–4 of the print. This phrasing is compatible with the marking in Brahms's piano-duet arrangement of the movement, where the legato slurs are preserved for the notes in the second half of bars 18 and 20, while the ascending notes in bars 17 and 19 carry legato slurs over staccato dots. By the time of the revised score prepared as engraver's exemplar, Brahms had decided on the simple marking *espress*. His later view, encapsulated in blue crayon in his personal copy, falls into the category of private improvement, and has its place in future editions of the symphony.

13 Private collection USA, photograph in Pierpont Morgan Library, New York.

GEORGE S. BOZARTH

Synthesizing word and tone: Brahms's setting of Hebbel's 'Vorüber'

The past decade and a half has witnessed a proliferation of studies on compositional process. Focussing for the most part on nineteenth-century composers, for with them the extant evidence tends to be more plentiful, scholars have produced a spate of papers, articles and dissertations in their effort to reconstruct the genesis of individual compositions and establish the general working procedures of composers from Beethoven and Schubert, through Rossini, Mendelssohn, Schumann and Chopin, to Verdi and Wagner, Debussy and Mahler, Schoenberg and Webern. Conspicuously absent from this list is Johannes Brahms. Hampered by the lack of an up-to-date source catalogue, discouraged by the scant source information in the Mandyczewski-Gál collected edition (Breitkopf & Härtel, 1926–8), and failing to challenge the traditional view that study of Brahms's compositional process was rendered impossible by his destruction of most of the relevant sources, scholars have long avoided venturing into this territory. It is indeed true that seldom can the scholar fully reconstruct the compositional history of a work by Brahms, for few sketches and drafts survive and the vast majority of his autographs and other primary sources disclose only the final, smaller-scale polishing of works. Still, as a number of recent studies, including some contributions to this volume, bear witness,[1] significant moments in the growth

1 On Brahms's symphonic music, see Robert Pascall 'Brahms's First Symphony, slow movement: the initial performing version' Musical Times 122 (1981) 664-7; on his chamber music, see Ernst Herttrich 'Johannes Brahms, Klaviertrio H-Dur, Opus 8: Frühfassung und Spätfassung: Ein analytische Vergleich' in Musik, Edition, Interpretation: Gedenkschrift Günther Henle ed. Martin Bente (Munich 1980); James Webster 'The C sharp minor version of Brahms's op. 60' Musical Times 121 (1980) 89-93; and the forthcoming work of Flynn Warmington on the Piano Quartet in G minor Op. 25 and other chamber works; on his songs and sketches, see my own papers and forthcoming publications, including Three Lieder on Poems by Adolf Friedrich von Schack, A Facsimile with Commentary (Washington, D.C. 1983) and The Sketches and Drafts of Johannes Brahms, A Facsimile with Transcriptions and Commentary (Vienna).

of a number of works are visible in the primary sources, and scholars should no longer hesitate to seek them out for study.

The present essay will discuss the compositional history of the word–tone synthesis Brahms achieved in his song 'Vorüber', the seventh of the *Lieder und Gesänge* Op. 58 (published in 1871), a little-known yet masterful setting of an intensely melancholy lyric-poem by the great mid-nineteenth-century dramatist Friedrich Hebbel (1813-63).[2] Beginning with a discussion of the reasons why Brahms chose to set this poem to music, an issue first raised by Max Kalbeck in his monumental biography of Brahms, this study will proceed to a detailed examination of the three extant versions of this song, two of which are found in sketches preserved in the Brahms estate at the Gesellschaft der Musikfreunde in Vienna (A 119), the third, the reading of the autograph manuscript, now in the Whittall Collection at the Library of Congress, Washington, DC.

Brahms's choice of Hebbel's 'Vorüber' puzzled Max Kalbeck:

The eight songs of Opus 58. . . stem from [1868 and before, the period of the first two Daumer cycles – the *Liebeslieder Walzer* Op. 52, and the *Lieder und Gesänge* Op. 57]; two of them, Nos. 7 and 2 ('Ich legte mich unter den Lindenbaum' [= 'Vorüber'] and 'Während des Regens') appear fragmentarily on the sketch sheets for the *Liebeslieder*. In contrast to the exclusive character of Op. 57, a lively, mixed company bustles about in Op. 58; poems of both light and serious character set it in motion . . . [yet] one would scarcely notice any of them had Brahms not set them to music, least of all the two poems taken from the cycle *Ein frühes Liebesleben* of Hebbel [Brahms's 'In der Gasse', and 'Vorüber', Op. 58 Nos. 6 and 7]. They are executed entirely in the style of Heine, [yet] without attaining the gracefulness of their model, and their point flashes not like a bolt from the blue, as does Heine's, but rather grows cold as the result of protracted and dull thought-processes which still betray in their expression the labour of their origin. [How] prosaic . . . the remark in 'Vorüber' that 'der süsseste Traum auch lange genug währte' (the sweetest dream lasted quite

2 For an accurate edition of this song, see the one by Eusebius Mandyczewski originally published in the *Johannes Brahms Sämtliche Werke* (Leipzig 1926) *XXIV* 126f., and recently reissued in *Johannes Brahms Complete Songs for Solo Voice and Piano* (New York 1979) II 126f. Only minor adjustments need be made to this edition, of which the most important are the addition of '*pp*' in the piano at bar 9, beat 4.5 (present in the Library of Congress autograph), of '*p*' in the piano at bar 25, beat 1 (present in all primary sources), and, possibly, of arpeggiation signs in the left hand on the third beats of bars 20 and 37 (present in the autograph).

long enough), [and how] dreadfully stilted and almost unintelligible
is the construction at the end of this poem: 'Und welk bedeckt mich
das Laub; doch leider noch nicht wie am dunklern Ort, verglühte
Asche der Staub'. Anxiously one looks about for the subject of the
sentence, perceives with shame that he has confused an adjective
with a verb, and at last discovers, slightly edified, that the poet
wanted to say: 'mich bedeckt welkes Laub, ich wollte es wäre der
Staub des Grabes, der die verglühte Asche meines Herzens
bedeckt' (wilted leaves cover me; I wish it were the dust of the
grave, which covers the ashes of my heart, which have ceased to
glow). How Brahms was inclined to make a song of this obstinate
text, how he wished to elevate this prose to poetry and to forge
[this] word construction into a decree of fate in order to produce
a . . . song, is worthy of wonder . . . the sobbing song of the
nightingale in 'Vorüber' was . . . placed in the accompaniment
and holds our attention so powerfully with the dissonant notes of
its sad chords that we can by no means take pleasure in him 'lange
genug', and the opposite is heard from that which the all-too-
satisfied poet says. Through the repetition of 'der währte' (which
lasts) the composer has given to the song of the bird that length by
which the poet shortened it. The ending, however, is saved by the
climbing of the melody, which must struggle through to the final
passage by means of extremely dense harmonies on the dominant
of F; with fatalistic urgency it sinks down onto the home key in order
to die out with the pointed words 'der Staub' (the dust).[3]

These are serious accusations indeed; in sum, Kalbeck is
maintaining that Brahms not only chose a poem of poor quality,
but also set it, either knowingly or unwittingly, in a manner
that contravenes the poet's intent, perhaps in an attempt to
cover up some of the poem's deficiencies.

In its final published form, the poem in question reads as
follows (see the Appendix for the earlier versions of this
poem):

Ich legte mich unter den Lindenbaum,   1
  In dem die Nachtigall schlug,
Sie sang mich in den süssesten Traum,
  Der währte auch lange genug.

Denn nun ich erwache, nun ist sie fort,   5
  Und welk bedeckt mich das Laub,
Doch leider noch nicht, wie am dunklern Ort,
  Verglühte Asche der Staub.

What is immediately apparent from perusal of this poem is
that Kalbeck, despite his self-confessed labours, has still not

3   Max Kalbeck *Johannes Brahms* II (Berlin [2]1910) 374ff.

achieved an accurate prose version, which, rendered quite literally, should read:

I lay down under the linden tree,
    in which the nightingale sang;
It sang me into the sweetest dream,
    which lasted quite long enough.

For now I awaken, now it [the nightingale] is gone,
    and withered leaves cover me,
But unfortunately not yet, as in the darker place,
    dust [covers] ashes that have ceased to glow.

The reasons for Kalbeck's problems with the second stanza are easy enough to discern. To begin with, his punctuation is incorrect: a comma, not a semicolon, follows 'das Laub', and another comma separates 'doch leider noch nicht' from 'wie am dunklern Ort'. The error in line 7 stems from Brahms; this comma is missing from the Library of Congress autograph and all subsequent sources, including the *Handexemplar* (personal copy) of the first edition (Gesellschaft der Musikfreunde, Vienna) and the manuscript engraver's models for both the original-key and the transposed edition (Brahms Archiv, Staats-und Universitätsbiliothek, Hamburg). The substitution of semicolon for comma at the end of line 6, however, is more difficult to explain. All primary musical sources I have seen contain a comma here, yet I suspect that one of the later editions, issued during Brahms's lifetime or shortly thereafter, but not necessarily controlled by him, may have introduced the semicolon; this variant punctuation is also present in Mandyczewski's edition of the song for the *Johannes Brahms Sämtliche Werke* (published in 1926, *after* Kalbeck's biography), and Mandyczewski's editions of songs were often inadvertently influenced by very late editions. Whatever the pedigree of these errors, though, their effect is to mask the syntactical parallel between lines 5–6 and 7–8, a construction which Hebbel had also employed in stanza 1, for the sake of simplicity and unity, and on which he quite reasonably relied when he omitted the redundant word 'bedeckt' from the last line (the parallels in stanza 2 were even clearer in the original version of the poem, where line 6 read 'und mich bedeckte das Laub'; cf. the Appendix). Surely adding to Kalbeck's confusion over these lines was his interpretation of this poem as a lament for lost love. There is no support for such a specific interpretation; *Weltschmerz*, not a thwarted affair of the heart, is the cause of the poet's anguish. Very likely Kalbeck was misled by his misattribution of this poem to Hebbel's poetic cycle *Ein frühes*

Liebesleben,[4] his incorrect placement of the composition of this song in the same period as Brahms's *Liebeslieder Walzer* Op. 52,[5] and possibly even the presence of 'Vorüber' amidst a number of settings of poems about love in Op. 58. Unfortunately, his erroneous interpretation has been reiterated and compounded as recently as the early 1970s, when one writer, in his zeal to relate Brahms's songs to his relationship with Clara Schumann, asserted without reservation that 'Vorüber' 'is about a broken love-affair . . . no doubt a memory of Clara was in mind; and most of these sad solo songs, as we know from the letters, were sent to her in manuscript'.[6]

As for Kalbeck's remarks on the fourth line of the first stanza, surely one must credit a poet of the stature of Hebbel at the time he wrote 'Vorüber' (1861) with meaning something more than a prosaic remark that the nightingale had sung long enough to satisfy him. If this was all he intended, then why does stanza 2 begin '*Denn nun ich erwache*'? It is clear, I think, that Hebbel deployed the closing line of stanza 1 to act as a *Stimmungsbrechung*, simply but forcefully to call for the end of the false dream-state and to begin the move back into the somber realm of reality. For a moment, when he likens 'Vorüber' to the poetry of Heine, Kalbeck seems to be on the right track, but he employs this comparison only to deride Hebbel. One must wonder whether Kalbeck has made a mistake common among musicians discus-

4 As noted in the Appendix to this article, 'Vorüber' first appeared in print in the periodical *Orion* in 1863 and was never part of either the original *Ein frühes Liebesleben* cycle of the 1842 *Gedichte* or the expanded cycle which appeared in later editions of Hebbel's poems. On the other hand, the poem 'Spuk,' which Brahms set as Op. 58 No. 6 and entitled 'In der Gasse', does appear in both versions of this cycle, as Kalbeck noted.

5 For the details of the problem of dating the *Liebeslieder Walzer* Op. 52 and the *Lieder und Gesänge* Op. 58, see George S. Bozarth 'The *Liederjahr* of 1868: Brahms research and modern musicology', to be published in the proceedings of the 1980 Detroit International Brahms Congress, ed. Ellwood Derr. Suffice it to say here that there is no reason to believe that the paper on which Brahms wrote his sketches for Op. 58 is the same paper, or was used at the same time, as the paper on which he wrote his sketches for Op. 52; and furthermore, most if not all of the *Liebeslieder Walzer* themselves probably stem from 1869 rather than 1868.

6 Eric Sams *Brahms Songs* (London 1972) 37. While Sams's last statement is true for certain songs, for example, 'Abenddämmerung' Op. 49 No. 5, and 'Herbstgefühl' Op. 48 No. 7, which Brahms sent to Clara Schumann in September 1867 (cf. Bozarth, *Three Lieder*), there is no evidence that it applies to 'Vorüber'. Brahms, in fact, gave the autograph of this song not to Clara Schumann, but to Ottilie Ebner, née Hauer, who in the early 1860s, shortly after Brahms moved to Vienna, had spent many hours with him singing his songs as well as those of Schubert. After she married in 1864 and moved to Budapest, she remained a close friend of Brahms, and all told received from him autograph manuscripts of sixteen songs. Cf. Ottilie von Balassa *Die Brahmsfreundin Ottilie Ebner und ihr Kreis* (Vienna: 1933).

sing songs: he seems to have read Hebbel's poem only in terms of his conception of Brahms's setting of it, a setting which one could possibly interpret in a manner that would support Kalbeck's misconception of the poem. One also detects in Kalbeck's remarks an echo of the criticism of Hebbel's poems prevelant in the late nineteenth century. As Albert Gubelmann has summarized: 'the charge has been made by men who admire Hebbel the dramatist that his songs are merely metricized reflections, that they bear evidence of labored workmanship and lack the freshness that marks the irresistible up-gust of strong feelings.'[7] To these charges, Gubelmann responded with an extensive and convincing monograph on the nature of Hebbel's poetry, emphasizing especially his use of sensuous imagery. Such critics do not understand Hebbel's muse, Gubelmann argued; Hebbel was not merely a 'speculative author', but a true poet:

With him living was essentially agitated thinking, and his most characteristic experience was the intense passion that such thinking aroused. Thus his reflections either sprang from high-wrought moods, or they superinduced such moods. The substance of his song is often the symbolized emotion or spell attending such intellectual travail. The sensuousness of his best poems points to a fine articulation of the reflective and the intuitive faculty; through this creative coalition his thought is transubstantiated, and is endowed as well with the graces of poetic form by the operation of a genuine and severely trained artistry.

The reflection that 'superinduced' the theme and mood of 'Vorüber' may well have been prompted by the event which Hebbel recounted in a letter to his wife, just before quoting for her his new poem, 'Vorüber'. From Dresden on 11 October 1861, on his way from Vienna to Hamburg, he wrote:

Safe and sound and not too weary, I arrived yesterday . . . in this beautiful city on the Elbe. En route, in fact between Prague and Lobositz, the same Lobositz in which we were once shown, as the sole curiosity of the town, the tree from which a night watchman had hung himself, I wrote three poems. One of them, a song, I set down here for you.[8]

Hebbel's relationship to nature, as revealed in his poems, underwent a series of transmutations.[9] In many of his earlier

7 Albert Gubelmann Studies in the Lyric Poems of Friedrich Hebbel: The Sensuous in Hebbel's Lyric Poetry (New Haven, London and Oxford 1912) 10.
8 Friedrich Hebbel Briefe ed. Richard Maria Werner (Berlin 1907) VII No. 735; the other two poems Hebbel mentions are no longer extant.
9 For a discussion of Hebbel's views on nature, see John Firman Coar 'The victory of democracy over partisanship: three democratic phases of poetic realism:

poems, as well as in his extensive diaries, he portrayed nature as incomprehensible and therefore threatening in its vastness, capable of making man feel infinitely insignificant and alone (cf. 'Nachtlied', one of his finest and best-known poems); however, in both his reminiscence about Lobositz and the poem 'Vorüber', nature is not threatening, but merely ineffectual: the night watchman finds himself amidst nature, but still sees suicide as his only recourse; the weary, anguished poet seeks solace and rest in the beauty and peace of nature, but soon realizes that that solution is but temporary, and only death will suffice.

The intensity and sincerity of feeling expressed in 'Vorüber' cannot be denied, nor should the simplicity of delivery be mistaken for 'merely metricized reflection', for these verses are cast in the image of folk- rather than art-song, an impression created by the extreme simplicity of the language, the uncomplicated though tightly organized formal structure – parallel constructions with the alternating rhymes and regular line-lengths of the *Volksliedstrophe* – and the unsophisticated but effective imagery: the gentle, hospitable, sweetly fragrant linden tree; the bittersweet song of the nightingale; the dead, dry blanket of leaves; and the image of ashes which have ceased glowing and turned to dust. Not all, though, is naive *Volkslied*; the hand of the 'severely trained' artist is evident in the careful variations of pace and modulations of sound introduced to reinforce the meaning, imagery and mood. In both stanzas, Hebbel employed amphibrachic feet to move the poem forward, emphasize important words, or increase tension at appropriate moments, while reserving measured iambic feet to slow the movement again and also to create a certain rugged bluntness (note the '*stumpf*' or 'masculine' closes on *every* line). Euphonious sound predominates in the first stanza, beginning with the mellifluous 'liquid' consonants (l, m, n) and 'long' vowels (e, u, au) which beckon the poet to rest, and passing on through an alliterative series of unvoiced 's' sounds, still supported by 'liquid' consonants, finally to linger on the sole 'ü' of the first stanza, as the poet is sung into a dream-state. Yet all of this is tempered by slightly cacophonous 'explosives' (primarily 'g', but also 't' and 'd') which have been pre-

Ludwig, Wagner, Hebbel' in *Studies in German Literature in the Nineteenth Century* (New York and London 1903) 254f.; for further information on Hebbel's poetry, see Louis Brun, *Hebbel, mit besonderer Berücksichtigung seiner Persönlichkeit und seiner Lyrik* (Leipzig 1922) and Edna Purdie, *Friedrich Hebbel: A Study of His Life and Work* (London 1932).

84   George S. Bozarth

sent throughout the stanza and come to the fore in the last line, together with the lone bright 'ä', to underscore the poet's restless rejection of nature. The sounds of the rhyming words summarize this progression – '-baum', 'schlug', 'Traum', 'genug' – the last of these ideally and most succinctly combining the euphonious and cacaphonous elements of the stanza.

Stanza 2 begins with the poet's actual awakening, which in his original version Hebbel had underscored not only with a pair of amphibrachic feet, but also with a marked shift to open 'a' and 'o' sounds: 'Denn als ich erwachte, da war sie fort' (cf. the Appendix, the versions in sources A^1 and A^2). For his final version, he retained the amphibrachic feet, but employed a change into present tense to denote the awakening. This then allowed him once again to employ euphonious 'n' and long 'u' sounds to darken the mood. The next line introduces into the poem for the first time bleak 'k' sounds and ends with the blunt but still slightly euphonious 'Laub', while the penultimate line, except for adding hollow 'o' sounds, duplicates the first line of stanza 2 in sound as well as in structure. For the final line, Hebbel vacillated between 'die glühende Asche', 'verglühende Asche', and 'verglühte Asche' ('glowing ashes', 'ashes ceasing to glow', and 'ashes that have ceased to glow'). All three employ the only 'ü' of stanza 2, which, with a touch of irony, links this final moment of despair to the moment of supreme bliss in stanza 1, 'den süssesten Traum'; the reading Hebbel ultimately chose, the bleakest of the three, only increases the poignancy of this association ('verglühte' also avoids the inappropriate lilt that the double amphibrachic feet of the other two readings would have created). Two pointed, single-syllable words, 'der Staub', now follow, providing the 'stumpf' rhyme with 'das Laub' (again, the sounds of the rhyming words summarize the progression of the stanza – 'fort', 'Laub', 'Ort', 'Staub') and closing the poem with a sense of unequivocal finality. Dust not only covers the ashes, but is all that is left of them; nothing more can be said.

That Brahms was attracted to the sombre theme of this poem should surprise no one familiar with his songs and choral works. Furthermore, one can easily imagine a composer like Brahms, for whom expression of strong emotion was always tempered by sound craftmanship, reacting favourably to the carefully controlled formal, rhythmic, figurative and sound-sensuous elements of this poem, those aspects of poetry which most closely approximate music.[10]

The two sketches for 'Vorüber' appear on the inner two pages of a bifolium which on its outer pages contains a short sketch for 'Unbewegte laue Luft' Op. 57 No. 8 (Daumer) and an 'accompaniment-realization draft' for 'Während des Regens' Op. 58 No. 2 (Kopisch).[11] Drafted on braces of two staves each, one for treble melodies, the other for the bass, the 'Vorüber' sketches (see the Facsimile and Examples 1 and 2) remind one of Brahms's advice to George Henschel in 1876 that, when composing songs, he should 'endeavor to invent, simultaneously with the melody, a healthy, powerful bass';[12] in a similar manner, Brahms explained to Max Graf why he covered the middle voices when examining one of this young composer's songs: 'I only want to see the melody and the bass; if these two are right, everything is right.'[13] Still, in these sketches much more is present than just the basic two-part contrapuntal framework. Explicitly written out, or implied by what is written, is much of the upper voice of the accompaniment, most of the harmonies (often designated by bass figures), and a good amount of the accompanimental figuration (in sketch 1, at bar 1 and, by implication, bars 2-22, and at bars 22, 31 and 34). Though these drafts may very well have been the first sketches for this song, they are

10 An *Albumblatt* from Hebbel to Brahms (in the Wesselburen Hebbel-Museum in 1943), dated 30 April 1863, reveals that not long after settling in Vienna the aspiring young composer sought out and visited the acknowledged dramatic master. The strong parallels between Hebbel's career and Brahms's own life and aspirations could not have escaped Brahms, for Hebbel was a fellow country-man (a native of the little Norderditmarsch town of Wesselburen and, as a young man, a resident of Hamburg) who, by the strength of his will and talent, had risen from crushing poverty and obscurity, eventually to become recognized as one of the foremost dramatists of his time, after achieving his first unqualified successes in Vienna, where his plays were produced at the royal Burgtheater. Cf. Kalbeck II 24f. and Victor Luithlen 'Hebbel und die Musik' in *Hebbel Jahrbuch 1943* (Heide in Holstein 1943) 37f.

11 For a detailed discussion of the sketches for Op. 57 No. 8 and 58 No. 2, see George S. Bozarth, 'The Lieder of Johannes Brahms - 1868-71: studies in chronology and compositional process' (Diss. Princeton University 1978) 85f.; for a brief overview of these and other sources that reveal aspects of Brahms's preliminary work on songs, see George S. Bozarth 'The musical and documentary sources for Brahms's *Lieder*: evidence of compositional process' to accompany the complete recording of Brahms's songs to be issued by the Deutsche Grammophon Gesellschaft in 1983.

12 George Henschel *Personal Recollections of Johannes Brahms* (Boston 1907) 44f.

13 Max Graf 'Recollections of Johannes Brahms' in *Legend of a Musical City* (New York 1945) 107f.; Graf also reported that when performing his own songs 'Brahms's accompaniment had a strong foundation of basses, even in sweet songs like the *Wiegenlied*, the accompaniment of which is usually sublimated and pampering. Brahms himself always used firmness in the basses' (103f.).

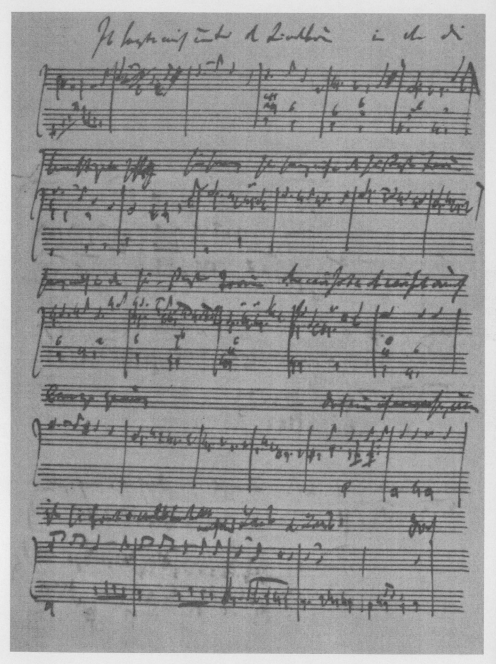

Plate 1 Facsimile. Sketches for Brahms's 'Voruber' Op. 58 No. 7

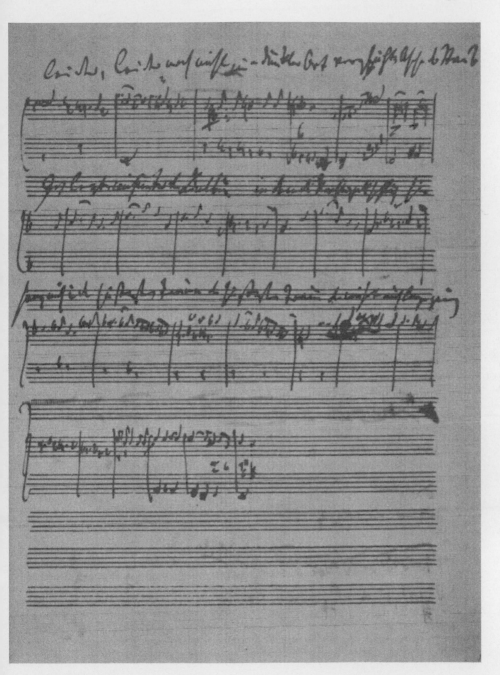

Ex. 1   Transcription of sketch 1 for 'Vorüber'

Ex. 2   Transcription of sketch 2 for 'Vorüber'

actually complete enough also to have served as the direct
model for the preparation of a fair-copy autograph like the
one in the Library of Congress.

In the first sketch, the final version of the A section of this
bipartite song is virtually in place (though here the song is in
E major; in Example 1 I have transposed this sketch into F
major to facilitate comparison to subsequent versions.) Like
the poet who uses a strict metrical scheme of accented and
unaccented syllables to provide the framework on which to
mount his poem, Brahms here has laid out a series of phrases
of predetermined lengths, which, in the number of measures
per phrase, directly reflect the number of metrical accents
per line of poem: 4 + 3 + 4(+ 4) + 3.[14] That Brahms was con-

14 One is reminded of Arnold Schoenberg's observation that 'Brahms's aesthetic
    canon demanded that the melody of a song must reflect, in one way or another, the
    number of metrical feet in the poem' ('Brahms the progressive' in *Style and Idea*
    (New York 1950) 75).

sciously planning this phrase structure is apparent in both of the sketches: he has methodically entered slanted lines above the final bar-lines of each of the initial three phrases to keep track of their length (bars 5, 8 and 12). (Such slanted lines, or straight extensions of bar-lines, are found in many of Brahms's sketches and drafts.) Within this structure, though, Brahms was no more constrained to slavish declamation and rigid phrase construction than was the poet to his underlying metrical scheme. For example, in the opening four-bar phrase Brahms compressed the final two feet into one bar in order to avoid undue stress on the last syllable, '-baum'; the one-bar piano 'interlude', however, extends the phrase back to its desired length. Similarly, for the third line of the poem, Brahms compressed two metrical feet into one measure to remove the word 'in' from an accented position, but maintained the desired phrase length by repeating a portion of the text – 'sie sang' – at the beginning of the phrase.

Brahms's effort to preserve this relationship between length of musical phrase and number of metrical feet is also evident in the next phrase, the second statement of the third line of the poem. Once again, he needed to contract the words 'sang mich in den' into one bar, but now found a new solution: he filled out the end of the phrase with text from the beginning of the fourth line of the poem – 'der währte', three syllables, one metrical foot set to one bar of music – which he then connected, without a strong caesura (and without a slanted line in the sketch) to his setting of the full fourth line, 'der währte auch lange genug'.

This solution is masterful, for it not only creates the necessary seven-bar phrase, but also renders in a most subtle and effective manner the point of *Stimmungsbrechung* in the poem. Recognizing that the third line of the poem can in fact be interpreted in two ways – the dream into which the poet has been lulled is not only a sweet, reassuring solution to his existential problem but also a false one – Brahms set this line twice. By extending the tonic major from the previous section, but mixing into it flattened $\hat{6}$s and $\hat{7}$s, with the nightingale's plaintive call above and a static bass pedal below, Brahms created a first statement which portrays the nature-inspired dream as a positive, peaceful, though somewhat melancholy, state. On the other hand, the second statement is restless and forward moving. For three bars the vocal melody seems to echo the preceding phrase, but now set over a bass that is transforming the flattened $\hat{6}$ of the previous phrase from a picturesque, melancholy detail into a new tonal centre. Then suddenly, while the piano's rolling arpeggios continue on toward the flattened submediant, the vocal line breaks off from its drowsy pattern of scalar descents, one bar before its expected close, and exclaims on a large melodic leap, 'der währte'. Far from extending the length of the song of the bird, as Kalbeck maintained, this initial statement of 'der währte' puts an abrupt albeit wistful end to the poet's involvement with the nightingale's song, though the piano accompaniment tells us that he has not yet fully left his dream-state. For a moment, we are startled and confused; but then the full final line of the stanza ensues, stated most forcefully over a strong descending bass and rising treble, and tempered only at the end by a retrospective tinge of scalar descent, before settling firmly on the dominant pitch and in the dominant key for the blunt word 'genug'. Then for four bars (three bars in sketch 2 and all subsequent versions) we hover on the dominant, as the last vestiges of the dream-state die away in the piano interlude.

The only large-scale compositional revision in the A section of sketch 1 occurs in the voice in the very first measure. Echoing the descending seconds of the piano introduction ($\hat{4}$–$\hat{3}$, $\hat{2}$–$\hat{1}$, $\hat{6}$–$\hat{5}$), the original melodic incipit not only perfectly portrayed its text, but also provided the germ motive (bb'-c''-a') from which much of the rest of the song, as it appears in sketch 1, grew. The remainder of the initial seven-bar phrase is derived directly from this motive (e''-g''-f''; d''-e''-c''; bb'-c''-a'; g'-a'-g'), as is also the repetition of 'sie sang mich in den süssesten Traum' (bars 13f.), the interlude between stanzas 1 and 2, and the setting of 'nun ist sie fort, und welk bedeckt mich das Laub' (bars 24f., both treble and bass). Moreover, underlying all other melodic figures, as well as the tonal scheme of both stanzas (F–Db–C), is the primary interval of this motive, the descending second (bb'-a'). Together, this germ motive and primary interval solve one of the fundamental problems a composer would face when setting Hebbel's poem: how to reflect and intensify both the unity and diversity between the two stanzas. Neither a strictly strophic nor a thoroughly 'durchkomponiert' setting would suffice; a bipartite strophic variation would seem most appropriate, but even this would present difficulties. For example, how could the music for the awakening at the beginning of stanza 2 bear any close resemblance to the music of the restful opening of stanza 1, or how could a setting tailored to the bleak, resigned closing of the poem also convey the impatience and disillusionment implied at the end of stanza 1? Literal repetition would thus, for the most part, seem out of place, but music has subtler means for establishing such relationships. What Brahms has done in sketch 1 to point up both the similarity and the individuality of the two stanzas is permeate them, on both melodic and tonal levels, with the germ motive and the principal interval, which, though always the same, appear in ever-changing musical contexts to mirror the variations of mood and content expressed in the poem.

While the purpose of the original incipit is unmistakable, the value of the revised reading is greater, for it establishes this opening measure as a major structural pillar of the song. Now the primary metrical stress falls on $\hat{5}$, rather than $\hat{4}$, before dropping to the secondary stress on $\hat{3}$, thereby laying out from the start the lower limit of the tetrachord span $\hat{8}$–$\hat{5}$ within which most of the melody and much of the bass for the rest of the song is arrayed and through which these two contrapuntal lines will often descend before achieving a final and full close at the end of the song (the last bars of the song are not, however, present in sketch 1, so it cannot, of course, be known exactly how Brahms intended to end this particular version of the song; for a summary of the appearances of the $\hat{8}$–$\hat{5}$ tetrachord in sketch 1, see Example 3). The vocal incipit

Ex. 3   Appearances of the upper tetrachord in sketch 1

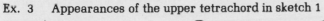

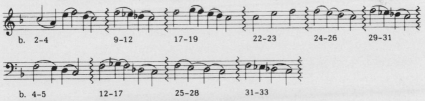

now gives over to the piano accompaniment the role of motivic generator. Furthermore, a new interval, the descending third from $\hat{5}$ to $\hat{3}$, momentarily comes to the fore, revealing the potential of the vocal melody to dwell in regions less tense than the upper tetrachord and to move downward toward its ultimate resting point, the tonic pitch. It is this potential that we shall see Brahms realize in his final version of the B section.

The second stanza begins in the same manner in sketch 1 as in the final version. To mark the awakening and its concomitant heightened level of emotional tension, Brahms shifted abruptly from dominant major to mediant minor, compressed 'denn nun ich er-' into the last half of its bar, allowing only two beats between the metrical accents on 'nún' and 'erwáche', and placed triplet octaves in the accompaniment. And though the next phrase progresses in a rather leisurely manner through a sequence that descends the tetrachord formerly associated with the dream-state, as the poet gradually becomes aware of his new waking state (bass in imitation of treble), a faster rate of declamation (*two* feet per measure) extends the heightened level of tension of the initial bar of this section and sets these lines off from the rest of the song. Note, however, that by repeating 'das Laub' and adding one bar of piano without voice, Brahms once again maintained an overall ratio of one metrical foot per bar (bar 22–8: seven bars = seven metrical accents); the B section actually progresses at the same pace as the A section. This, together with the melodic and harmonic similarities between the two stanzas already noted and the literal repetition at 'doch leider noch nicht' of material used in stanza 1 for the first 'sie sang mich in den süssesten Traum', reinforces the impression that stanza 2 is a strophic variation of stanza 1.

Before writing out the final bars of sketch 1, Brahms broke off and began his second sketch. Set now in F major, surely because of this key's pastoral connotation, the first eight bars, taken over *in toto* from the revised reading in sketch 1, again lay out a broad phrase which sets the scene and then comes to a full close (the only tonic in the voice before the very last note of the song). What follows, though, is not the dreamy setting of line 3 found at this point in sketch 1, but rather an expansion of the second, modulatory setting of this line (cf. sketch 1, bars 13f.). The extension of this phrase occurs at bars 12–13, where a reiteration of 'den süssesten Traum' replaces 'der währte'. Then, after considering two variant readings, Brahms closed the A section with the same three-bar unit as in sketch 1.

What prompted Brahms to recast the first stanza? Very likely, he simply wanted to try out a shorter reading, one that would balance the length of the B section in sketch 1. To achieve this he tried eliminating the A section material which he had duplicated in the B section. There are severe problems with this solution, though. First, the revised second phrase is five, rather than the requisite four bars long – a fact Brahms methodically registered with the slanted line he entered over the barline at the beginning of the final bar of this phrase. Second, this version extends to five bars the harmonic progression originally designed for four, causing a serious slackening of harmonic rhythm at bars 12–13. And perhaps most crucial, this version does away with the very passage

that, together with its varied repetition, had revealed and expressed the dual nature of the third line of the poem. To compensate for the loss of the first statement of 'sie sang mich in den süssesten Traum', Brahms tried to include both restlessness (bars 9–11) and tranquility (bars 11–13) in one phrase. But this was a poor substitute for a passage of such harmonic and motivic richness. Furthermore, this new reading makes the moment of *Stimmungsbrechung* most awkward, for the poet is still amidst his dreams (bar 13) when suddenly he must sing this crucial line. Brahms's struggle with this problem can be seen in sketch 2 (bar 14): first he tried rising out of the dream-stage gradually; then he sought to recapture something of the wistfulness of his original setting; but finally he realized that to be effective the vocal line must still declaim its text in a high register, however musically abrupt this might be.
abrupt this might be.

In the end Brahms left the version of section A found in sketch 1 unaltered, and instead solved the problem of balance by recasting the B section. The sketches shed very little light on this process, for only the beginning of the B section is present in sketch 2, and this reading is still quite different from the final version. Yet two significant changes in approach are already in evidence. To isolate the poet's awakening as a local event, as did Hebbel in the final version of his poem, and to follow this excited moment with a steadier, more resigned mood, as the poet accepts his return to reality and surveys his surroundings, Brahms rejected the immediate modulation away from the mediant minor found in sketch 1 and instead constructed an opening phrase for section B which ends on the verge of a fully established new key area, the mediant minor. Furthermore, he abandoned the two metrical feet per measure ratio he had employed in sketch 1 for 'nun i̇́st sie fört', and returned to the slower pace of the A section. Similarly, in his final version of section B, Brahms capitalized on the series of iambic feet which end line 5 and begin line 6 ('nu̅n i̇́st / sie fört, / u̅nd we̅lk') to create a broad, harmonically rich passage. In the Library of Congress autograph we can see that Brahms initially thought to maintain this slower pace at least until the first 'verglühte Asche', for he originally notated the voice part for the repeat of 'wie am dunklern Ort' as in Example 4. But even before entering the text and accompaniment he changed his mind, smeared out the still wet voice notes, and wrote the revised and final reading, now with text and piano. would have intensified the climax on these words; but by

Ex. 4   Original reading in the Library of Congress autograph of
'Vorüber', bars 35f.

changing the rate of declamation one bar earlier, Brahms was
able to move this phrase forward toward the climax even more
powerfully by adding quickened rhythmic and harmonic pace,
as well as syncopated rhythm, to the crescendo which had
begun in the preceding measure. This quickened pace Brahms
then maintained through the climax on the first 'verglühte
Asche', after which he resumed his original metrical ratio,
allowing the energy to dissipate as the vocal line makes one
last descent through the upper tetrachord (appropriately
using flattened 7̂ and 6̂, for, as in the poem, 'verglühte' equals
'süssesten') and the poet's thoughts turn to his final state, 'der
Staub'.

Harmonically, the version present in the autograph and in
all subsequent sources avoids the premature return to the
tonic area which had occurred in sketch 1 at 'doch leider noch
nicht' and, after the broad mediant minor area, moves strongly
toward the flattened submediant (bars 31–6) which now
sounds like a long-range tonal goal rather than a mere
harmonic digression. Only then does the tonic area return.
Although sketch 2 does not yet reveal Brahms's intention to
extend the mediant area to such lengths, one element that
Brahms used to maintain harmonic interest in this large tonal
plateau is already present, albeit in a slightly different guise.
At bar 25 of the final version, and again at bar 28, Brahms
substituted a diminished chord for the expected tonic, creating
a delayed cadence which at one and the same time expresses
the poet's confusion as he awakens from his dream and propels the music forward into the next phrase. This diminished
chord is already present in the last bar of sketch 2, deployed,

however, only as an accented appoggiatura to the E major chord which follows.

The result of all these revisions is a setting of the second stanza that functions more openly as a strophic variation of the first stanza while still retaining its own integrity. Both stanzas progress with the same overall ratio of metrical feet to measures of music; both begin with a stable tonal plateau (F major vs. A minor) to express the poet's static physical and emotional state; both modulate through the flattened submediant as tension mounts; both again achieve stability via the dominant; and, at the appropriate moments, both stanzas employ the descending tetrachord motive. Yet, in the second stanza, new accompanimental figurations and local harmonies are deployed to illustrate the meaning and mood of the text; the words and phrases chosen for repetition fit the new context; and, perhaps most significantly, both to unite and to distinguish the two stanzas structurally, the interval of the third (5̂-3̂), which had only appeared momentarily at the beginning of the first stanza (revised reading of vocal line, sketch 1, bar 2), now comes to the fore as the structural pole of the melody during both the A minor plateau (c″-a′) and the subsequent modulation to D♭ major (c″-a♭′). Thus, just as the poet's thoughts pass from his dream, through his awakening, and finally settle on the only true solution to his anguish, the grave, so too does the overall melodic contour of the song leave the upper tetrachord of stanza 1 and move downward through the 3̂ to its final, inevitable resting place, the tonic. This musical metaphor is then reiterated and reinforced by the plagal postlude, where a true and full resolution of the poet's existential quandary and of the music's bleak open octaves and strong dissonances – *simultaneously* sounding flattened 6̂ and 5̂ – is finally found in deep, sombre Picardian tonics.

Appendix: The various versions of Hebbel's 'Vorüber'

The sources

According to *Friedrich Hebbel Sämtliche Werke* ed. Richard Maria Werner (Berlin 1904) VII 379–80, 'Vorüber' exists in three autograph manuscripts that predate the sole publication of this poem during Hebbel's lifetime:

A¹: The original manuscript which Hebbel wrote while on his journey from Vienna to Hamburg in October 1861; written in pencil on a small sheet from a writing tablet, without title or date, but labelled 'Bodenbach'

A[2]: The version found in the letter which Hebbel sent to his wife Christine from Dresden on 11 October 1861 (cited in the body of this paper)

A[3]: An autograph copy written on a small sheet and dated 'Oct. 1861' (once owned by Stefan Zweig)

A[4]: An autograph copy entered into Hebbel's 'Grossquartheft' and dated 'Oct. 1861'

P: Printed edition, in *Orion, Monatsschrift für Literatur und Kunst*, Adolf Stradtmann, ed. (Hamburg, 1863), I/2: 84

Also published shortly after Hebbel's death in *Friedrich Hebbel Sämmtliche Werke* ed. Emil Kuh (Hamburg 1865–7) VII 20, of which Brahms owned a copy (this copy now in the Archive of the Gesellschaft der Musikfreunde in Wien)

The versions

Stanza 1 (in all sources):
> Ich legte mich unter den Lindenbaum,
> In dem die Nachtigall schlug,
> Sie sang mich in den süssesten Traum,
> Der währte auch lange genug.

Stanza 2:
In A[1]: Denn als ich erwachte, da war sie fort,
> Und mich bedeckte das Laub,
> Doch leider *nicht so,* wie am dunklern Ort,
> *Verglühte* Asche der Staub.
>> Orig., *noch nicht* and *Die glühende*

In A[2]: Denn als ich erwachte, da war sie fort,
> Und mich bedeckte das Laub,
> Doch leider nicht so, wie am dunklern Ort,
> *Die glühende* Asche der Staub.
>> Orig., *Verglühende*

In A[3]: Denn nun ich erwache, *nun* ist sie fort,
> Und welk bedeckt mich das Laub,
> Doch leider noch nicht, wie am dunklern Ort,
> Verglühende Asche der Staub.
>> Orig., *da*

In A[4], P, Kuh and Brahms:
> Denn nun ich erwache, nun ist sie fort,
> Und welk bedeckt mich das Laub,
> Doch leider noch nicht, wie am dunklern Ort,
> Verglühte Asche der Staub.

JAMES WEBSTER

Brahms's *Tragic Overture:*
the form of tragedy

The *Tragic Overture,* one of Brahms's longest and most complex instrumental movements, occupies a peculiar and somewhat obscure place in the canon. Its companion-piece, the
Academic Festival Overture, has become part of our received
picture of Brahms's musical personality: the boisterous trans-
mogrification of student songs into high art. But our work
enjoys no comparable status; it is not often performed and has
not been much written about. Many authorities, for example
Karl Geiringer and Edwin Evans, dislike the work or view it
with ambivalence;[1] others do not discuss it at all.[2] Formally, it
has never been adequately described; critically, Brahms's
appellation 'tragic' has elicited serious comments only from
Tovey and Arno Mitschka.[3] In the following, I will discuss the
first group and especially the opening motto, and then the form
of the whole, with some attention to Brahms's other orchestral
music and the instrumental traditions in which he worked. I
will next assess certain musical aspects in which the work can
be said to be 'tragic'. Finally, I will compare it to other comparable nineteenth-century overtures. The outward form is
diagrammed in Example 1 (boldface numbers and letters there
and in the text refer to the extensive Thematic Appendix given
at the end of this chapter).

I

The opening motto is extraordinary, and its implications for
the form as a whole profound; yet not one description or analysis of the movement takes the slightest account of its special

1 Karl Geiringer *Brahms: His Life and Works* tr. H. B. Weiner and Bernard Miall
(London 1936) 261; Edwin Evans, *Handbook to the Chamber & Orchestral Music of
Johannes Brahms* second series (London [193–]) 77–84.
2 E.g., Rudolf von Tobel *Die Formenwelt der klassischen Instrumentalmusik* (Berne
1935) mentions the work only in passing.
3 Donald Francis Tovey *Essays in Musical Analysis* II (London 1935) 151–4; VI
(London 1939) 55–7; Arno Mitschka *Der Sonatensatz in den Werken von Johannes
Brahms* (Gütersloh 1961) 287–91.

Ex. 1 *Tragic Overture*: overview of form (Motive-, theme-, and passage-designations in bold-face type refer to the Thematic Appendix)

features, and most ignore it altogether, concentrating instead on the 'theme' in bar 3. Before examining it, however, it will be helpful to look briefly at the structure of the first group. It is long and complex; the last tonic full cadence comes in bar 68 (still echoed in 77), and the second group proper does not begin until bar 106. Its pace never slackens. It is constructed of three paragraphs, bars 1–20, 21–41, and 43–68, each ending with a full cadence. The first paragraph is described below. The second introduces several new ideas (see the Thematic Appendix, Passage **2**), leading eventually to the double cadence in bars 33 and 41. The third (Passage **3**) develops motives from the opening, until the climax at bar 59 reverts to the opening material in something like its original form.

The two abrupt fortissimo chords which open the work – the motto (**a** in Passage **1**) – constitute an atypical beginning for Brahms. Ordinarily he opens a movement directly with a theme. In the exceptions, like Symphonies Nos. 1 and 3 and the Andante to No. 4, the motto is continuous in character, dynamics, rhythm etc. with the main theme to follow. But in the *Tragic Overture* the motto erupts from nowhere, and before we have quite grasped what is happening the reverberations of its bare fifth are already dying away over ominous timpani. The continuation avoids 'explaining' this; the motto remains unexplained psychologically. (The closest parallel in character among Brahms's other mottoes is that in Symphony No. 3; but its integration into its larger context indicates how radical is his procedure here.) Nevertheless, its massive orchestration and the length of the following diminuendo establish at once the vast scale and the unsettled, rapidly changing pace of the work, its struggle among opposing and in part 'mysterious' forces.

And, strange as it may seem in view of his richly chromatic harmony, Brahms almost always begins an orchestral movement squarely on a root-position tonic in the bass; or perhaps (in chamber works) on a clear local dominant. Real ambiguity occurs only in shorter works, such as the piano pieces Op. 76 Nos. 4 and 8 and Op. 118 No. 1. When he begins a large work 'off' the tonic, as in the Clarinet Quintet or the Finale of the String Quintet in G, the growth into the tonic is seamless and continuous. (In the Double Concerto, the opening on the dominant serves the special purpose of preparing the two huge introductory cadenzas, which themselves prolong the dominant, before the ritornello proper establishes the tonic.) But in the *Tragic Overture* the opening is as ambiguous and unstable tonally as it is abrupt.

The motto comprises a falling fourth a″–e″ in the melody over a rising third f–a in the bass, **a1**. The contrapuntal combination of two skips in contrary motion is already unusual. From a local harmonic point of view, the first-inversion triad on F and open fifth on A do not conclusively establish any key; they could appear (in descending order of probability) as diatonic triads in D minor, A minor, F major, or C major. Taking a Schenkerian view, the only tonality in which the melody can constitute a single part is A (major or minor); but if this were so, the bass would enter on and leap away from a non-tonic-triad pitch (see Example 2a). The bass equally clearly implies F; but then the melody must skip to the leading-note (2b). In either case the chord on A would have to be understood as subsidiary to one which will follow – an interpretation completely incompatible with what we hear. Since the most natural tonal interpretation of each part contradicts that of

Ex. 2   Motto **a** (a) (b) (c) Various tonal interpretations (d) Implied dissonance F–E (e) Beethoven, Quartet in E minor Op. 59 No. 2, opening motto (f) Brahms, Quintet in F major Op. 88, Finale, opening motto

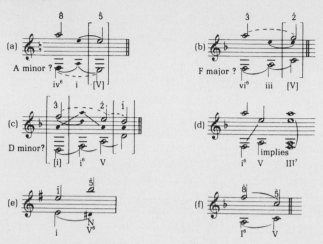

the other, we may as well accept the motto as a half-cadence in D minor. But now the bass must be understood as arising out of a notional initial root-position tonic, or pointing towards one to follow; and the melody still lies askew on the dominant (2c – a coherent, but largely fictive progression). (To grasp how difficult this motto really is, one may compare the gesturally identical opening of Beethoven's Quartet in E minor Op. 59 No. 2, in which melody and bass create a coherent progression in the tonic; in the Finale of Brahms's Quintet in F, the two leaps are even identical but, owing to the different vertical intervals, they clearly express a single key; cf. Examples 2e–f.)

And what are the implications of **a** for larger-scale structure? If A ($\hat{5}$) is to be the head-note of an *Urlinie*, it is peculiar to present it here as something to be skipped away from; but if not (that is, if it is thrown up from a middle register, as implied in Example 2c), then F ($\hat{3}$) must be the head-note – but F is conspicuous by its absence. The motto strikingly fails to establish any clear musical relations between E and F; indeed, by not 'displacing' either soprano or bass of the first chord to an adjacent pitch by step, it implicitly places E and F in dissonant relation to each other, as shown in Example 2d – a relation which will prove significant later on. These tonal and motivic implications of the motto in the context of D minor govern much of the course of the entire work.

The continuation contrasts with the motto in expected ways, but also maintains the air of ambiguity and instability. As so often in Brahms, expressive contrast is based on continuity of motivic development.[4] As shown in Passage 1, the contrasting theme **b** harbours **a** within it, and the upward third **b4** replicates (indeed continues) the initial arpeggiation **a1**. At the same time **b1** produces an F major triad in first inversion over A; the initial six-three sonority thus continues to govern in other contexts. More than this, the second phrase **b3** 'inverts' the structural interval from a fourth to a fifth, filling in the span e″–a′ which lies between the higher and lower statements of **a** just heard. This relationship develops further with the important dotted motive **c** (bars 6–7) which, though apparently introducing yet another contrasting idea, actually descends e″–a′ again.[5] This now turns into a new 'jousting' motive **c1** – note f′ vs. e″ again – which leads to a dominant cadence in bar 10; this cadence brings the first raised leading-tone, c♯, whose absence to this point has materially increased the tonal ambiguity.

The counterstatement, forte throughout, balances the first phrase and creates a large-scale antecedent–consequent period. It favours the tonic, first through its complete-triad dominants (in place of the open fifths) in bars 14 and 16, then through the altered harmonic orientation of **c1**, which now lies on the tonic fifth D–A (the dissonance, now a‴ vs. b flat, still does not resolve); this latter reorientation decisively affects the form of the movement. The phrase ends with an extraordinary cadence in bars 20–1 (see Example 3, which also shows **c1**). Is this a half-cadence in bar 20? The goal seems to

Ex. 3   *Tragic Overture*, bars 19–21

4 I take for granted – cf. the Thematic Appendix – Brahms's powers of thematic transformation; for references to this topic within works on Brahms's form, see James Webster 'Schubert's sonata form and Brahms's first maturity' *19th Century Music* II (1978–9) 18–35; III (1979–80) 52–71; esp. III 62, n.61. Three recent dissertations exploring the Brahms–Schoenberg relation and thematic transformation are Michael Musgrave 'Schoenberg and Brahms: a study of Schoenberg's response to Brahms's music', Diss., U. of London 1980; Jonathan Dunsby *Structural Ambiguity in Brahms* (Ann Arbor 1981); Walter M. Frisch 'Brahms's sonata structure and the principle of developing variation' Diss., U. of California at Berkeley 1981 (announced for publication in 1983).
5 This point is made in Oswald Jonas *Einführung in die Lehre Heinrich Schenkers: Das Wesen des musikalischen Kunstwerkes* rev. edn (Vienna 1972) 116–7.

be this climax on the motto – that is, a half-cadence – by virtue of the parallelism of the two phrases, the recurrence of the motto itself (which we have learnt to hear as abruptly segregated from whatever follows it), and the disjunction in material and register from the new beginning in bar 21. Or, despite all this, does the harmonic continuity between bars 20 and 21 create a functional progression from dominant to tonic, supplying that stable root-position D minor which has so far been withheld? One cannot say: the cadence is rhythmically ambiguous, and hence maintains the tension and instability that constitute the primary aesthetic mode of the first group. Passage 2 is thus psychologically as well as tonally necessary. Its material has already been described; for the first time, bars 21–4 relate the tonic-triad pitches F and A in the melody to D in the bass, albeit indirectly.[6] Nevertheless, the actual harmonies remain dissonant, and there is no stable middle-ground $\hat{3}$–$\hat{2}$–$\hat{1}$ until the cadence in bars 33–40–41.

To have two successive large and eventful paragraphs close in the tonic is already unusual, and the ensuing paragraph, Passage 3, is refreshing in its modulating sequences and its development of motive **b**. But its impression of transition also proves to be illusory: the bass can still do no more than move once again from F (bar 43) to A (bar 51), in a gigantic augmentation of **a1** (cf. Example 1); and it still generates first-inversion harmonies exclusively. Having thus landed on the dominant, it refuses to budge, despite continuing developments of **b** and accelerating repetitions of **a1**. Worse, the unresolved ambiguity of relation between E and F has become acute: various new motives **b5–b7**, featuring this half-step, become increasingly difficult to parse – which is 'harmonic' tone, which 'non-harmonic'? – and the implied dissonance of bars 1–2 (cf. Example 2d) now manifests itself objectively in bars 56–8, transformed into an excruciating dissonant clash between first horn and trumpet on E vs. third and fourth horns and lower strings on F (still insisting on **a1**). But with the climax on **a** in bar 59, this E resolves unambiguously down to D, implying that it is in turn subsidiary to the tonic-triad pitch F ($\hat{3}$) – for the motto does finally align f''' with D in the bass (although the actual sonority and the bass arpeggiation in bars 59–60 still

6 That is, this is not a mere non-simultaneity of the initial tones of the *Urlinie* and the structural bass, as would be the case if one equated the melodic f''' or a''' in bar 23–4 with the bass d from bar 21–2. (For the technique in question, see Schenker *Free Composition* tr. Ernst Oster (New York 1979) I 46–7 §124, 127.) Those melody notes are in the wrong register; worse, such a step would turn a problematical opening into an all too comfortable one.

maintain a first-inversion triad). The forms **a3** and **a4** in bars 59–60 grow out of **b5–b7**, just as originally **a** and **a1** were embedded in **b**. The continuation restates **b**, transposed to D and with clear and forceful $\hat{2}$–$\hat{1}$ closure on **a2** (bar 62), and repeated not only in register but in the d''' and d' octaves as well. The bare fifths on these dominant chords explicitly recall the motto itself and thus strengthen the sense of 'rounding off'. The harmonic and rhythmic closure in bar 41 was thus insufficient; only now is the tension between E and F resolved in favour of the latter; only now is D established as a tonic with sufficient stability and intelligibility to serve as the basis for wide-ranging modulations and large-scale form.

Not without a price, however. Ordinarily, a sonata-form first group becomes *less* stable as it progresses, in order to generate momentum for the modulating transition to follow. Conversely, strong tonic closure so far into a movement is ordinarily found only in ternary and rondo forms. Thus, in his symphony first movements Brahms either closes only the first paragraph in the tonic (No. 1, bar 70; No. 3, bar 15; No. 4, bar 19) or, as in No. 2, the two cadences (bars 44, 59) create elisions, and the whole builds continually to higher dynamic levels and greater rhythmic activity. (Particularly effective rhythmically is the reinterpretation in Symphony No. 1 of the apparent full cadence in bar 89 into a three-chord motive extending to the dominant in bar 90.) Yet the *Tragic Overture* is clearly in sonata style, not to say in a heroic vein. What formal principle can govern a work so vast in scale, so hectic and so varied in pace, so serious in tone, which nevertheless has so early on been fully rounded off in the tonic?

II

The transition (Passages 4–5) introduces a plaintive motive **h** alternating with the bleak cadential **a2**, but rising sequentially towards C, the dominant of F; from there, however, two descending steps (**h1**) lead to the solemn, mysterious pianissimo trombone theme **5** in the 'vastly remote' key (Tovey) of A flat (locally, the perfectly intelligible relation ♭III of III). (Was the unexplained passing six-four sonority on A flat in bars 37–8, also in a local context of F, a covert preparation for this key?) Such themes – all in A flat – were becoming something of a 'topos'; the idea recurs in the first group of the Finale of Symphony No. 3, bar 19, where the larger context is also F; both passages recall the original stroke of genius of this type,

Schubert's 'purple patch' in the second group of the first movement of the 'Great' C major Symphony. But the theme itself also recalls Mendelssohn's *Hebrides Overture* – a work Brahms admired – at bars 39ff.; that is, also in a transitional context.[7] Brahms's descent of a third from V to ♭III also resembles the beginning of the recapitulation in the Finale of the Schubert symphony. This unexpected appearance of a remote flat-side key recalls Schubert's and Brahms's three-key expositions; Schubert's four-hand Sonata D 617 and Brahms's Sextet in B flat resemble our work in this unusual procedure of establishing V of V before moving to the remote key.[8] Following the theme, a series of impressively beautiful sequences, still developing **a5**, leads back to C (bar 100) and thence to the second group.

Compared to the violently active and unstable first group, this entire transition, composed entirely of two- and four-bar phrases and pianissimo throughout, is remarkably relaxed. Its extraordinary calm also contrasts with the second group.[9] Even the somewhat sweetly yearning second theme (Passage **6**), though eight bars long, is restless and asymmetrical (2 + 4 + 2); and its rising sequence (bars 108–10) directly prepares the much longer chromatic rising sequence at 118–25, which decisively returns to the realms of action and, by turning F major into its parallel minor, sets up the major–minor alternations which pervade the remainder of the second group. In this realm new ideas, each introducing a new section, enter with increasing frequency (cf. Passages **7–10**), the restless activity never slackens, the surface rhythm becomes increasingly active, and F major and minor interpenetrate more and more thoroughly. The syncopated chords at bar 181 strip away everything extraneous (the bare F and A in the extreme high register recall the end of Beethoven's Symphony No. 8), and nothing can withstand the terrific culmination of this cumulative momentum on the motto **a**, scored even more brilliantly than at the beginning. (This function of **a** as climax has already been prepared at bars 20 and 59–60.) Despite the closing character of Passages **9–10**, especially bar 177, Brahms's entire second group is thus a preparation for the reprise of the motto; indeed, its tonal function is yet another augmentation of **a1** – F

7 I owe this observation and a number of others to my colleague Edward Murray; I have also benefited from comments by William W. Austin, Shirlene A. Ward, and Matthew G. Brown.

8 On these topics cf. Webster 'Schubert and Brahms' II 26–31; III 61–8.

9 For this article I have ignored the draft of the second group, apparently from the late 1860s, first described by Geiringer *Brahms* 260–1.

to A (cf. Example 1). In turn this unceasing crescendo partly explains the calm of the transition – there was no other locus for this *Affekt*, so necessary not only for contrast but to allow the music to gather strength for the second group crescendo itself. Far from following any schematic or 'classicizing' notion of sonata form, Brahms's unique procedure makes his tonally most unstable section in A flat his point of greatest repose.

The motto thus erupts at the beginning of the development as a second beginning.[10] In a first movement, a return to the main theme in the tonic at this point always constitutes something of a special effect, because a false impression arises that the exposition is to be repeated, as in the well-known examples of Beethoven's Quartet Op. 59 No. 1, or Brahms's Symphony No. 4. In the *Tragic Overture*, however, the motto's status as the climax of a long crescendo (rather than a lowering of the temperature), and the distinction that it is repeated softly and with a different continuation, show at once that it cannot be a plain repetition (in the latter respect it is more closely analogous to Beethoven's Symphony No. 9). Mysterious, unhurried developments of **b** move in new directions (see Passages **11–12**); the bass sonorities F and A still return (bars 196, 201); but the bass then descends slowly on **h1** to F sharp, the *raised* third degree of D. (This descent mimics the end of **4**, where **h1** also established a remote key a third below a structural dominant.) The surprising new sonority of F sharp minor leads to repetitions of **a** in the winds and trumpet on D major (bars 205–7), but its rhythmically odd transformation into an upbeat motive in bars 206–7 and subsequent augmentation in the horn – cf. the alternative notation suggested above the staff in Passage **12** – restores the minor, deflected however so as to impinge on E, the dominant of A. Just as F, the first bass note of the motto, generated the second-group key, so A now likewise generates the development.

In the dominant minor, then, the Molto più moderato (Passages **13–14**) begins its plaintive course. As has often been noted, it is based on **c**; the succession **a b c** (bars 185–189–211) thus reflects, in 'augmentation', the material of Passage **1**.[11] It develops in two sections, first homophonically in A minor, leading to a half-cadence at bars 230–1; then contrapuntally, with independent countersubjects, of which **c1**, stated first at bar 236, should be especially noted. The latter section moves

10 It is curious that the first chord of the motto in bar 185 (but only there) has D rather than F in the bass.
11 E.g., Tovey and Jonas as in nn. 3, 5.

systematically upwards through the circle of fifths, until a cadence on C sharp (bars 253–5) leads to an abbreviated repetition of **13**, now in F sharp minor. And it is thus as nearly 'inevitable' as such surprises can be when, through the most direct of false cadences, the expected resolution to F sharp in bar 264 yields instead to the transition theme **5** in the tonic major. As noted, the major has been adumbrated at bars 205–7, and in relation to F sharp minor; moreover, unlike the earlier cadence in bar 230-1, bar 263 is an almost literal repetition of **a** and **a1**. Structurally, the bass arpeggiation $\hat{5}$-$\sharp\hat{3}$-$\hat{8}$ (bars 211-64; cf. Example 1) develops the original generating progression $\hat{3}$-$\hat{5}$-$\hat{8}$ (bars 1-21, etc.).

Tovey links the Moderato section to other passages in Brahms's developments in which the tempo slackens and all outward brilliance disappears, such as bars 206ff. in the Finale of Symphony No. 2.[12] In those cases, however, the passage represents only a portion of a larger section (usually towards the end), and the ideas on which it is based often return in a coda; the closest approach to a separate section in a 'normal' work is the development of the first movement of the D minor Violin Sonata, cast entirely over a dominant pedal (which also returns as the second half of the coda, over a tonic pedal). In the *Tragic Overture*, however, the doppio movimento relation, not to mention the 'tragic' intent of the whole, preclude any such later reprise of the moderato. Nevertheless it is integrated into the movement by virtue of its material, rhythmic preparation and denouement, and links to other transitional sections. (Mitschka, oddly, interprets the entire span from bars 189 to 319 [sic; including the recapitulation of the second theme] as a 'middle' section, contrasting with the activity before and after.)

As in a number of Brahms movements, the structure resembles Mozart's favourite sonata-rondo, $\overset{A}{\underset{I}{}}\ \overset{B}{\underset{V}{}}\ \overset{A}{\underset{I}{}}\ \overset{C}{\underset{X}{}}\ \overset{B}{\underset{I}{}}\ \overset{A}{\underset{I}{}}\ \overset{Coda}{\underset{I}{}}$. But this form often seems as much or more a sonata without development, $\overset{A}{\underset{I}{}}\ \overset{B}{\underset{V}{}}\ \ \overset{A}{\underset{I}{}}\ \overset{(C)}{\underset{X}{}}\ \overset{B}{\underset{I}{}}\ \ \overset{A}{\underset{I}{}}\ \overset{Coda}{\underset{}{}}$, with a developmental section (c) inserted into the recapitulation.[13] With respect to Brahms, Mitschka analyses this type as 'kontrahierter Sonatensatz' (roughly,

---

12 *Essays in Analysis* VI 55-6; cf. I 105-6; also 'Brahms' in *Cobbett's Cyclopedic Survey of Chamber Music* I (London 1929) rpt. as 'Brahms's Chamber Music' in *Essays and Lectures on Music* (London 1949) 220-70, esp. 255 (on the Finale of the C Minor Piano Quartet).

13 See, for example, Tovey 'Brahms' *Essays and Lectures* 244; 'Rondo' in *Musical Articles from the Encyclopaedia Britannica* (London 1944) 193. Charles Rosen's recent *Sonata Forms* (New York and London 1980) offers numerous insightful discussions particularly of the 'second development', as he calls it, inserted into the recapitulation; e.g. 106-8.

sonata without development), Pascall as 'sonata with displaced development or conflated response'.[14] For some slow movements, finales and overtures these concepts clearly apply; but it does not follow, especially in large movements, that the mere absence of a literal reprise of the very first idea at the very beginning of the recapitulation abrogates the 'double return'.[15] (A separate study of this whole question is sorely needed.)

In fact, however, the recapitulated 'transition' harbours considerable reference to Passage 1. Theme 5 itself develops motive **a**, while from bar 274 on **b** appears in the bass, combining with fragments of and then an extension of 5. And the climactic apotheosis in the brass (Passage 15) is nothing more than an augmentation of **b**, supported by the new variation **h2** in the bass – F sharp and A yet again, inverting bars 201–3 and filling them in chromatically. Moreover, the absence of a literal reprise is well motivated. The halting plaint of the moderato could hardly have been linked directly to the violent activity of the main sections (this was not done in its preparation either). And since the motto can only function as abrupt initial gesture or as climax, and must serve this function once again at the beginning of the coda, a reprise here would have necessitated another large-scale preparation; but such a preparation could only lie stupidly on the dominant or, redundantly, once again on F.

As was common throughout Brahms's career, the second group returns without significant change until a point shortly preceding the equivalent to the end of the exposition,[16] where (bar 365) it breaks off and leads seamlessly into the coda.[17] That we should return to the motto (bar 379) was doubtless predictable; its omission from the recapitulation makes its reappearance almost obligatory. But the crescendo *to* the motto (bar 367), with the rising chromatic progressions over first-inversion harmonies created by **b1** in the bass, recalls the transition-like Passage 3 (bar 43). The motto leads directly to

14 Mitschka 273–92; Robert Pascall 'Formal principles in the music of Brahms' (Diss. U. of Oxford 1973) 60, 125–35; cf. his 'Some special uses of sonata form by Brahms' *Soundings* IV (1974) 58–63.

15 See my comments on the recapitulation of the G minor Piano Quartet in 'Schubert and Brahms' III 64; cf. II 33–4.

16 See Mitschka 197–9; Pascall 'Formal principles' 154–6; Webster 'Schubert and Brahms' III, 58, 68–9.

17 The nature, construction, and artistic purpose of codas remain one of the great unexplored topics. An essay by Joseph Kerman on Beethoven's codas is scheduled for publication in *Beethoven Studies* III ed. Alan Tyson (Cambridge 1982) 141–59. See also Peter Cahn 'Aspekte der Schlussgestaltung in Beethovens Instrumentalwerken' *Archiv für Musikwissenschaft* 39 (1982) 19–31.

the c motives, with a strange new climax on the 'jousting' form
c1 (bar 386ff.), based on its tonic, 'final' form from bar 19
rather than bar 9. The biggest climax now follows (bar 394), on
b and a, but (once again) using the forms these assume at the
end of the first group (bars 61–8). (The double statement of b in
long notes, quasi *stile antico*, recalls the end of the first movement of Schubert's 'Great' Symphony and the return of the
'chorale' theme in the coda of the Finale of Brahms's Symphony No. 1 – as Tovey continually insisted, and as we have
already seen at 5, Brahms's use of trombones illuminates both
the form and the aesthetic intent.) An 'exhausted' postlude on
b1 and b2 recalls Passage 3 even more distinctly than before,
but also (in the descending crotchets) the transition to the
Moderato, Passage 11; moreover, the thirds and the suspensions in the winds summon up the ghost of the Moderato itself
– cf. bars 225–6 and 229–30 vs. 415–17. The final cadences
refer to Passage 2, motives c2 and e, used however in the
cadential form they assume at the end of the exposition, bars
177–8 (Passage 10).

As a whole, then, this coda does not have the function of
'thematic completion' (Kerman) so familiar from Beethoven.
Save for four bars on the motto, it derives entirely from other
first-group material, principally the later Passage 3. Most
significantly, this material has not been heard since the first
group. The form defined by the appearance of 'closing'
material at the beginning, preceding any significant modulation and rounding off the opening section in the tonic, when it
returns at the end of the work, creating a parallelism between
the end of the first section and the end of the work as a whole,
is the *ritornello* principle. (The term derives from Baroque
models, of course; I am using it here to describe these more
general aspects of form.) The *Tragic Overture* is so aesthetically distant from Baroque style, and it so thoroughly recom-
poses and rearranges this material at the end, that it may at
first seem odd to describe it as a ritornello-based work. But
there can be no doubt of the recall of bar 19 in the last 'jousting' passage, nor of the strong and repeated sense of closure
at the end of the Passage 3, returning to round off the work at
the climax. Nor is such a procedure unprecedented in sonata
style (again, a separate study is sorely needed). I would cite
just one other, perhaps equally startling, example: the Finale
of Mozart's 'Jupiter' Symphony, in which the purely homophonic concluding passage (bars 402ff.) is a literal repetition of
bars 13–29; this passage too is omitted from the recapitula-

tion. Brahms however provides an additional subtlety by closing with **e** and **c2** in the forms they assumed at the end of the exposition. Such an ending is drawn from sonata style after all, specifically the binary principle in which the two sections end symmetrically, the conclusion in the tonic balancing the earlier one in the foreign key. In form the *Tragic Overture* thus incorporates sonata-without-development, sonata-rondo, *ABA*, and ritornello principles, even though the sonata idea remains paramount. Example 4 attempts to indicate these various overlapping relationships. The totality of these seems far more significant than any question as to the supposed 'episodic' nature of the Moderato section.

Ex. 4   *Tragic Overture*: formal principles

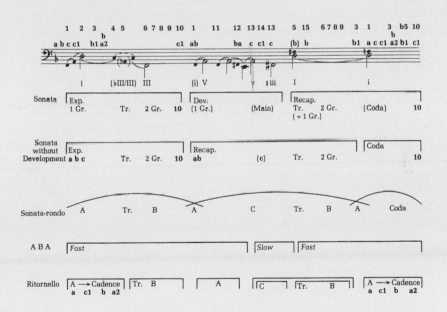

III

I propose here neither an attempt to divine a possible 'programme' for the *Tragic Overture*, nor a discussion of the possible meanings of the 'tragic' in music, or of the implications of discussing a work of music with the kinds of language of which 'tragic' is a natural part. Brahms himself was uncertain about his title (nor was this the only case of its kind). He suggested

'Trauerspiel-Ouvertüre' ('overture to a tragedy', not the same as 'tragic overture'), 'dramatic overture' etc., and he remarked that while the *Academic Festival* 'laughs', our work 'weeps', before he settled on the familiar title.[18] I know of nothing in his correspondence or in reminiscences of Brahms by others to suggest how he might have reacted to the kind of interpretation that follows.

The 'tragic' (or any comparable concept) in music would be hollow, if it could not be shown, 'documented' one might almost say, *in* music; that is, in the same relations among the notes that are elucidated by technical analysis. If the monuments of Western music are as great as we like to think, there must be some 'objective correlative' between these two domains. I believe that this may be so in the *Tragic Overture*. I would therefore like to experiment with an interpretation of the 'notes themselves', in their 'purely musical' meanings, as embodying or articulating relationships which can be understood as analogous to tragic ones. In this, one must 'personify' the notes, along lines suggested by Victor Zuckerkandl:

> Tones in music [are] things existing by themselves . . . doing this and doing that, moving here and moving there, attracting and repelling . . . behaving altogether not like artifacts, the man-made things that after all they are, but rather like things of nature, grown things, living things . . . strictly subjected to the laws of an all-embracing order, at the same time exhibiting an almost unlimited degree of freedom under these laws, in fact existing by the constant interaction between their freedom and their law – a mode of existence strangely reminiscent of that of man himself.[19]

So: let us interpret the opening motto **a** as 'tragic'. Its character is established at once as decisive, resolute, defiant (it not only enters *ff*, but arpeggiates forcefully in both outer parts in contrary motion). But these sterling qualities contain a 'tragic flaw': its tonal instability dooms its attempts to function in the world of D minor to failure and incoherence. Nothing so vulgar as that it is not 'of' this world; as the continuation of **b** plainly shows, the elements of its character spring from the world and belong to it; but this relation is ominous, highly charged, mysterious. He – let us personify – strives to bend D minor to his will, but passes too quickly from one desperate

18 Brahms's few surviving comments are assembled in Max Kalbeck's biography and in Wilhelm Altmann's preface to the Eulenburg miniature score.
19 Victor Zuckerkandl *The Sense of Music* (Princeton 1959) 244–5. I prefer this unsentimental approach to that in Deryck Cooke *The Language of Music* (London 1959).

remedy to another (**a** to **b** to **c**); the 'jousting' motive **c1** storms the two-octave height too precipitously. His next attempt (bars 11-20) rights itself tonally and is under better control (compare bar 19 to bar 9), but now his sense of timing is out of joint: he (the motto) wants to become a goal in bar 20, but the real world's rhythm compels it to proceed without halt to bar 21, where his tribulations begin anew (or perhaps it is that he wishes to anchor his passion in a 'realistic' V-i cadence at bar 21, but fails to see that his own character, compulsively fixated on his motto in bar 20, undercuts this aim). He is a man of action, and his repeated attempts to deal with his dilemma (Passages **1-2-3**) are superficially effective: by the end of the first group (bars 62-8) his motto repeatedly takes the conclusive and coherent form **a2**. Yet this only removes his dilemma to a 'higher' level: all his stormy activity accomplishes nothing, for he remains all too firmly rooted in his problematical D minor, prevented from fulfilling a destiny in the sonata world of modulatory action.

If one accepts the premise of 'personification' at all, this account should have been relatively straightforward so far. But it would be dangerous and silly to extend it mechanically through the entire work. One recoils from the vulgarity of interpreting the transition as a depiction of our hero setting out on knightly adventures, or the varied and active second group as 'recounting' these; so complex and tough-minded an artistic personality as Brahms will hardly have composed an entire large work merely as a gloss on some interior drama. And in any case, the motto is now abandoned until bar 185.

A more adequate interpretation, doing justice to the specially temporal nature of music (which cannot be equivalent to the rhythm of a staged drama, even if dramatic 'realism' is understood to be problematical), as well as to the psychological implications of 'tragedy', is suggested by the preternaturally remote trombone theme **5**. Given an unresolved conflict between the desperate heroic motto **a** and the real world of D minor, this 'otherwordly' theme cannot be Tovey's 'message of peace' (which anyhow ignores the dark minor subdominant of bars 86-7 and the complexity of bars 92-9). It seems rather to evoke the hero's vision of an ideal world, one which he once inhabited or cherishes for the future. (Because it is *his* vision, motive **a** still animates this theme.) But theme **5** is 'unreal', both in its rhythmic calm and in its impossibly remote key (reckoned from the tonic). This is quite right: such a vision is illusory and can never become reality. The second group which arises out of this transition therefore does not 'depict' or 'recount' the hero's adventures but rather, continuing a progression of mental states, represents his *memory of past action*, when he was whole, perhaps, before his tragic flaw was revealed. (Just so, the second group restores the rhythmic basis of the first group and is in the ordinary relative major.) As memory, idealized and transfigured, we can accept (if we like) the second theme as feelings for a lover, the ensuing procession of active themes as a review of campaigns past. But the reverie gradually becomes penetrated by present reality (motives from the first group appear in the closing groups 9 and 10) until, having 'come to', the hero realizes that his dilemma has not disappeared, that indeed it gnaws ever closer to the bone (the desperate syncopated chords, then the reprise of the motto itself, 'scored even more brilliantly').

The same approach may help with the Moderato section, which Tovey interprets sentimentally, invoking the Fool in *King Lear* and several varieties of children's terror. But as he himself points out, the musical substance is based on the first group, chiefly motive c. The entire passage retains something of the march-like character of the c motives, more particularly when the 'jousting' motive c1 enters (bar 236); but this is now veiled, distanced, as if a world, a cherished object, were physically near at hand but the mind unable to focus on it. Hence any personifying interpretation must see this section as another state of mind of the hero – childlike, perhaps, but rather to be understood as a sort of *Angst*, or more precisely that sort of 'childish' fixation on familiar things, as if talismen, that constitutes our chief defence against *Angst*. (Again, one may never insist on such an interpretation; Brahms may have intended nothing more than a cool, reserved discussion of his familiar material.)

The formal and psychological reasons for omitting any return to the motto following this section have already been described. But what can be the meaning for a 'tragedy' of the return of the trombone theme 5 in the tonic and the literal recapitulation of the second group? Merely to repeat such 'mental states', as if they still could retain their original artistic significance in this new context, would of course be trivially simple-minded. Tovey liked to interpret such recapitulations in the major, within works destined to end in the minor, as 'tragic irony': the illusion of hope is given, of a happy ending in the major, but in the end Fate is stronger than our hopes.[20] In any case, despite the wonderful effect of Brahms's initial D major sonority, the transition as a whole is not firmly in the major; as soon as the bass moves (bar 270), major and minor interpenetrate once more in unstable ways, and the final triumph is withheld until the 'apotheosis' on the augmentation of **b** in the brass (Passage 15). Its chief expressive correlative seems to be that of pathos: the world itself (**b**) now appears in the major, shining through poignant descending sequences of consolation. This cannot mean that it has become a friendly place; rather, the hero presumably attempts to accept the world's law as his own, he acknowledges his tragic flaw; the poignancy is the emotional upwelling that accompanies admission of error, renunciation of pride, heightened consciousness of one's own humanity. Strong sentiment – too strong, perhaps; particularly in the falling sequences, the passage hovers dangerously close to sentimentality.

With respect to the literal repetition of the second group, Tovey spoke coyly of 'principles of form which . . . are to this music what the laws of human probability are to the dramatist'. But the fact that a work in sonata style must ordinarily observe the 'sonata principle', recapitulating material which originally appeared outside the tonic, does not compel a composer to repeat every paragraph literally. The 'pathos' of the tonic major has already been exploited, and the additional nuances in Passages **6, 8** and **9** do not compensate for the redundancy or the loss of psychological cogency. It is a pity here even more than elsewhere that Brahms did not take lessons in the free recapitulation of second groups from Haydn. Even Beethoven proceeds differently in Symphony No. 9 (in the same key): his second group stood originally in the submediant major throughout, so that his mixture of tonic major and minor in the recapitulation (which additionally is more thoroughly recomposed than usual for him) throws an entirely new light on the material. And Brahms himself had long since achieved subtler and more compelling recapitulations in mixed major and minor, notably in the G minor Piano Quartet and the Piano Quintet.[21]

But the denouement in the coda is compelling. The world, motive **b**, presses about the hero still more urgently, and his last defiant gesture (bar 379) dissolves abruptly into uncontrollable plunging diminutions (380–3). The extraordinary

20 See, for example, with respect to Brahms, once again a discussion of the C minor Piano Quartet, here the Finale, in *Essays in Analysis* (supplementary vol.) *Chamber Music* (London 1944) 214.

21 See Webster 'Schubert and Brahms' III 64–5, 68.

'jousting' climax **c1** is shorn of its foundations: there is no 'middle' between it and the distant bass; its harmonic basis eludes intelligibility. It is as if the hero 'breaks his lance' and, having no recourse, bares his breast to the fatal counterstroke in bars 394–400. This climax lends retrospective poignancy to the Moderato section, based on **c**, particularly to the appearance of this very motive in its contrapuntal section. Perhaps the difficulty of bars 386–93 is related to Brahms's refusal to resolve the high a''' (see Example 5): A ($\hat{5}$) over F (bars 386–9, equivalent to motive **a**) must move to F ($\hat{3}$) over D (bar 393), be-

Ex. 5   *Tragic Overture*, bars 378–407, voice-leading analysis

before the conclusive $\frac{3}{1} - \frac{2}{V} - \frac{1}{i}$ can follow (bars 394–407). The analysis shows in particular the weak harmonization of the putative structural $\hat{4}$ (g'''), which must lead to $\hat{3}$; only its status as the resolution of a dissonance (a''' to g''' over B flat; see '(7–6)' in the example, and compare bar 19 in Example 3) gives it any strength; but the B flat is not a structural bass pitch. On the other hand, this 'unintelligibility' correlates poetically with the sense of catastrophe and dissolution which must attend the death of any 'tragic hero'. Perhaps the ambiguities and incoherence of this motto should never be comfortably resolved.

The world now seals his fate, returning to the remorseless version of **b** from the end of the first group; the solemn augmentation in the trombones explodes the illusion of Passage **15**, and perhaps also signifies that his idealistic vision (Theme **5**) harboured, ironically, the seeds of his own destruction. The broken and pathetic recollections (bars 409–23) of his strivings in Passage **3** and of his terror in the Moderato serve movingly as the equivalent of the hushed shock and mourning onstage that accompany such a demise. Mitschka's not unattractive interpretation is that the tragedy lies in the failure of cantabile melody, represented primarily by the second theme **6**, to main-

tain itself against forces of unrest and destruction; this contrasts with Brahms's occasional endings of other 'tragic'
works in consolation, notably the Finale of Symphony No. 3.
This is then taken as a symbol of the human individual (melody), unable to maintain his integrity in a chaotic and amoral
world. But Mitschka does nothing with the motto, the second
theme's unstable character and relatively modest role in the
whole seem poorly designed to bear this weight of interpretation, and the 'symmetrical' ending frankly baffles him. Here,
Tovey must be right: the quotidian busyness of the closing
theme (c2 and e) from Passage 10, its lack of emotional re-
sonance, and its symmetrical formal role as a parallel to the
end of the exposition represent the 'restoration of the moral
order' with which all great tragedies end. D minor is the real
world, in which everyday sonata actions as well as heroic ones
will long continue to take place. Finally, the ritornello and
binary aspects of the form are also psychologically appropriate: the catastrophe and in particular this restoration have
been *foretold* by the appearance of these very acts of closure
in the exposition. Musically and dramatically, the outcome is
'inevitable'. Such inevitability is characteristic of tragic art.

IV

Like the *Tragic Overture* itself, the nineteenth-century overture in general has been analytically and critically under-
valued. A recent study by Susanne Steinbeck gives a comprehensive survey according to types such as 'programmatic-
dramatic', 'scenic-lyric', and 'independent' (of plot or programme), etc., and discusses how various examples do or do
not conform to (rather stereotyped) notions of sonata form. She
points out that very few overtures actually end in the minor,
and suggests plausibly enough a connection between these and
'tragic' subjects; but this topic is not followed up.[22] It may be
interesting, in conclusion, to compare the *Tragic Overture*
briefly with this modest nineteenth-century tradition.

The most obvious work is *Coriolan* – an overtly tragic subject, and Beethoven's only independent orchestral composition
that ends in the minor. Astonishingly, despite its universal pres-
tige and the precedent of interpretations by E. T. A. Hoff-

---

22 Susanne Steinbeck *Die Ouvertüre in der Zeit von Beethoven bis Wagner* (Munich
   1973); see 29 and n. 5. Despite advances on earlier works by Hugo Botstiber and
   George J. Durham, Jr, this volume leaves much to be desired critically and analytically.

mann and Wagner himself, no serious modern study has been devoted to this masterpiece.[23] Beethoven's tremendous opening achieves a monumentality entirely beyond Brahms's powers. His motto develops at once into a complete paragraph, with its own internal dynamic: the long-held unison tonics in the strings vs. the explosively unstable full-orchestra chords, whose harmonically unexpected contents combine with their brevity to force us to hear them primarily in reverberation, to grasp their meaning 'out of thin air' (this effect is like that of Brahms's motto, taken for itself). Yet the *piano* theme which follows (bar 15) relates just as clearly to the protagonist, the alternation of staccato skip and legato steps perhaps signifying inner conflict, and the ensuing crescendo to the offbeat forte chord prolonging the tension and instability. At the same time, bar 15 links up to the original motto: both begin on a bare c–c' octave in strings alone, and the outline of an upward fifth, c'–g', relates directly to the leap of a sixth (thirteenth) at the opening, c'–a♭ ", a relation made explicit in the proper register in bars 19–20. And by their similarity in scoring, brevity, dynamics, and in being followed by long pauses, the offbeat cadential chords in bars 20 and 27 reflect and develop the explosive chords of the motto. Yet these crescendos simultaneously introduce the alternating dotted rhythms (bars 19–20 etc.) which play such an important role throughout second group, development and coda. Uncharacteristically, Beethoven's concentrated motivic development is (one is tempted to say) worthy of Brahms himself.

As is well known, *Coriolan* sets up a confrontation of this heroic, 'masculine' material with the pleading, 'feminine' lyrical second theme. Here Beethoven's programme has decisively influenced the composition; Brahms, having no such programme, also eschews the contrast. The two works also differ decisively in gross form. Beethoven includes a clear development growing out of the end of the second group, which leads quickly (as in most of his overtures) to the reprise. This, again, is notorious for standing in the subdominant; but far from being a mechanical procedure it breaks off almost at once and, hurrying through a tonally ambiguous, abbreviated recapitulation of the twofold *piano* theme, moves directly to

23 Brief essays by Paul Mies, in *Beethoven-Jahrbuch* VI (1965–8), and by Willy Hess, in his *Beethoven-Studien* (Bonn 1972), are chiefly concerned merely to establish that it was Collin's treatment, not Shakespeare's, that Beethoven had in mind. Alan Tyson offers some provocative hints in 'The problem of Beethoven's "First" *Leonore* Overture' *Journal of the American Musicological Society* XXVIII (1975) 326–9.

the transition and thus to the second theme in the tonic major. Here is one of the clearest manifestations in all music of Tovey's 'tragic irony'; indeed Beethoven cannot forbear to repeat it 'one more time' in the coda. But now it leads, terrifyingly, through remorseless rising sequences and new dotted motives on the subdominant to the climactic 'thematic completion' and the return of the motto theme (bars 270, 276). This climax on the main theme, with repeated strong $\frac{3-2-1}{1-V-1}$ motions in various registers, thus differs decisively from Brahms's. The famous 'dissolution' of the theme (death of the hero) follows directly. Aside from obvious things like its dynamic and rhythmic power and motivic concentration, one may note the rule of the 'dark' subdominant in this work, from the opening bars through the reprise (in this respect well motivated) to the dotted passage just cited; and the extraordinary role played by rising sequences – perhaps signifying the hero's striving, the victim's pleading; in any case, moral passion which is doomed to failure.

No other 'tragic' overture before Brahms approaches this intensity or concentration. Cherubini was influential on Beethoven in his 'heroic phase',[24] but his overture to *Medée*, though remarkable for its insistence on a tragic ending, is otherwise simply not adequate to this great subject. Weber's *Die Beherrscher der Geister* impresses, but, as in *Egmont*, *Freischütz*, and many other works, its coda in the major removes its from consideration. In Mendelssohn's *Hebrides*, the astonishing originality of material and mastery of form and orchestration only exacerbate the customary gap between facility and genius, allowing even so fortunate an opportunity to expire in picturesqueness. Perhaps in part because it attempts less, his attractive and formally most original *Melusine* is less troubling; but in that the proto-Rhinemaidenly water music surrounds the four-square 'knightly' music on every side, there can of course be no question of tragedy.

Perhaps the only two concert overtures between Beethoven and Brahms which can lay claim to 'tragic' status both conceptually and compositionally are Schumann's *Manfred* and Wagner's *Faust Overture*. (Schumann's *Die Braut von Messina* exhibits the requisite high seriousness and minor ending, but is a much less interesting composition.) *Manfred* is even closer to Brahms's *Tragic Overture* than is *Coriolan* in beginning with a provocative, violent, unstable motto, whose only weakness (if

24 For this concept, see Tyson 'Beethoven's heroic phase' *Musical Times* 110 (1969) 139–41.

that is the right term) is that it is abandoned for the rest of the composition. Nothing could be more effective than the evocation of dark, brooding, inner conflict in this work, nor the many formal strokes of genius: the gradual coalescing of the main fast section out of the mysterious introductory ideas; the second group in the slightly remote key of F sharp minor (iii), whose closing theme in the major, upon its return in the recapitulation, gives just the right touch of 'tragic irony'; and especially the coda, from the climax on the march-like dotted motive, through the profound and original descrescendo on the combination of a chief second-group theme in the strings and the augmented dotted theme in trumpets and winds, to the chromatic second theme itself which, because of its origins in the harmonies of the slow introduction, foreshadows and justifies the latter's surprising return at the end. The 'inevitability' of tragic fate has rarely been so effectively suggested through purely musical means.

As for the *Faust Overture*, it is less often performed and, despite Tovey's substantial laudatory essay,[25] forms less a part of accepted critical opinion even than the *Tragic Overture*. (The standard Wagner literature seems hardly to notice it.)[26] Yet it is difficult to imagine a work better suited to literary and psychologizing criticism, or better calculated to illuminate the boundary between musical and extra-musical significance. If perhaps ultimately conventional in psychology, it is nonetheless constructed with imposing skill and consistency; the slow introduction and main movement are unified thematically; the eighth-note motive ideally fills its 'obsessive' role; the sonata form is handled conventionally enough, but with uniquely personal phrase-rhythms and developmental processes. New in technique are the repeated crescendos and continual beginnings of the first group (bars 31–50, 50–63, 63–69, 69–73, 73–80); the transition theme (bar 80) and second theme (118) each sound new, but each is closely related to a familiar idea (the main theme and the 'Gretchen' idea from bar 19, respectively).[27] Effective, too, is the large-scale elision on

25 *Essays in Analysis* IV 117–22.
26 It receives no musical discussion, for example, in Ernest Newman *Wagner as Man and Artist* (New York 1924); in Curt von Westernhagen *Wagner* (2 vols.) trans. Mary Whittall (Cambridge 1978); or in the musical sections by Carl Dahlhaus in the Wagner article in *The New Grove* (London 1980).
27 Wagner argued that Gretchen is not 'depicted' in the work (planned originally as the first movement of a symphony, in which the second movement would be 'hers', as in Liszt's *Faust Symphony*), but the identification seems difficult to resist nonetheless.

the 'Gretchen' theme in bar 167, at once the closing theme of the exposition and the beginning of the development.[28] The development proper is effectively constructed as a double progression: first an episodic modulating section (characteristic for an overture) on the 'Gretchen' theme, gradually building up to a terrific climax of *Verzweiflung* on the leading-note of the dominant (first notated as A flat), bars 248–75; then a long passage of dominant preparation on the main theme. The recapitulation is considerably rearranged and drastically compressed. (The dotted-rhythm triadic theme, often cited as generically resembling Beethoven's Symphony No. 9, which Wagner had had 'revealed' to him under Habeneck shortly before composing the *Faust Overture*, is not incidentally the blandest in the entire work. In its extension here, bars 342–8, it reveals the only clear compositional reference to Beethoven, namely the similarly inflected rising sequences tending towards the subdominant in his Scherzo, bars 288–96.) This rearrangement allows the plaintive transition theme from bar 80 to reappear at the end of the recapitulation (bar 385), and so lead directly to the final apotheosis. The ending is remarkable in Wagner for its terseness and economy, and only the high winds, chromatic sweetness, and $^{6}_{\mathrm{ii5b}}\text{-I}$ plagal cadence of the final visionary drawing up to heaven strike a false note. It is the same sentimental, unearned progression of salvation which ends many of the 'tragic' operas and music-dramas, including the *Dutchman*, *Tristan*, and *Götterdämmerung* (even the *Meistersinger* and *Parsifal* end similarly except that, as befits their societies made whole, the progression is diatonic).

It was thus a noble, if modest, tradition within or against which Brahms wrote the *Tragic Overture*. But Brahms's originality and cogency surpass all of these examples save *Coriolan* itself. On superficial acquaintance a little bland, even opaque, his overture constitutes the only real counterpoise to Beethoven within the nineteenth-century German tradition – a familiar enough historical conclusion for the symphony, but not yet so for this more limited genre. Brahms seems more profound not only in compositional technique, which might have been taken for granted, but as well in his psychological sensitivity towards the tragic implications of his theme. Many other interpretations might be offered in place of the ones at-

---

28 This was a typical large-scale formal device in Wagner. See Anthony Newcomb 'The birth of music out of the spirit of drama' *19th Century Music* V (1981–2) 38–66.

tempted here, of course, and I am aware that they will seem inadequate, even bizarre, to some readers. That seems a risk worth running for the sake of focussing attention on this remarkable work.

Thematic Appendix

123

124

SIEGFRIED KROSS

Brahms the symphonist

When Brahms, just twenty years old, visited Robert Schumann in Düsseldorf on 30 September 1853 and played some of his first works, Schumann interrupted him after only a few moments in order to fetch Clara. He presented the young man to her with the words: 'Here you shall hear music such as you never heard before.'[1] Some time later Schumann, who was precise and analytic in his diction, described more exactly what he had heard, in his famous article 'Neue Bahnen'[2]; this did as much harm as good on Brahms's behalf, because its effusive enthusiasm could not be verified by the critical public. Schumann had recognized that Brahms's piano style had gone beyond the boundaries of traditional piano writing. He wrote that Brahms 'made an orchestra of lamenting and loudly jubilating voices out of the piano'. The pianist Clara saw it from another point of view: 'Here and there the sound of the instruments was not suitable to their characters, but these are trifles in comparison with his rich imagination and feeling.'[3] It did not remain hidden from the Schumanns that Brahms in his earliest works, though conceiving from the piano, in fact thought orchestrally. Once, Clara heard piano playing from outdoors, and asked who were playing duets, but she found that it was Brahms alone (Kalbeck I 218). Robert Schumann therefore predicted: 'If he should point his magic wand to where the masses of choir and orchestra will lend him their powers, we anticipate wonderful views of the world of spirits'. But in spite of his rhapsodic enthusiasm, Schumann was not blind to the problems resulting from this mixing of genres: Brahms's sonatas for piano seemed to be 'more disguised symphonies' to him ('Neue Bahnen').

Indeed, only a short time later Brahms began working on a

1 Max Kalbeck *Johannes Brahms* I (Berlin [4]1921) (hereafter Kalbeck I) 115.
2 *Neue Zeitschrift für Musik* 39 (28 October 1853).
3 Diary entry 4 October 1853. See Berthold Litzmann *Clara Schumann. Ein Künstlerleben nach Tagebüchern und Briefen* II (Leipzig [5]1918) 282.

composition which reached still further beyond piano writing and piano sound than his Third Sonata in F minor, which had been created during his close friendship with Schumann. At first he tried to accommodate this by expanding it into a sonata for two pianos; but this too proved unable to support so demanding a conception – a conception which was already so pronouncedly symphonic that – earlier than he himself had intended, and for purely musical reasons – Brahms was compelled to fulfil Schumann's predictions: he began his first symphony. For the first movement he had chosen a main theme of truly symphonic size with extraordinary potential for symphonic development. Its chains of trills are perhaps a result of his study of Hamburg musical history in the figure of Carl Philipp Emanuel Bach.

It begins with a tympani-roll on the tonic D. The expectation of the hearer of a piece in D is not fulfilled however, for Brahms introduces the main theme with a first inversion of the submediant, B flat major. In bar 4 he even adds an A flat as minor seventh, which he clearly emphasizes as the peak of the melody by means of a trill. Now the listener believes that he is hearing a first-inversion dominant seventh chord in E flat major. But Brahms does not cadence onto E flat, but onto A major (the dominant chord of the main key, again in first inversion) and immediately adds a repetition of the main theme on the dominant. Thus he has exploited the Neapolitan relation between B flat major and A major.

This was musical material enough for a symphonic development broad as well as deep. But it then became apparent that his knowledge and practical experience did not yet suffice to fulfil Schumann's predictions: an orchestrally conceived piano sonata cannot yet become a symphony after all. So his first attempt to master the formal problems of the post-Beethovenian symphony failed in the small tasks of not-yet-mastered instrumentation as well as in the greater one of mastering cyclic form, although he had so successfully developed the style of middle Beethoven in his earlier piano sonatas. He returned at least partially to the piano texture better known to him: he reworked the unmastered symphony into a piano concerto, which was published as his Opus 15. This composition became his problem-child and for months it claimed attention in his correspondence with his friends Joseph Joachim and Julius Otto Grimm. The work grew to a monster in his hands. The cyclic structure of the work, in the shadow of Beethoven's example with his compelling 'logical' forceful intensification to a climax, proved the most difficult problem. At last Brahms himself had to admit: 'I have no judgement and no power over the piece anymore... It never will turn into anything good', and he spoke of its 'unfortunate first movement which could not be born'.[4]

The remodelling of the symphony into a concerto had its consequences: the already completed Scherzo could not be used in a concerto. It was used, however, as the second movement in the *German Requiem* Op. 45, and, even without the gloomy chant-like unisono song composed into it for the Requiem, it shows the dark character Brahms had intended to give the scherzo of his first symphony, thus demonstrating a certain threat to the traditional cyclical procedures. But the problem of the cyclical structure of a symphony in succession to Beethoven, with his intensification towards the final movement, touched Brahms even in the modification of his symphony into a piano concerto, although in a different way: a symphony finale is too weighty to permit the insertion of brilliant solo passages such as are demanded of the final movement of a piano concerto. Brahms therefore had to compose a completely new finale.

After these experiences with his first attempt at the symphony, Brahms prepared his main approach with unparalleled care and thoroughness. He gathered his next experiences in orchestral technique – beyond the Piano Concerto – in the relatively free style of his two serenades, whose imperfect instrumentational technique can clearly be heard. Musically more substantial is his solution to the problem of musical texture. This was, I believe, the real legacy of Schumann, who used to recommend to young people the study of Renaissance vocal polyphony 'in order to capture the spirit of song'. Brahms did not apply this to the vocal style of individual voices, but to the texture and the equality of each part in it. He studied strict counterpoint to such an extent that for five years not a single newly composed work appeared. The critics, having had their expectations raised so high by Schumann, were forced to consider him a will-o'-the-wisp rapidly burnt out. His studies in texture were oriented exclusively to choral sound, but they, too, went so far beyond a cappella practicalities that complications were inevitable, as with his first attempts at symphony. Until his last years it was his habit to test new compositional techniques in a choral setting. He was especially fascinated by the phenomenon of the canon in all its

4 *Johannes Brahms Briefwechsel V: Johannes Brahms im Briefwechsel mit Joseph Joachim* ed. Andreas Moser (Berlin ³1921) (hereafter *Briefwechsel V*) 194-6.

various forms, to the extent that he planned to compose a complete canonic mass, an idea which was not at all progressive for his time.

Not until he was sure that he had mastered all the technical means did he begin to produce again, and to publish. Two different directions are clearly distinguishable: one leading from his chamber music with piano (Trios Opp. 8 and 40, Quartets Opp. 25 and 26, Quintet Op. 34) and his reductions of fuller scorings (Sextets Op. 18 and 36), to the smaller and most difficult, since most transparent, genre, the string quartet; the other leading from his choral works with different instrumental scoring to the German Requiem and from the whole group of choral–orchestral works around the Requiem (cantata Rinaldo Op. 50, Alto Rhapsody Op. 53, Song of Destiny Op. 54 and Song of Triumph Op. 55), pointing to the symphony. The conjunction of the two fields of experience, choral writing and orchestral technique, evidently resulted in the choral–orchestral works as emancipatory steps on the way to the symphony. At almost the same time he began work on his first two string quartets (later published as Op. 51, although they were written after Opp. 58 and 59) and also on his First Symphony Op. 68. These three instrumental works are closer to one another in time of composition than the opus numbers show.

But, while he finished the two string quartets without delay, he evidently needed yet another emancipatory step in order to complete his First Symphony: in September 1872, after a long struggle, he became 'artistic director' of the Gesellschaft der Musikfreunde in Vienna and for three years conducted its orchestral and choral concerts. As a result of these new experiences he wrote the so-called Haydn Variations Op. 56; even these were in a double version for two pianos and for orchestra. Just as in his (symphony) Piano Concerto Op. 15 and Piano Quintet Op. 34, which was originally intended as a string quintet, setting for two pianos was again involved.

In texture and structure the so-called Haydn Variations do not add anything to the Schumann Variations Op. 23 or the Handel Variations Op. 24. So it is clear that Brahms, even after the choral–orchestral works, still wished to study purely orchestral setting in the form of variations, with which he was familiar and always with the piano version as a control in the background. His progress in instrumentation, in comparison with his earlier works for orchestra, cannot be ignored. In the Haydn Variations the characteristic Brahms sound is already apparent, less determined by instrumentation in a pure sense than by the linear construction, which has often led to the surely false accusation of 'thick' orchestration. One should not fail to notice that Brahms closes the work with a passacaglia, in which the recurring bass is as much determined by the theme as are the upper parts.

Immediately after having mastered the powerful textural rarefication in his first string quartets (completed 1873), Brahms returned to the completion of his First Symphony. But its origins go back to the time of the *German Requiem*. As early as the summer of 1862, the First Symphony was mentioned in his correspondence with friends (*Briefwechsel* V 320), but it was not finished for another fourteen years. The choral–orchestral works and the orchestral variations created in the meantime were indeed emancipatory steps. As he now began to elaborate and finish the work, the rhythm of his life was running smoothly: in winter he gave concerts, busied himself with editorial work and reading proofs; the summer was his creative season. Usually he went to agreeable highland regions, such as Baden-Baden, or to the Lake of Starnberg near Munich, to Heidelberg or to Carinthia. He was very dependent on his scenic environment; only once did he change this favourite habit. In 1876 he was evidently looking for a wilder and more original landscape, and he found it in the steep coasts of the island of Rügen. He himself alluded to the connection between the symphony and the wild landscape of the chalk cliffs of Rügen: the symphony 'clings to the cliffs of Wissow'.[5]

The work had scarcely received its first performance when the great conductor, Hans von Bülow, who was never at a loss for an *aperçu*, made the famous statement which has caused misunderstanding to this day, that Brahms's First Symphony was 'Beethoven's Tenth'. This claim, though made without any Brahmsian support, has become an established critical position. It is mostly founded upon the assumption that the themes of the final movements of Beethoven's Ninth Symphony and of Brahms's First are related. Bülow's claim clashed with Wagner's postulate that Beethoven's step from purely instrumental towards text-generated music in the finale of his Ninth was a necessary consequence of the historical development of the genre, and that it must in turn necessarily lead to Wagner's conception of the *Gesamtkunstwerk*. But in no way does Bülow's claim do justice either to the historical position of

5 *Johannes Brahms Briefwechsel X: Johannes Brahms Briefe an P. J. Simrock und Fritz Simrock* ed. Max Kalbeck (Berlin 1917) (hereafter *Briefwechsel X*) 13.

Brahms and of his First Symphony, or, more especially, to his consciousness of the problems of the post-Beethovenian symphony.

Under the weight of the difficulties surrounding his projected D minor Symphony, Brahms had doubted whether he would ever indeed produce a symphony. Once he told the conductor Hermann Levi: 'I shall never compose a symphony! You don't have any idea how it feels if one always hears such a giant [Beethoven] marching behind one' (Kalbeck I 165). All the greater must have been his annoyance at this emphasis on a continuity from which he wanted and had to separate himself!

Brahms reacted with irritation to allusions to this presumed continuity between the themes of the final movements of his First Symphony and Beethoven's 'Ode to Joy'. During his twenty years of wrestling with symphonic form, he had become very conscious of the problems of the post-Beethovenian symphony. Already in connection with the composition of the serenades, a statement of his is preserved: 'O God, if one dares to write symphonies after Beethoven they must look very different' (Kalbeck I 339). Brahms's friends, too, saw the continuity with Beethoven more as a danger. In a letter to Otto Dessoff, music director at the court of Karlsruhe, Brahms reports: 'Hanslick admits that he looks forward to my symphony with fear. [The art-historian Wilhelm] Lübke talks too much of late Beethoven.'[6]

He had learned from the projected D minor Symphony that the grandly conceived intensification from the first movement to the finale was no longer practicable. But the renunciation of this intensification towards the apotheosis of the finale had the consequence, firstly, of adding to the weight of the first movement within the cycle and thus upsetting the balance between the movements, and, secondly, of threatening the unity of the whole work. The change of emphasis towards the first movement was mainly to the disadvantage of the finale. Brahms tried to counterbalance this temporarily by the unsuitable means of shortening the middle movements: 'I hope that it is not perceptible that there is violent shortening. This was done with respect for the finale!' But after protests by Dessoff he restored the cuts (Briefwechsel XVI ii 146–8).

Dangers of losing the unity of the work as a consequence of the renunciation of the continuous intensification, and the concomitant problem of maintaining the cyclical connection of all four movements seems to have occupied Brahms substantially.

6 Johannes Brahms Briefwechsel XVI Teil II: Johannes Brahms im Briefwechsel mit Otto Dessoff ed. Carl Krebs (Berlin 1922) (hereafter Briefwechsel XVI ii) 153.

This thought-process, as well as his studies of the counterpoint of the Netherlanders and of the period of Palestrina, belonged to the heritage of Schumann (which influenced Brahms when he arranged and studied Schumann's library after Schumann's breakdown). Schumann had undoubtedly considered these structural problems very substantially himself, especially in his own Symphony in D minor with the belated opus number 120. Brahms owned the autograph of the earlier version of this Symphony (1841). It was originally the second symphony, which Schumann later modified in the light of experiences (not totally beneficial) with the municipal orchestra of Düsseldorf, and which he then published as his Fourth. Brahms, however, after careful study, decided he preferred the original version, and while composing his own symphonic works he resolved to let this version be published by Franz Wüllner. For the sake of this publication of his preferred version, he even accepted long-lasting discord with Clara Schumann.[7] Indeed Brahms's First Symphony is scarcely imaginable without this careful study of the creative problems in Schumann's Fourth, with its technique of thematic connection between the individual movements. In comparison with this, the similarity of the final theme with the 'Ode to Joy' from Beethoven's Ninth pales to mere superficiality.

Brahms's creative problem in his First Symphony was not the maintenance or emphasis of continuity with Beethoven, but how to find his own identity and preserve it, on the basis of the knowledge reached by Schumann, and with his own failed D minor symphony in the background. In contrast to the style of Beethoven, who set up clearly defined themes, the first few bars of the slow introduction of Brahms's First Symphony begin a very complex process. The introduction is dominated by two pre-thematic lines, one directed upward in the violins and cellos, and one moving in contrary motion in the woodwind and violas. This two-part counterpoint unfolds over a pedal bass, while the second part of each woodwind instrument and the second viola form a supplementary part in thirds below the falling line. The beginning of the movement is therefore thematically and texturally complex, all the more since Brahms darkens the tonality by introducing the minor seventh as the first step of the theme and thus turns the initial tonic into a dominant. The real thematic nucleus of the movement

7 See: Max Kalbeck *Johannes Brahms* IV (Berlin [2]1915) 123ff.; and *Clara Schumann-Johannes Brahms: Briefe aus den Jahren 1853–1896* ed. Berthold Litzmann (Leipzig 1927) (hereafter *Schumann–Brahms Briefe*) II 464ff.

lies in the violin and cello line: this material will have thematic as well as harmonic function. But the contrary motion of the wind, here harmonically motivated, develops its own formal energy. Real thematic contours can first be heard in bar 9 with its descending diminished seventh, expanded into a sequential motive.

What the listener experiences at first as a gradual preparation for the repetition of the introductory complex (bars 21-4), reveals itself later as an allusive anticipation of the main theme, which unfolds stage by stage – in a manner very unlike Beethoven. But when it appears for the first time in its definite form (bar 42), it proves to be a mere 'secondary artificial product of counterpoint' (as Kretzschmar called it) to the cello part, formed – hardly perceptibly to the hearer – from the thematic nucleus in the slow introduction. The main theme of the leading movement of Brahms's First Symphony thus proves to be a mere derivative of a motivic nucleus which does not appear itself as a theme, but which is the true constitutive basis for the structure of the themes and the form. It is of course no serious objection to this analysis that Brahms composed the slow introduction after the allegro (as we know from Clara Schumann); rather we may thereby detect a positive intentionality behind the veiling and complication in the thematic structure of the movement. Such analysis of the process of the thematic construction already sufficiently demonstrates how far the aphorism of 'Beethoven's tenth symphony' fails to hit the mark: the structure of themes is simply not comparable. Furthermore, thematic exposition has another function for the structure of a movement. In Beethoven's symphonies, the motivic development and treatment of themes in the development section had required the broadest space, moreover, it had penetrated the other sections of each movement and had finally led to the apotheosis of a theme; see for instance bar 632 of the first movement of the 'Eroica' Symphony. In Brahms's symphonies, however, the centre of gravity shifts back to the exposition: the development section is no greater in length and content than the exposition, as it is in Beethoven.

The fact that the themes develop stepwise out of the structure, and are, as such, not the primary constructive basis of the whole movement, creates a function for the ending other than that which developed within the Beethovenian structure. The endings in Brahms's works are signalled not by the resolution of conflicts and liberation, which revealed themselves in Beethoven's works through an acceleration of inner tempo and a

texture becoming more and more simple, but rather a con-
densation and, in contrast to Beethoven, therefore, a concentration of all technical means. Intensification of motivic
elaboration and of textural elements forms a summation of the
formal development of the whole movement. It adds further
elements to the structure of a movement, beyond those of the
exposition and development section – though these are not
elements such as the further breaking up of motivic material,
but those of concentration, such as insertion of canonic forms.
Brahms himself was very conscious of the fact that his
technique of ending did not correspond to the expectations of a
public oriented to Beethoven and to the form-ideal of the
sanctified Classical symphony. So in the early performances
he persistently took pains to prevent the First Symphony being
placed at the end of a programme.[8]

The thematic nucleus of the first movement exerts its power
beyond the end of this movement, however.[9] In the second
movement, which, like that of Beethoven's C minor Piano Concerto, is in E major, the slow introduction of the first movement
appears in bar 5, seamlessly woven into a thematic development. This is followed in bar 6 by a variation of the main theme
of the leading movement in its rudimentary form, as it
appeared in bar 21 of the slow introduction, before it had
taken thematic shape. The slow movement is thus bound into
the cyclical form through its thematic substance.

Both elements are also present in the third movement; but as
they come from the slow introduction, they naturally have an
effect of severity on the character of a movement with scherzo
function. The chord separating the first phrase of the theme
from the second is expanded step by step, until the two
characteristic lines in contrary motion from the slow introduction are audible in bars 23 and 29. Previously (bar 11) the first
theme of the symphony in its emergent state of the slow
introduction had been introduced pianissimo in the strings as
an accompaniment to the falling dotted quavers in the woodwind, binding them, too, into the common thematic substance
of the Symphony. The use of common thematic material not
only in the slow introduction and the main theme of the first
movement, but also between first movement, slow movement

8 *Johannes Brahms Briefwechsel XV: Johannes Brahms im Briefwechsel mit Franz
Wüllner* ed. Ernst Wolff (Berlin 1922) 68; and *Johannes Brahms Briefwechsel III:
Johannes Brahms im Briefwechsel mit Karl Reinthaler . . .* ed. Wilhelm Altmann
(Berlin [2]1912) 141.

9 R. Klein 'Die konstruktiven Grundlagen der Brahms-Symphonien' *Österreichische
Musikzeitschrift* 23 (1968) 258.

and scherzo demonstrates Brahms's strong interest in cyclical binding. However, it also reveals the danger that too close a connection between the different movements through common thematic material can hinder the forming of contrasts which maintain the necessary state of tension between the parts of a cyclic work.

Even the slow introduction of the finale reveals allusions to the introduction of the first movement. Twice these interrupt the main theme, which at first appears in the minor key, and hinder its unfolding. It is delayed, too, by the famous horn episode above the tonic six-four chord, which Brahms had notated during a tour of Switzerland, calling it an Alpine horn melody; he had sent it to Clara Schumann with greetings for her birthday and had set to it the text 'Hoch auf'm Berg, tief im Tal grüß' ich Dich vieltausendmal!' (High on the mountain, deep in the valley I greet you many thousand times!) (*Schumann-Brahms Briefe* I 597). Even if one does not go so far as to explain the main theme (which is repeatedly compared to Beethoven's 'Ode to Joy') as developed from the main theme of the first movement by inversion, the finale shows, however, the same type of movement: the main theme is but gradually emancipated. One needs only to think of Beethoven's Symphony in C minor, where the dynamic of development from the scherzo to the finale theme is so dominant that Beethoven repeats this transition again before the recapitulation, and to compare it with Brahms's gradual emancipation of themes, to understand how superficial is the thesis of continuity between Beethoven and Brahms in the concept of symphony.

But Brahms's formal conception proved able to sustain the whole work; the thematic connection of the movements did make of them a unity. From a concept of form quite different from Beethoven's, Brahms's creative power had so convincingly interrelated the movements of the Symphony that even a man like Bülow could nevertheless unhesitatingly link the Symphony to Beethoven's formal effects. But in contrast to Bruckner, for example, his solution did not give rise to a new type of symphonic form; on the contrary, even the striking inner logic of Brahms's First Symphony cannot obscure the fact that, similar to Schumann's Symphony in D minor, it was only one particular solution to the formal problems of the genre bound to specific thematic material. In his attempt to keep his work distinct from the Beethovenian tradition, he even set a high value on his spelling 'Sinfonie' rather than 'symphony': of the Second he said, 'It is no symphony (he more than distinctly pronounced 'Sümphonie') but only a Sinfonie.'[10]

Brahms often wrote two similar works within a short space of time. In most cases the earlier one is the more spontaneous and immediate work, the later the more elaborated and artificial. Already, prior to the printing of the First Symphony and the completion of the arrangement for piano duet, he began to draft his Second Symphony. In contrast with the other double works, the first of these two symphonies is the more strictly elaborated. It seems as if Brahms, having proved the possibility of composing symphonies after Beethoven without slavishly copying their style, had won the freedom to compose without fears about his stylistic identity. After the long struggle for the final structure of his First Symphony, he produced his Second, in only a few months. Moreover, the serenity of the work is clearly stamped by the scene of its creation, Pörtschach at the Lake of Wörth in Carinthia, which Brahms had chosen in 1877 for his summer residence, in contrast with the wild, harsh landscape of Rügen: 'here the melodies are flying so thick that one must be careful not to step on one',[11] he enthused in a letter to Eduard Hanslick in Vienna. The final revision of the Second Symphony was done in Baden-Baden, as had been that of the First.

The Second Symphony is Brahms's 'Pastoral', glowing with the Carinthian sun: and this image harmonizes with the second subject's allusion (bar 82) to the famous lullaby 'Gut'n Abend, gut' Nacht' from Op. 49; hardly anyone hears that it is developed from a variation of the main subject (bar 44) (see Example 1). How much Brahms in composing it was guided by emotions, and had thrust aside the rational superstructure otherwise so clearly to be seen in his work, was demonstrated

Ex. 1

10 *Johannes Brahms Briefwechsel I: Johannes Brahms im Briefwechsel mit Heinrich und Elisabet von Herzogenberg* ed. Max Kalbeck (Berlin [4]1921) (hereafter *Briefwechsel I*) 32.
11 Alfred v. Ehrmann *Johannes Brahms: Weg, Werk und Welt* (Leipzig 1933) 287.

shortly after finishing it by the ironical manner with which he treated it. Brahms usually reacted with irony and self-parody towards works that touched him more than the consciousness and self-control of his working-style seemed to allow. 'The new symphony is so melancholy it is unbearable. I never wrote anything so sad, in such a minor character: the score must be printed with a mourning border' (thus to Simrock; Briefwechsel X 56-7). He refused a performance in Munich where the First Symphony had been rejected: 'This one would be enjoyed [there] even less than the first one.'[12] To Schubring he wrote the ironic advice: 'Don't expect anything and don't drum anything other than Berlioz, Liszt and Wagner for a month before you hear it, and then its charming sound will do you good.'[13] He warned his publisher: 'In any case it will totally fail and people will think that I took it easy. But I advise you to be cautious!' (Briefwechsel X 55). And even after the first performance, when the fame of the work began to spread, he continued the camouflage: 'Here the musicians played my new one with mourning bands on their arms, since it sounds so very lamentable; it will be printed with mourning border.' (Briefwechsel I 41, and similar in Briefwechsel X 65).

Disregarding the irony that tries to cover just that joy which stands out in this symphony (and other works of the Pörtschach summers – in particular the Violin Concerto, but also the Violin Sonata Op. 78) and which separates them from most of his other works, one indeed must listen very closely in order to discover here too his strict formal logic, especially in the outer movements. Only in the course of the first movement does it become apparent that the initial motive of the basses, which at first looks like a mere introduction and which is lost in the shining melody of the wind, is the constructional basis of the whole movement. The informing motivic material is pre-thematic here also, and forms the basis of the first movement as well as of the finale, whose subject is developed from the contraction of the initial bass-motive and the beginning of the main subject. Thus it is again a unifying factor in a cyclic work.[14]

But Brahms's creative discipline in his Second Symphony is so wrapped in peace and serenity that it belongs among his

12 Johannes Brahms Briefwechsel VII: Johannes Brahms im Briefwechsel mit Hermann Levi . . . ed. Leopold Schmidt (Berlin 1910) 200–1.
13 Johannes Brahms Briefwechsel VIII: Johannes Brahms Briefe an Joseph Viktor Widmann. . . ed. Max Kalbeck (Berlin 1915) 230.
14 Alfred Heuss 'Innerer Betrachtung gewidmet' Zeitschrift für Musik 89 (1922) 164.

most approachable works. 'The orchestra here rehearsed and played with pleasure and praised me as it has never happened to me before' (*Briefwechsel X* 65), and ' . . . I think that this particular work or some of it can be brought to sound well',[15] he himself conceded. So the first performance under Hans Richter in Vienna became one of his greatest triumphs.

While the first two symphonies were composed within two years, between these and the Third Symphony there was a period of six years, not perhaps an extraordinarily long time. But between his Second and Third Symphonies there are several choral works (Motets Op. 74, *Nänie* Op. 82, devoted to the memory of Anselm Feuerbach, and *Parzengesang* Op. 89) and one recalls that between his first symphonic attempt and first finished symphony Brahms had studied choral writing and had composed a series of choral – orchestral works. A similar process, especially the experiment of the *Parzengesang* with its one pervading rhythm throughout, signals the 50-year-old composer's transition to his late style. Nevertheless, the Third Symphony lies structurally nearer to the Second than one might think, particularly in the stamp of its expressive character.

When Brahms went to Wiesbaden in 1883 to complete his Third Symphony, he did so primarily because he wanted to be near the contralto, Hermine Spies, whose interpretation of his songs expressed his intentions more closely than most other singers of the time, and who also knew well how to accommodate herself to his boisterous and grumpy nature. Brahms, though already 50 years old, is said to have wanted to marry her. This atmosphere of tenderness and, at the same time, of mild resignation determined the character of the Symphony, therefore making it hard for it to compete for the estimation of the public, and still more of conductors, against the glowing Second.

Similar to the Second, the Third Symphony begins with a short introduction which seems only to lead to the main subject, but later on it becomes clear that it, like the introductions of the preceding symphonies, is the true source of the thematic and formal power of the whole work. The motive f″ – ab″ – f‴ in the upper parts, of which the listener is hardly conscious, becomes support as bass for the true main subject (bars 3–6). The strange iridescence of the subject oscillating

---

15 *Johannes Brahms Briefwechsel VI: Johannes Brahms im Briefwechsel mit Joseph Joachim* ed. Andreas Moser (Berlin ²1912) (hereafter *Briefwechsel VI*) 139.

between F major and minor is implied in this motive. Shifted back to the upper parts, the same motive closes the first thematic complex (bars 21–3); it not only frames the thematic complex, but also forces it into fixed progressions, and therefore determines it horizontally and vertically. As is usual with Brahms, the symphonic conflict lies less in the relatively short development section than in the structure of the themes. It is an expression of its function of delimitation when this motive, transfigured and extended into a reconciling horn melody closes the development section with its conflicts and leads to the recapitulation (bars 101–8).

The phlegmatic serenity of the Second Symphony, with an added trace of resignation, radiates from the slow movement of the Third, while the Poco Allegretto develops its uncommon charm from a changing rhythmical combination of anapestic and dactylic motives bringing the dotted semiquavers alternately onto the up-beat and the down-beat (♫|♩.|♫ ♪|); the tempo does not allow this to become truly scherzo-like. That which in the phlegmatic-sweet melodic delight of the Second Symphony is thrust into the background, i.e. the absence of development and tension between true contrasts, becomes obvious in the Third, making its generally episodic character clear – not only in the inner movements. Its pervading serene melancholic character as well as the constructive motivic basis of the subjects in the first movement hinder the forming of thematic contrast, which is a prerequisite for the creation of great cyclic forms with interrelated parts.

This has nothing to do with a decrease in Brahms's creative power or with a manifestation of the 'melancholy of impotence', as Nietzsche believed.[16] Rather one must recognize here the limits which are logically set to the possibility of fresh and new solutions of the general problems of the genre and form in a production so very oriented towards an individual structure, as was Brahms's idea of form. But when in the Finale of the Third Symphony contrasting subjects break up (see, for example, bars 19–40), it proves yet again that Brahms's idea of form did not intend the shaping of final movements in accordance with a progression from conflict to triumphant solution. Here Brahms, on the contrary, lets his finale return to the initial motive of the first movement, and lets it die away in a pianissimo in the wind and pizzicato in the

16 Friedrich Nietzsche Der Fall Wagner; see Friedrich Nietzsche The Birth of Tragedy and the Case of Wagner trans. Walter Kaufmann (New York 1967) 187.

strings. That is, I admit, an emphatically stated closed form, but it is rather more in opposition to Beethovenian practice than continuing his tradition.

Between his Third and Fourth Symphonies Brahms wrote songs full of a very personally felt deep resignation, which he compiled as Op. 94, and which were evidently grouped together on account of their common spiritual attitude. The next opus, again a collection of songs is opened by a song which he no doubt consciously placed as a new beginning after all those resigned and depressed texts. It is determined by a strange technique of variation from one single motive which dominates the whole song. Characteristically, this technique of total variation appears also in connection with studies in choral writing, for the same song from Op. 95 exists in a choral version in Op. 93a, which together with the strict canonic setting of 'Beherzigung' by Goethe from the Op. 93 set shows yet another piece of unusual technical concentration. One may, therefore, assume that this remarkable experiment in texture and form, which at first did not allow anything other than very short structures, demonstrates a fundamental exploration of technical possibilities and their consequences for form.

Brahms composed his Fourth Symphony in the summers of 1884 and 1885 in Mürzzuschlag, to the south of the Semmering. Once again he connected the character of the work with the scene of its creation: 'Usually pieces by me are unfortunately more agreeable than I am, and one finds less to correct in them?! But in this region cherries don't become sweet and edible.'[17] In a letter to Hans von Bülow he expressed his fear even more concretely as to 'whether it will reach a greater public. I fear namely, that it tastes of the climate here, cherries here don't become sweet, you would not eat them!'[18] After returning to Vienna, Brahms played the work to friends, on two pianos with Ignaz Brüll, and disconcerted perplexity spread through the group. Eduard Hanslick, who never tired of presenting Brahms as the antipode of Wagner, simply capitulated before that very work of Brahms which comes nearest to his polemically formulated statement of formal aesthetics: 'During the whole first movement I felt as if I were being beaten soundly by two terribly clever people' (Kalbeck

17 *Johannes Brahms Briefwechsel II: Johannes Brahms im Briefwechsel mit Heinrich und Elisabet von Herzogenberg* ed. Max Kalbeck (Berlin [4]1921) (hereafter *Briefwechsel II*) 73-4.
18 Max Kalbeck *Johannes Brahms III* (Berlin [2]1912-13) (hereafter Kalbeck III) 447.

III 452). Kalbeck urged Brahms not to publish the work as it was, in order to prevent him from destroying his artistic reputation (Kalbeck III 453ff.) Clara Schumann was totally dumbfounded, as were most other friends who were confronted with the work before its first performance. She, who otherwise judged so surely, avoided taking a clear position (*Schumann–Brahms Briefe* II 293).

Elisabet von Herzogenberg, Brahms's gifted friend, had similarly tried to avoid a clear position. But Brahms nevertheless provoked her to show her colours: he wrote 'My recent attack [i.e. his sending the manuscript of the first movement] throughly failed and a symphony too' (*Briefwechsel* II 79). Not until four weeks later did she dare put her impressions into words. But she was honest enough to send also an earlier letter not previously dispatched, which indeed showed the complete perplexity even of this sensible friend but at the same time is also one of the most ingenious documents of the reception of this symphony:

I have had a strange experience with the work, the deeper I look into it, the more the texture deepens, the more the stars appear in the twilight which at first hides the sparkling points, the more pleasure I have, either expected or unexpected, and the clearer becomes the continuous tension, which makes a unity from the multiplicity. One does not get tired of listening to it and looking upon the wealth of ingenious ideas, of strange lights of rhythmic and sonic nature which are scattered all over the work . . . ; and so much is contained there that one rejoices like an explorer or scientist if one finds out all the tricks of your creation! But there is one point, too, where a certain doubt remains, which for me is so difficult completely to understand that it is impossible for me to know how to say anything reasonable about it. It seems to me that this creation is calculated too much for the eye which sees through a microscope, that its beauties do not lie open for every simple admirer, and that it is a little world for the discerning and learned, and that they who walk in the darkness could only have a small part in it. I discovered a number of points first with my eyes, and I must confess that I would have understood them only with the ears of my intellect, not with the senses or feeling, if my eyes had not come to my aid. Lay the blame for this on my abstract acquaintance with the work, which of course must be heard in order to manifest its whole power . . . – I would think that if in its total impression it nevertheless appears simple and immediate, that this can only happen at the expense of the mass of detail which one must overlook in order to taste and enjoy the essence completely. One is hunting after a bit of this or that theme, one suspects it also where it is not and becomes worried. One desires to be allowed to fold one's hands, and shut one's eyes

and to be naive, to rest on the heart of the artist and not to be so rest-
lessly driven by him . . . (*Briefwechsel II* 86f.)

But Brahms stood firm: it is true that he showed occasional
scepticism about the capability of the public, even of well-
meaning friends, to grasp the novelty of the work. He announced the planned performance in Frankfurt to Clara Schumann,
'. . . perhaps it will be a dubious pleasure for you!? . . . But
will you go to the concert? . . . but I beg you to tell me simply
whether the whole affair is not too disagreeable for you?' and
then eight question marks and four exclamation marks follow,
the number of the question marks clearly preponderant
(*Schumann-Brahms Briefe* II 294). But except for discarding
the slow introduction, he left the work unchanged. Carefully
rehearsed by himself and Hans von Bülow, it even made a
concert tour of the Meiningen Court Orchestra a triumph.[19] But
in Vienna the public reacted helplessly after a performance
under Hans Richter; some even hissed. Among musicians in
Vienna the main subject of the first movement was underlayed
with the text: 'Es fiel ihm wieder mal nichts ein!' (He once
again had no ideas!) The opposition was not mainly directed
against the grand but unusual chaconne-finale, those incredi-
bly compact 'variations on no theme' (although that again was
no classic symphony finale in the sense of the Beethoven tradition) but against the first movement – as indeed had been the
case with the opposition of his own circle of friends.

The mockers obviously had discovered that the main subject
of the symphony – ignoring for once the octave transpositions –
is a compulsive sequence of equal intervals, seven thirds in the
same direction. Seven thirds enclose all degrees of the diatonic
scale. They appear in descending as well as in ascending
order, so that no note occurs more than once initially and that
each reappears only after all the others of the scale have been
heard. One may doubt that Brahms engaged in this strict constructive obligation because 'he once again had no ideas', or
because the 'melancholy of impotence' determined the character of the work; but surely this was no symphonic theme in
the sense of the Classic–Romantic formal tradition. There are
good arguments, however, that with this symphony Brahms
had come to the point within strict tonal music where he was

19 25 October and 1 November 1885 Meiningen; 3 November Frankfurt/M.; 6 Novem-
    ber Essen; 8 November Elberfeld; 11 November Utrecht; 13 November Amsterdam;
    14 November The Hague; 21 November Krefeld; 23 November Cologne; 25 Novem-
    ber Wiesbaden.

compelled to draw similar conclusions to those Schoenberg drew much later, after his advance into atonality.

Brahms must have been conscious of the fact that with this work he had thought to the very end the tradition of the Classic and Romantic symphony with a thoroughness which was only understood a generation later. Schoenberg himself was the first who, against the image of Brahms as academic composer, the traditionalist captive within historicism and classicism, placed the image of a thoroughgoing innovator.[20] From this clear consciousness of having come to a final point probably resulted his doubts whether the work would be at all comprehensible to the contemporary public. Even to Elisabet von Herzogenberg he put the question seriously: 'Are you at all able to endure the finale until the end? . . . It is very uncertain whether I shall burden the people with the work any more.' (Briefwechsel II 89-90). He took precautions for the publication of the work in the case of his death, but he himself hesitated to publish it immediately.[21] The startled perplexity of even his nearest friends when faced with the work did not cause him to make substantial changes, thus far he was completely sure of his ground, but it did make him very cautious about publishing. He only resolved to publish it after convincing himself with careful rehearsal that his Fourth Symphony was really comprehensible. The concert tour with the Meiningers proved this so unmistakably that the set-back in Vienna did not carry much weight with him (Kalbeck III 456f.).

Even if the opposition of contemporaries was at first provoked by the opening movement, this should not obscure the fact that the finale also made the reception of the work difficult for an audience which was fixed on Beethoven's radiant conclusions. Max Kalbeck recommended that he make the chaconne into an autonomous work and replace it in the symphony with a final movement in the manner of the Beethovenian tradition (Kalbeck III 454), and Joseph Joachim, who – as Elisabet von Herzogenberg said – 'had achieved incredible things in the rehearsals' (Briefwechsel II 115) in order to guarantee the success of the symphony in its first Berlin performance, not only put a note in the programme that it was a variation – movement, but also had the theme printed (Kalbeck III 478).

20 'Brahms, der Fortschrittliche' in Stil und Gedanke, Gesammelte Schriften I (Frankfurt/M. 1976) 35.
21 Johannes Brahms Briefwechsel XI: Johannes Brahms Briefe an Fritz Simrock ed. Max Kalbeck (Berlin 1919) 103-4.

In 1884 there appeared in volume 30 of the Bach Complete Edition, which Brahms himself owned, the Cantata 'Nach dir, Herr, verlanget mich' (BWV 150), the authenticity of which is however often doubted.[22] It is not clear whether Brahms was acquainted with the cantata prior to this but there is a recorded discussion between him, Hans von Bülow and Siegfried Ochs, the founder of the Philharmonic Chorus of Berlin, about the final movement of the cantata, whose passacaglia subject indeed shows a close connection with the chaconne by Brahms. He is said to have agreed with Bülow in his doubts about the effectiveness of a vocal passacaglia and to have said: 'What would you think if someone were to write a symphony movement on the same theme? But it is too bulky, too straight; one must change it somehow.'[23] What Brahms then composed is certainly not a passacaglia with the perpetual presence of the bass theme, but a chaconne. Very soon he must have become conscious of the possibility of combining the chaconne theme, as found in Bach, with his own chain-of-thirds subject from the first movement, which – if the detailed dates are correct, as we must presume – was already finished and whose theoretical implications were in the forefront of his mind.[24]

In the final movement of his Fourth Symphony, which even in its first movement had already reached the limits of formal possibilities under the preconditions set by the material, he intended more than just a clear nod in the direction of closed forms. The principle of the chaconne, with its regular construction which nevertheless dispenses with the continual actual presence of the theme, led him to formal possibilities such as those he had tested in the small songs Op. 93a/95. That he did not intend a theme with variations, as Joachim had described, is clearly shown in the segmentation of the movement into 4 + 8 + 4 and 8 + 8 = 32 transitions. Step by step he approaches the chain of thirds from the first movement until it appears in full in the thirtieth transition (bar 233), and in the thirty-first transition (bar 241) (see Example 2), a truly Brahmsian moment, it is intensified by a canon between bass and violins. The point directly before the coda (transition 32, bar 253), is according to Brahms's idea of

22 A. Dürr *Die Kantaten von J. S. Bach* (Kassel 1971) 628ff.
23 A.v. Ehrmann *Johannes Brahms: Weg, Werk und Welt* 366.
24 Autumn/Winter 1884, publication of the Bach Cantata. Brahms's Notizkalender: Summer 1884 composition of the first movements; Summer 1885: composition of Finale und Scherzo.

Ex. 2

form always a very exposed moment where canons are often found. The chain of thirds taken from the first movement and openly laid upon the chaconne model in the thirtieth transition, only demonstrates how far the dominance of this material in the work goes. To begin the chaconne with the subdominant instead of the tonic is not at all a free artistic decision, but is already determined by the chain of thirds which appears concretely only at the end: the chain also determines the vertical layout of the chords,[25] which Brahms himself demonstrated in the canonic stratification of the thirty-first transition. The rigorous form of the chaconne did not only enable Brahms to remain consistent until the end of the symphony, but also enabled him to pursue further that which he had begun with the main subject of the first movement. For the present it solved the difficulty that the persistent pursual of this track would only allow the production of small forms. Though, indeed in his late piano works small forms preponderate.

Brahms did not finish any further symphony. He was too conscious of the fact that with his Fourth he had already reached a point beyond which the further composition of symphonies as before would have cost him his inner credibility. When he had set an end to his life's work with the seven-times-seven arrangements of folk songs, he wrote to his publisher: 'Did you realize that as a composer I definitely have said farewell?! The last of the folk songs and the same one in my Op. 1 are the serpent which bites its tail and say nicely, symbolically, that the story is over. If I should compose anything for fun, . . . I shall take care that publishers will not be tempted.[26]

25 cf. R. Klein 'Die Doppelgerüsttechnik in der Passacaglia der IV. Symphonie von Brahms' *Österreichische Musikzeitschrift* 27 (1972) 641–8.
26 *Johannes Brahms Briefwechsel XII: Johannes Brahms Briefe an Fritz Simrock* ed. Max Kalbeck (Berlin 1919) 151.

That means: composing and experimenting for himself, yes, but a thorough prevention of anything reaching the public.

The Fourth Symphony became his last and greatest musical triumph in Vienna. On 7 March 1897, less than four weeks before he died, it was performed under Hans Richter in the Philharmonic Concerts. Conductor, orchestra and public had been converted to the work, and thus after the excellent performance of the once so controversial first movement and especially after the monumental chaconne-finale truly thunderous applause broke out until Brahms, who had sat hidden in the depths of the director's box, presented himself to the shocked public, hopelessly ill and bearing the mark of death. His farewell from the world of music therefore was with that very work in which he, as no other composer of his time, had brought the tradition of Classic and Romantic music to its logical conclusion.

DAVID OSMOND-SMITH

The retreat from dynamism:
a study of Brahms's
Fourth Symphony

Beethoven dominated the aspirations of his successors as
have all great teachers of the imagination: by proposing an
ideal that was so vivid, and yet proved so resistant to more
general realization that neither the rapid evolution of musical
circumstance, nor the mummifying effect of general adulation
could prevent it from looming large in the bad conscience of
subsequent generations. Although on a conceptual level that
ideal demanded an organic rather than an episodic vision of
musical structure, and an indissoluble relationship between
the individual detail and the wider whole, this in itself was not
sufficient to impose so sweeping an authority. (Had it been so,
the market for plaster busts of Haydn should have proved
equally brisk.) What assured Beethoven's unique place within
the pantheon was his capacity to body forth this organic vision
in a powerful rhetoric that could capture the imagination of
music's new, middle-class patrons, irrespective of their willingness to delve into a score. Beethoven himself was by no means
insensitive to the musical priorities of his widening audience:
in addressing his Ninth Symphony to 'der ganzen Welt' he
opened with a movement whose comparatively conventional
and loosely argued tonal framework was a direct corollary of
its overwhelmingly powerful rhetorical resources – in direct
contrast to the fierce structural logic of the last quartets and
sonatas, and indeed the previous symphony. But he thereby acknowledged a dichotomy to which nineteenth-century musicians were to find no unanimous solution. If they sought to
emulate the 'Classical' pursuit of organic coherence, they
were maintaining an *ars occulta* from which those of their
listeners unable or unwilling to study scores were barred. But
if they freed the new harmonic and tonal rhetoric of its obligations to structural logic, they were relinquishing a tension
between concept and percept peculiar to notated music, that
had been a necessary precondition for the tonal control of

large spans of musical time (and previously for almost all of
Europe's rich contrapuntal tradition). Even Berlioz, pursuing
this latter option to its radical limits by generating a kaleido-
scopic pattern of tension and release as a self-sufficient
musical proposition could not restrain himself from the odd,
reverential bow in the direction of a seemingly moribund
sonata principle.

This dichotomy was all the more keenly felt by such compulsive Classicists as Schumann and Brahms because of the
uncomfortable example posed by Schubert, to whose lyrical conception of instrumental form both composers looked for a congenial model. For alongside the expansive idiom of his later
chamber works, Schubert had been coming to grips with a
vocabulary of spare, abstract thematic building-blocks that focussed the ear squarely upon larger structural energies. This
sometimes arduous progress[1] reached fruition in his Ninth
Symphony D 944 – an extraordinary, almost encyclopaedic
essay in the structural potential of third-based modulation
chains that was obtained by Schumann from Schubert's
brother Ferdinand for a first, possibly abbreviated, performance under Mendelssohn at the Leipzig Gewandhaus Concerts of 1839. The example of this work proved both decisive
and disastrous to Schumann when he embarked upon his own
career as a symphonist a year later, for without having yet developed any very marked feeling for the generative potential of
tonal logic, he grasped at the repetition of small, abstract thematic units as being in itself a guarantor of symphonic integrity – a particularly persistent feature of the outer movements of his Fourth and Second Symphonies (of 1841 and
1845–6 respectively). The resultant tendency to short-winded-
ness was compounded by his ill-judged transposition into a
symphonic context of the block repetitions within development
sections that Schubert had employed in several of his late
chamber works.[2] Schumann was never to overcome the latter
problem entirely convincingly, despite permutational experiments in the first movement development of his final, 'Rhenish',
Symphony of 1850. But in one respect this movement was to
provide Brahms with a crucial example, for in it Schumann

1 Which can be traced through several of his later piano sonatas, notably those in
  A minor D 784 and 845, and in D major D 850, as well as the Sonata in C for
  piano duet D 812 and the Piano Trio in E flat D 929.
2 Notably, as far as Schumann was concerned, the String Quartet in D minor D 810,
  the Sonata in C for piano duet and the Piano Trio in E flat. Other equally germane
  examples such as the String Quartet in G D 887 and the String Quintet D 956 had
  not yet been published.

finally found the courage of his lyrical convictions and produced an expansive, self-regenerating melodic idiom that
could fill out the symphonic mould without resort to uncongenial abstraction.[3]

It is no unreasonable hypothesis that the forbidding achievements of Schubert's Ninth Symphony, and the problems that
Schumann had encountered in attempting to respond to them
served to compound Brahms's notorious reticence as a symphonist. His disquiet was in part well founded – like them, he
was by instinct a lyricist, and although his attempts to discipline such impulses in the interests of Beethovenian cogency
were a good deal more assured than those of his mentor Schumann, they resulted in an idiom so highly wrought as to be far
better suited to the self-conscious sophistications of the
chamber-music recital than to the democracy of the symphony
concert. It was only once his intensive cultivation of thematic
development and transformation had matured into a melodic
language of deceptive ease and directness, compatible with
the models provided by Schubert's 'Unfinished' Symphony
(which had been published in 1867) and Schumann's 'Rhenish'
Symphony, that he felt able to move beyond the tortuous idiom
of his own First Symphony's opening Allegro[4] to an unapolo-
getically lyrical form of symphonic writing that was nevertheless able to placate the Beethovenian moral imperative of conceptual coherence between tonal planning and melodic detail.

Although this ideal underlies all of Brahms's symphonies, it
is nowhere more overtly and systematically pursued than in
his Symphony No. 4 in E minor, written in 1884–5 and first
performed by the Meiningen Orchestra. For in this work he
chose to confront the tradition, established with particular
clarity by certain of Beethoven's later quartets and sonatas
and by Schubert's Ninth Symphony, of using chains of thirds
as a common element unifying thematic materials and tonal
ground-plan. Beethoven's frequent recourse to this device was
not surprising, for there was no other material that could fulfil
this function with equal flexibility. Extended diatonic third-
chains provided a malleable basis for generating melodic
materials; while sequences of third-based modulations offered

3 Brahms's debt is particularly obvious in the opening subject of his Third Symphony
  – itself conceived on a trip to the Rhine. Furthermore, the triadic progression
  I–iii–V underlying Schumann's exposition is reworked by Brahms in the first movement of his Second Symphony (though the ancestry of this device stretches back
  through Schubert's Ninth Symphony to Beethoven's Fourth).
4 Whose first version was produced between 1855 and 1862.

resources ranging from an enriched cycle of fifths (e.g. I–iii–
V–vii–II etc.)[5] to vivid clashes between non-diatonically related
keys (e.g. I–III– ♭VI) – though the latter could be rendered more
fluent by major/minor shifts on the same tonic (e.g. I–i–♭III–
♭iii–♭V etc.) – or from the rapidly closed cycles represented by
either of the last two examples to the endless meander generated by an irrational mixture of major and minor thirds.

But although, as any ass could see, Brahms opened his symphony with a Beethovenian *hommage* – a figure used in the development of the 'Hammerklavier' Sonata's third movement
(cf. bars 78–84), though here reharmonized to affirm the tonic
– he held back from the dangerous territory into which such
models might have led him. For Beethoven's use of third-chains
in his later works implied an organic vision of sonata form
within which all sections were bound together by an overriding process. This is particularly evident in the two great
B♭-based works, the 'Hammerklavier' Sonata (first subject:
B♭; second subject: G; Development E♭–B) and the Quartet
Op. 130 (first subject: B♭; second subject: G♭; Development D).
The same concern for a unifying dynamism prompted Beethoven to review the function of recapitulation, reworking the
materials of the exposition in the light of the processes un-
leashed by the development. A simple instance is provided by
the opening movement of his Sonata in A flat Op. 110, where a
single descending chain of thirds provides the tonal plan for the
development, and is answered by a recapitulation that reworks its materials around a single rising chain. More complex versions of the same device may again be found in the
first movement of the Op. 130 Quartet where, as a counter-
tension to the falling third-chain summarized above, an
extended development episode in G (bars 113–21) establishes
an upward thrust through the recapitulatory B♭ and on to
D♭ (bars 150–70) before resolving back to the tonic, and in the
'Hammerklavier' Sonata.[6]

But although in his earlier chamber works Brahms had en-
thusiastically adopted the reworked recapitulation as a further aid in maintaining dynamic flow throughout the movement,[7] his use of the device in a symphonic context had become

5 Here, as elsewhere throughout this study, upper case indicates major keys, lower
  case minor keys, whether they are expressed numerically or alphabetically.
  Roman numerals indicate keys or chords; arab numerals indicate degrees of the
  scale. Individual notes are represented in lower case.
6 Of which a lucid analysis may be found in: Charles Rosen *The Classical Style*
  (London 1971) 409–14.
7 A radical example may be found in the Piano Quartet in G minor Op. 25; James

a good deal more circumspect (mainly serving to abbreviate
the recapitulated 1st subject, as in the Second Symphony, first
movement, or the Third Symphony, fourth movement) – and in
the Fourth Symphony he rejected it altogether. This was not
for lack of precedent – the first movements of both Beethoven's and Schubert's Ninth Symphonies have tonally fluid recapitulations precipitated by third-chains spilling over from
the developments – nor necessarily because the concert-hall
demanded broader, simpler forms. But regression to a more
rigid and sectionalized view of sonata form was Brahms's wry
(and perhaps overdue) declaration of autonomy from the overwhelming obligation to dynamism that Beethoven had imposed
upon his youth. By employing a strictly ternary version of the
form, in which an expository mosaic of lyrical units governed
by a wider tonal logic is reworked in recapitulation only as
much as is necessary to bring the second subjects to the tonic,
and third-based sequences are moulded into a meticulously
symmetrical structure in the development, Brahms placed a
question mark against the symphony's traditional celebration
of dynamic growth, that could then be turned into a fierce af-
firmation of stasis – or rather of the 'still point of the turning
world' – in the final passacaglia.

Brahms favoured an idiosyncratic synthesis of the expository practice of Beethoven and Schubert. Although his expositions were frequently tripartite, as were many of Schubert's,
he showed a marked predeliction for placing the second and
third groups in minor and major (or vice versa) versions of the
same key. This practice derives from certain of Beethoven's
piano sonatas, notably Op. 2 No. 3 and Op. 13 and – pre-
eminently – his F minor Sonata Op. 57, whose expository key-
scheme, I–♭III–♭iii minus Neapolitan inflections, Brahms
adopted for his First Symphony's opening Allegro. For his
Fourth Symphony, however, Brahms returned to the i–v–V
scheme that he had used, although with radically different
consequences, in his Piano Quartet in G minor. But whereas in
the quartet the obligation to dynamism welds the sections
together into a continuous sweep, here, on the contrary,
Brahms spaces out his three subjects, setting between them
tonally ambivalent materials so as to give the scheme outlined
in Example 1. The linking episodes each pivot upon ambiguous
versions of G and C – in the first instance tempered by
sharpened fourths, as in Example 2a, and resolving into b and

Webster gives a useful analysis of this in the second part of his 'Schubert's Sonata
Form and Brahms' first maturity' *19th Century Music* III (1979–80) 62–5.

Ex. 1

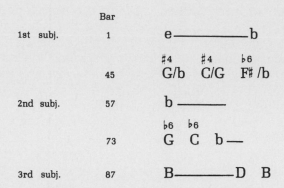

	Bar			
1st subj.	1	e————b		
		♯4	♯4	♭6
	45	G/b	C/G	F♯ /b
2nd subj.	57	b ————		
		♭6	♭6	
	73	G	C	b—
3rd subj.	87	B————D B		

Ex. 2

G respectively, in the second by flattened sixths, as in Example 2b. The ambivalence of the latter figure is exploited structurally. It first appears immediately after Example 2a on the triad of F♯, functioning as the dominant of b – into which it leads for the second subject (bar 53) – and then reappears at bar 73 to assert the tonic in both G and C. The distorted versions of these keys recur throughout the movement, anticipating more solid counter-assertion to the tonic E in the second movement, and complete autonomy as the principal keys of the third.

The three subjects thus insulated from each other have certain elements in common. The first subject, although a continuous lyrical statement, is itself tripartite – each element within it pursuing a different trajectory. The first of these, Example 3a, based upon a chain of descending thirds and answered in this instance by a complementary rising chain, will reappear in more basic form as a counterpoint to the second subject (bar 57) and as an epilogue to Example 2b (bar 80), before finally being absorbed into the third subject. It is only once these third-chains have played out their thematic potential that Brahms permits the same principle to invade the level of tonal organization, with the B/D contrast of bar 125 heralding the development's systematic use of this device. The second element, a chromatically moving bass, Example 3b, is likewise to be left in abeyance until the development. But the filled third above it crystallizes into a process that is to unify much of the rest of the exposition. It is followed immediately by falling fourths (bar 13) and then by filled fourths which provide the first subject's final element, Example 3c. These are taken up in diminution as a counterpoint to the repeated first subject, extended to filled fifths in the first connecting episode (Example 2a) and finally, after temporary abeyance, generate the filled sixths and sevenths of the third subject; Example 4 – the latter descent emphasizing the latent chain of thirds by its dotted rhythm.[8] Falling intervals then give way to rising ones as filled thirds borrow the upbeat pattern of Example 2b in order to open out the comparatively circumspect range of modulation so far used by a direct confrontation of B and D.

Ex. 3

Ex. 4

By contrast, the second subject (bar 57) shares rather more modestly in this game of thematic genetics. Its angularities serve as a necessary foil to the easy contours (upward leap/ slow fall) of the first and third subjects, and its minims pivoting around dominant and tonic give a modest foretaste of the extensive use of melodic pivots in the second movement. But, even so, Brahms cannot resist the pleasures of systematicity, and having used the falling thirds of the first subject as foil to this theme, now reshapes elements from it to provide a descant for the repeat of the third subject (bar 95).

The distance that Brahms has set between himself and his Beethovenian models is most readily measured in the development section. For while the tonal scheme employed is recognizably indebted to Beethoven at his most logical,[9] the musical surface, on the contrary, proclaims Brahms's unabashed affiliation to a lyric conception of the sonata process. A restate-

8 The figure is a reminiscence of Brahms's Violin Sonata in G Op. 78, third movement, bar 87.
9 Notably to the opening movement of the *Eroica*. The comparison will be pursued below in note 13.

ment of the opening theme in the tonic (a play upon the convention of the repeated exposition)[10] is followed by two transposed variations upon the same theme – and a further variation emerges to end the section several tonal skirmishes later. Each proposes a new version of the filled thirds first heard in the repeat of the first subject. Brahms thus stamps upon the first movement a process that is to make an increasingly central contribution to the surface of the two subsequent movements, before taking over as the effective structural principle of the finale.

The initial restatement of the opening theme and its two subsequent variations stake out a tonal progress of unequivocal clarity: a chain of rising minor thirds. The second variation, which uses only the first four bars of the theme twice repeated, finally exploits the modulatory potential of falling thirds – twice rising from b♭ to D♭, and each time falling back rather than close the cycle on the tonic. Instead, Brahms allows the fall to continue through an 'enriched cycle of fifths' third-chain to B which, becoming b, closes the process with a cadence into G. The tonal argument thus far established is summarized in the initial stages of Example 5; the remainder of Example 5 presents the consequences that flow from it – for the G chord articulates the familiar, equivocal ♭6 of Example 2b, multiplied through the octaves in imitation of bar 107, and it resolves into c, quietly asserted by projecting the rhythm of bar 110 onto rising and falling third-chains.

Ex. 5

Bar	
	┌────── minor thirds ↗ ──────┐
145	e ──────── g ──────── b♭ /D♭

	┌──── alternate ────┐ ♭6
176	D♭ b♭ G♭ e♭ B b G ── c ──
	└── major ──┘
	thirds

| | c — chromatic bass — d♯ |
| 195 | (D♭ A: D B♭ : E♭ B) |

| | ┌ major thirds ↘┐ |
| 206 | e   C A♭ /g♯ ──────── |

| | d♯ — chromatic bass ──── b |
| 227 | (A♭ F: B♭ G: C A : D B : E) |

10 Of which a further example may be found in the first movement of Brahms's Violin Sonata in G.

At this point, the first subject's chromatic element comes into its own. Bars 9–15 saw a rise from d♯ to c: here it is complemented by a rise from c to d♯, underpinning a series of interrupted cadences (V⁷ – ♭VI). These tonal shifts rehearse in miniature what is to follow, for having arrived on the dominant of e with a repeat of the figure from bars 184–7, an emphatic reworking of bars 188–91 affirms the home key without stating the tonic chord, and promptly cadences into C. This is complemented two bars later by a drop into A♭ – and the logic of Brahms's tonal plan falls into place. For if the first half of the development began with a rather more leisurely chain of minor thirds rising from the tonic, the second is to be set in motion by major thirds abruptly falling from the tonic. Melodically, the move to A♭ also introduces an inversion of the filled thirds from bar 110, and these are now taken up to provide the final, and most subtle variation upon the first subject. But when this variation reaches the appointed place for a chromatic bass, it offers the chance of a progression to match the one that ended the first half of the development. This time, Brahms protracts the process by altering each dominant seventh to a diminished seventh and back again, before resolving onto the dominant seventh a minor third below. The resultant implication is of minor-third-related keys shifting upward by tones, as opposed to the previous major-third-related keys moving by semitones. The chromatic line, tossed between bass and upper parts, moves from d♯ up to b – balancing the exposition's second chromatic passage at bars 27–31, which moved from d♯ down to b – and ushers in a slow motion reprise of the first subject. For one troubling moment this summons up a familiar ghost – C with its ♭6 – before proceeding to a recapitulation whose adroit and unproblematical reworking of the transition (at bar 285) allows for a near facsimile, save for the appropriate transpositions and some swapping of woodwind roles in the second subject.

The Beethovenian coda – a contained review of some of the energies that ran through the development – is all the more necessary after so faithful a recapitulation. Appropriate impetus is provided by the third-based modulation at the end of the third subject – the exposition's leap from B to D (bar 125) here being replaced a move from E to g♯ (bar 369).[11] This provides a convenient subdominant from which to recapitulate

11 Since the E/G contrast is to be used to trigger the brief, third-based development, inserted into the second movement's recapitulation (bars 76–7), it would have been inappropriate to anticipate the device here.

the development's descending major-third-chain down a semi-tone, thus moving from e♭ through to G; G, as always, retains its ambiguous flattened sixth, enabling it to act as a pivot that leads first to B♭ and then to e – thus encapsulating the minor-third-chain that started the development section.[12] The gravitational pull of the tonic having been reasserted with a final, almost hectoring version of the first subject in close imitation upon itself, all the ambiguous tonal inflections at large within the movement are drawn back into it: first C with its ♭6, then the sharpened fourth, disconcertingly projected onto the traditional tonic/subdominant tension of the classical coda, and finally G, likewise retaining a flattened sixth to the last.

Although this gravitational force is a necessary presence at the end of any movement, it has governed this one throughout its duration. With a third subject that ended in B, and resolved easily back to e for a play upon the conventional repeat, and a development that proceeded to use this key as its pivot, the point of departure for both chains of thirds and the goal for both responding chromatic ascents, the influence of the tonic is pervasive.[13] By the time that Brahms reaches his last movement it will have become all-engulfing; meanwhile, the central movements play out tonal tensions familiar from the first movement in more dispersive form, while allowing surface energies to move to the forefront of musical attention.

The second movement is thus able to enrich its traditional slow movement form – two lyrical episodes, one in the tonic major, the other in the dominant, both immediately repeated in the tonic – with a series of third-based relations that once more imply an upward rising chain. The resultant pattern is outlined in Example 6. Its first bars reactivate the familiar counter-tension of C. But it is no longer this key that bears a flattened sixth, let alone seventh, but the tonic major itself into which the movement opens, as into virgin territory, four bars later. In the interplay between third-related keys thus initiated, the contrast between diatonic and non-diatonic relation-

---

12 And anticipating the major third pivots around E of the second movement.
13 The distance that this establishes from classical precedent can be gauged by a brief comparison with the first movement of Beethoven's *Eroica* Symphony, where the development is likewise based upon two complementary third chains. Although the scale is much broader, the principle is the same: a descending chain of major thirds, spaced out by two cycles of fifths, one descending, the other ascending, (bars 166, 220, 284) is answered by an ascending chain of minor thirds (bars 292–330). But Beethoven's concern for large-scale tonal tension forbids him the use of the tonic save as a final goal – overshot, and then regained at the end of the second chain.

Ex. 6

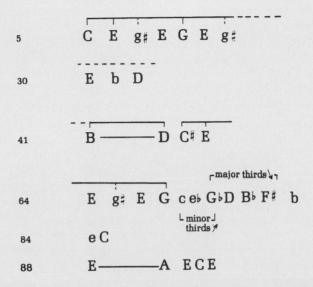

ships is crucial. Thus the E/g♯ tension upon which the first subject's progress is based gives way to a fiercer contrast when, at bar 18, the dominant is transformed into G. Similarly, the b/D contrast that provides a prelude to the second subject is capped by the move from B to D that follows on from it (bar 59–60) – this in turn being answered by a move from C♯ to E that starts the recapitulation's third-chain from a somewhat different perspective. Without an intervening development, literal recapitulation of such closed, lyrical units would make for undue rigidity, for all the ingenuity that Brahms naturally brings to the reworking of the music's surface. Accordingly, he uses the moment of maximal tonal disruption in the first subject, when G challenges the tonic, to launch a miniature development that reworks the familiar gesture of rising minor thirds answered by falling major thirds in microcosm (bars 78–82). After such an episode, the prelude to the second subject naturally avoids reasserting G, and instead gravitates towards C. The second subject is repeated, and the second time round veers towards the subdominant traditional at this juncture – though in beautifully oblique fashion – before resolving through the familiar descent from g♯ to E. C reappears as an undertow to the final bars in recollection of the opening of this movement, and in anticipation of the next.

Within this parsimonious framework, Brahms is able to expand upon some of the lyric processes adumbrated in the first movement. A rather freer version of interval expansion within successive materials is in evidence here, moving from the filled thirds of the opening through to the sevenths and final octave that define the gamut of each succeeding phrase of the second subject – as in Example 7. Equally evident are the expanding pivotal figures that open each section of the exposition, set out in Example 8.[14] As for variation, already an unusually strong presence within the first movement, the slow movement recapitulation offers a traditionally congenial context for displays of skill. Both principal subjects undergo extravagant heterophonic elaboration built on octave displacement, as in Example 9. Furthermore, since the first subject is played twice in exposition and once in recapitulation (the inserted development obliterating the second opportunity), and the second subject vice versa, there is ample opportunity for varying harmony and texture. Both subjects are recapitulated in mellower form – the first without its ♭6 (and without ♭7 either for the first two bars), the second without the moments of harmonic tension that had appeared at bars 41 and 43. Similarly, although the first subject's initial statement establishes a steady flow of low woodwind and pizzicato strings, on its return at bar 22 the woodwind come and go, underlining the theme's irregular use of repetition. Regularity is restored in the recapitulation, but with wind and timpani establishing a counter-accent on the final beat of each two-bar phrase. The second subject, first stated in a restrained string and bassoon texture, with a soaring countersubject from violins (bar 41) returns amidst lush divisi strings, but devoid of countersubject, before launching into the syncopated heterophony noted above.

Although the C major scherzo opens up a wider frame of tonal reference, thematic variation assumes an even more central role within it, for it is here used to generate almost all materials from a single source. The family tree is traced in Example 10, and the only thematic element absent from it is the fanfare that establishes E♭ 's opposition to C in bar 10. The opening proposition (bars 1–6) is answered by a two-bar

---

14 There are also a number of more straightforward correlations, both within the movement (the falling triads that close both first and second subjects, bars 28–9 and 48–9, or the chains of interlocking thirds that fall at bar 42 of the second subject, but rise at bar 52), and with the first movement (the falling chain of thirds underlying bars 46–8 of the second subject, or bar 30–1 expanding upon bar 9 of the first movement) – but discovery of the more detailed instances is best left to the diligent score-reader.

phrase that complements bars 2 and 4 by inversions – pivoting upon g in the first instance, literal in the second – and is immediately repeated in ornamented form. Each of these materials now pursues a separate transformational fate: the

Ex. 7

Ex. 8

Ex. 9

Ex. 10

opening gesture being subjected to the linear manipulations of retrograde inversion in the transition (bar 44) and inversion in the development (bar 139), while its answer provides all the remaining materials through deletion and addition. In contrast to the heterophonic accretions of the second movement, it is the process of deletion that proves most congenial here. Thus bar 18 offers a more skeletal version of bar 6 – and when, by a neat *tour de main*, this is transformed into a second subject juxtaposing the three principal triads of G^{15} (bar 51), it is immediately repeated, reduced to bare bones (bar 62). A further transformation occurs during the development at bar 155 where the melodic shape first introduced at bar 18 is permutated and inverted.

The third-based relationships that so strictly governed the conceptual framework of the first movement have by now assumed a more purely rhetorical role. The ♭III contrast reserved for the end of the exposition in the first movement (bar 125) is here deployed immediately as a local energizer (bar 10) – but with no long-term implication other than that we are headed for G in due course. The second subject (bar 51) confirms Brahms's intention to play down tonal drama by circumspectly refusing to establish G too firmly, being forever tempted by the gravitational pull of the tonic – to which, as in the first movement, it reverts to start the development. Although a single rising chain of thirds still structures this section, its internal relations are not dramatized in any way comparable to the previous exercise in full sonata form, and instead create a fluid tonal structure within which Brahms can concentrate upon his *tour de force* of thematic ingenuity and local harmonic daring. After some aggressive play with the hiatus in the first subject (bar 93), the music slips into a, and from there, via E to cushion confrontation, into c♯ (bar 139). This turns into D♭ (bar 168), pushes quietly up to F to complete the chain of thirds, but immediately reverts to D♭ for a more expansive episode that carries the music back to the tonic by a Neapolitan shift (bar 189). The E♭ interruption then propels the first subject into renewed life, and a straightforward recapitulation follows, modified only by the necessary reworking of the bridge (bar 224) and a new variation upon the second subject. A brief, third-based development upon this deposits the listener upon a pedal G (bar 282), whereupon Brahms proceeds to juggle with phantom oppositions (d/g, d/f and, more pertinently, d/E♭) before loosing a grandly affirma-

15 And containing a hint of the first subject's opening phrase.

tory crescendo towards C that capsizes, at its climax, into F. Flatward gravitation increases in the direction of B♭ (bar 315 and 325) – with the tonic in strenuous opposition. Escape from the impasse is provided by combining the two most striking tonal manoeuvres to date. B♭ slips into A, by analogy with the Neapolitan shift preceding the recapitulation (bar 189), and A is interrupted by the familiar ♭III fanfare that up to now has thundered opposition to C, but here at the last affirms it.

This release of tonal energy within the C/G axis allows the finale to take up the tonic fixation, already prepared in the first and second movements, in absolute form. That Brahms should have sought retreat from tonal dialectic, with all its temptations to mock heroics and dramatic posturing, in the austere intricacies of a passacaglia was a revealing valediction. It was also an original solution to a long-standing problem. Only Mozart really knew the art of balancing a minor first movement with a minor finale – Beethoven found constant difficulty with it, all too often returning, as Joseph Kerman has noted, 'more grossly to the feeling of the opening movement',[16] The problem was avoided altogether in his two minor symphonies, the blinding conviction of whose tonic major apotheoses Brahms could not easily emulate when he adopted the same device for his First Symphony. (Much more true to the genuine Brahmsian spirit was the ironic reversal of this procedure – major-keyed work with minor finale – in the Third Symphony.) Schubert's disconcerting solution in the last two quartets, where the broad perspectives of the first movement give way to spiralling hysteria in the last, was equally uncongenial – and the *Quartettsatz* and 'Unfinished' Symphony provided mute testimony to the difficulties that he had encountered in achieving it. So instead Brahms, like Beethoven in his final years, looked for a sense of ending beyond the dynamics of sonata form. In Beethoven's case the solution had been variously found in fugue and variation. But just as he had been constrained to transform the tonal obligations of fugue to fit it for its new role, so Brahms could not simply emulate the great chaconnes and passacaglias of Couperin, Bach or Rameau, that dominate preceding movements (often a string of binary dances) by sheer extent. He therefore adapted to more flexible structural use the Baroque convention that linked together two succeeding versions of the theme (or alternatively employed an 8 or 16 bar theme whose second half restated the first save for a more final cadence). Working with the eight-bar theme set out

16 Joseph Kerman *The Beethoven Quartets* (London and New York 1967) 266.

Ex. 11

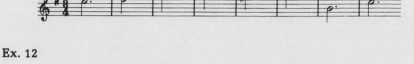

Ex. 12

Harmony

$$\begin{smallmatrix}3\\2\end{smallmatrix}\qquad\begin{smallmatrix}3\\4\end{smallmatrix}$$

1·2·3·4·5·6·7·8·9·10·11·12│13│14 15·16│(1) 17·18·19·20·21·22·23·24·25·26·27·(2 · 3 · 4) 28·29·30·31│32 →

Melody

in Example 11,[17] he coupled certain successive statements through either harmonic structure or melodic features, or both, to create the pattern set out in Example 12 (where the solid lines indicate nearly exact repetition and the dotted lines indicate a degree of variation). The theme's 32 statements[18] divide into two groups of 16, of which the first subdivides into 4 groups of 4, and the second into an elegant retrograde. Of the first group of 16, statements 1–4 and 5–8 pursue the same pattern of an initial coupling of harmonic and thematic materials, followed by a third statement that retains only thematic links with the previous two, and a fourth that is independent. The first group uses the theme as a melodic line, passing it down through the octaves and up again; the second uses it as the bass line, as do most of the remaining statements in the first half[19] – though with a variety of modifications to the final bars. Statements 9–12 consolidate the coupling principle before the final group, 13–16, whose metre expands from $\frac{3}{4}$ to $\frac{3}{2}$. Statement 14 reproposes the harmonic content of 13 in the tonic major,[20] which continues through the thematically coupled 15 and 16, mirroring the late Baroque practice of a major episode in the middle of this traditionally minor form.

Having reached the half-way mark, Brahms re-establishes the original metre and key with a harmonic variation upon statement 1. The symmetrical structure that he imposes upon the second half by couplings of harmonic and/or thematic con-

17 Whose much-emphasized derivation from the ciacona in Bach's Cantata No. 150 is of comparatively little relevance, granted Brahms's substantial modifications to the rhythmic cast of the original.
18 Of which 8 are simply implicit in their harmonic progressions.
19 Save for statements 13, 14 and 16, where it is absent in explicit form, and a brief upward migration during the course of 11.
20 Though there are variants in the final bars.

tent hinges upon statement 25 which, although linked to previous statements by the persistent triplet figure, initiates a recapitulation of statements 2–4, each transformed as it is restated in a manner not unlike the varied recapitulation of the slow movement. In particular, the respective dynamic weights of 3 and 4 is reversed in 26 and 27 – and the latter is also varied harmonically by being worked out over a c pedal. A more general balance between the two halves of the movement is established by again having the theme shift registers at the start of the second half, as at the start of the first – but this time, from statement 20 onwards, it settles for the treble register (although with rather more frequent disappearances).

With so static an overall form, and one so symmetrically proportioned – even the free coda is balanced to a considerable degree by the double duration of statements 13–16 at the end of the first half – attention is naturally focussed upon the amount of variety that can be achieved within each eight-bar statement by means of phrase-length and harmony. Phrase-length in particular is not a notably flexible parameter under these circumstances. The division into two four-bar phrases, although softened in statements 2 (plus its recapitulation at 25), 11, 13, 15 and 16 by the use of one-bar units, is never contradicted save in statement 3, which is phrased as $3 + 3 + 2$ bars – thus serving to underline its recapitulation at statement 26 in particularly striking fashion. This constant focus is underlined by the comparatively stable harmonic treatment meeted out to the theme's a♯ and b (bars 5 and 6). The a♯ is almost invariably identified with $F\sharp^7$ or a diminished seventh (occasionally a German sixth), and resolves onto I with only two exceptions in the first half – though in the second III and V become equally possible. The phrase structure is made the more rigid by the strongly predominant tendency of the first four bars to divide into $2 + 2$ from statement 4 onwards, and it is only the careful leavening of $1 + 3$ or $1 + 2 + 1$ phrase structures employed every so often in the second half of the theme that prevents the rigidity from becoming overwhelming.

An enormous musical onus is therefore placed upon the variety of harmonic inflection and thematic material that Brahms can deploy. But his harmonic fertility serves more than local ends. Although all statements are subject to the gravitational pull of the tonic in their final bars, inventive harmonization may temporarily imply other keys, or confuse the ear with rapid tonal shifts. These, too, can be used to larger structural purpose, and a summary of the resultant formal

Ex. 13

G G !   E   !   g ! ┌Ped. e┐- ┐ Ped. C/G
                                    c
1·2·3·4·5·6·7·8·9·10·11·12│13│14·15·16│17·18·19·20·21·22·23·24·25·26·27·28·29·30·31│32 →

! = rapid modulation

balances is set out in Example 13. Statements 5–10 are quite closely integrated in terms of harmonic content so as to provide a stable sense of growth: indeed, 5 and 6 are harmonic first cousins of 9 and 10, save that the g is harmonized as Ib in the former and as IIIa in the latter. This move towards the relative major in 9 and 10 is anticipated in 7. But the e/G axis thus established is immediately dissolved in 11 and 12 by one of Brahms's most disruptive gestures, whereby the first 5 notes of the theme are treated as a chain of sevenths.[21] It has already been noted that the ⅔ section sets e against E; but as soon as the tonic minor is restored by statement 17 we hear two more statements devoted to rapid tonal shifts followed, in 20 and 21, by implications of a shift to g. Thus another retrograde is established around the E major section – one whose last element also initiates a further group of relations pivoting around the move to recapitulation.

A single, rapidly modulating statement clears the air, ushering in the oscillating e/d♯ pedal that unites 23 and 24. This stabilizes as e in statement 25, underlining the recapitulation of 2, and extends through much of 26 before dropping to a pedal c in 27. This prepares the way for the C/G tonal axis of statements 28 and 29 – a counterweight to the tonal excursions of 20 and 21. Having evoked the tonal axis of the third movement immediately after recapitulating the opening of the last, Brahms now reintroduces the thematic descending thirds of the first movement in statements 30 and 31[22] in order to ground the music firmly back in the tonic.

The sheer variety of melodic invention bodied forth by these carefully controlled harmonic fields needs little analytical commentary. But it, too is put to structural use. For although in the first half the theme assumes a traditional role as ground bass, the sequence of melodies written above it germinate from one another. Thus 6 is a variation of 5, and 7 borrows the

21 A memory, perhaps, of the seventh chains over a rising bass in the first movement's development.
22 A gesture already familiar from statement 23.

rhythm of 6 to articulate a new melodic shape whose appog-
giatura-laden harmonies herald those of 8. When, on the contrary, the theme assumes the role of a variable melody in the
second half, a predictable premium is put upon contrast. Thus
20 and 21 are quite contradicted by 22, whereupon the theme
disappears, only to re-emerge in another new form in 24 in
preparation for the recapitulation.

The frame within which these various processes have inter-
acted is finally broken when a four-bar extension to statement
31 gives notice of disruption. Statement 32 then starts, 'piu
allegro', with a reharmonization of the theme that again
evokes a G–Bb progression, but pauses on the a♯ (now written
as bb). This is interpreted first in g, and then in its familiar
guise of a German sixth, before forging on up the chromatic
scale – and out of the confines of the passacaglia into a free
coda. The scale is harmonized with the pattern of dominant
sevenths resolving onto flattened submediants first heard in
the opening movement (bars 195–202),[23] and having reached f
gives way to a speedier version of the passacaglia theme. This
is repeated over c to recreate the German sixth, which this
time resolves into a concluding peroration in the tonic using
opposing filled thirds derived from statement 3. The passacaglia theme makes a final appearance reworked as a cadential formula, and at its third statement pushes on up through
the chromatic scale to final and absolute closure.

23 Though here moving from tonic to tonic rather than mediant to mediant.

JONATHAN DUNSBY

The multi-piece in Brahms:
Fantasien Op. 116

This study is directed towards an historical end: the better
understanding of an aspect of Brahms's form. In considering
form the analytical literature on Brahms has maintained a
long-standing tradition by concentrating on whole pieces of
music. This concentration has diverted our attention from an
interest in music in sections which do not make a whole in
every sense but which are not entirely unconnected. Music of
that type may even constitute a genre in the nineteenth-
century repertoire. If so, our understanding of nineteenth-
century genres is inadequate in an important area.

The concept of whole pieces informs all analytical 'sys-
tems' for tonal music, that is, all theories about the nature of
tonal structure that are sufficiently rich to embrace different
pieces in the same terminology. The Schenkerian system is
well known for offering the chance to analyse pieces in different styles – by Bach and Chopin for instance – in comparable ways. It is also well known for being preoccupied with
musical wholes. That characteristic, however, is by no means
restricted to the work of Schenker and his followers. Certainly
the Schenkerian tradition represents a high point in the concern with 'organic' unity, but it is the high point of an attitude
that has crossed many scholastic boundaries. The concept of
'organic' unity is the aesthetic premise of virtually all discourse that would nowadays be considered analytical, whether by Riemann, Tovey, Schoenberg or Meyer, or in Brahms
studies from the earliest to the most recent.[1]

The concept of whole pieces is a crude premise about
musical structure, if only because the archetypal presentation
of Classical and Romantic instrumental music is inherently
sectional. Most composers of the period concentrated on writ-

---

1 See for example Edward Evans, Snr *Historical, Descriptive and Analytical Account of the Entire Works of Johannes Brahms* 4 vols (London 1912–36) and Robert
Pascall 'Formal principles in the music of Brahms' (Diss. U. of Oxford 1972).

ing multi-movement pieces. Yet the concept of the multi-movement piece was not consistent from the early Classical to the late Romantic periods. Common knowledge about performance practice is evidence enough. Whereas it was tolerable, even desirable, and certainly the case, for Classical movements from multi-movement pieces to be performed separately, this was no longer either Brahms's or his audience's expectation. Common understanding of the history of composition would also suffice to show this trend. It is generally believed that Beethoven's multi-movement works were more structurally integrated than those of his predecessors: we may even want to assume – against the Schenkerian view – that the movements in Beethoven are therefore 'less whole' than the earlier, Classical aesthetic permitted. It is also understood that the development of relatively extended single-movement works, on a well-charted course through Schubert's *Wanderer-Fantasie* and Liszt's symphonic poems, led to what amounted to a new standard practice in Strauss and Schoenberg. All these points are in themselves coarse, subject to notable exceptions, and culturally restricted – it is less easy, for example, to describe French Romantic music in the same manner. Nevertheless, they demonstrate the poverty of the proposition that music either does or does not make a whole.

This poverty is even more apparent in the face of the novel aspects of nineteenth-century composition. The miniature, above all, the short piano piece, became a significant genre. The miniature was the province not only of the salon and the benefit concert where the virtuoso-cult was nurtured, but also of the serious composer pursuing his art for art's sake. This genre was not merely a kind of *Gebrauchsmusik* for Mendelssohn, Chopin or Schumann. Brahms learned from his predecessors that the short instrumental piece was among the highest forms of expression. It was as valid to make 'great' music in this genre as it was to make it in the *Lied*. In Hoffmannesque terms, it was even better to do so, since only instrumental music could express the 'truly characteristic spirit of music itself'.[2] The combination of miniaturism and a continuation of the Classical tradition led to the investigation of a new form of musical connection, the connection of small, heterogeneous pieces to make a large homogeneous work. Although little attention has been directed towards the history of this development, few doubt that its existence is confirmed both in histori-

2 R. Murray Schafer *E.T.A. Hoffmann and Music* (Toronto 1975) 83.

cal authenticity and in our current perception of some Romantic music. For example, song-cycles like Schumann's *Frauenliebe und -leben* were always intended to be and are comprehended as musical structures rather like multi-movement instrumental works. In instrumental music, this genre goes back at least as far as the late Beethoven *Bagatelles* and continues beyond the nineteenth century into post-tonal composition. It is most conspicuous in Schumann's piano works. We may question whether *Kreisleriana* makes a whole in just the same way that *Carnaval* makes a whole; but the performance of separate items from either of those pieces is not considered by many musicians to be entirely satisfactory. No body of evidence will be presented here to support the idea that a genre of 'multi-pieces' can be identified in many areas of nineteenth-century music. It will be important to assert that idea, however, and to distinguish it from the notion of a 'collection'. Schumann may have denied the relevance of the concept of the whole in *Carnaval*, yet we would lose a critical tool in our understanding of Romantic form if we therefore equated the overall structure of *Carnaval* with that of, say, Chopin's Op. 17 Mazurkas.

In order to ask useful questions about Brahms's practice in this respect, a familiar distinction – between pieces, including multi-movement pieces, and collections which are not wholes – is being set aside in favour of new distinctions – between pieces, multi-movement pieces, multi-pieces and collections. The new categorization is really as coarse as the old one, but it has the merit of including, within the scope of the analysis of unity, music which has traditionally been ignored. To make this point by analogy, it is necessary only to ask how useful are existing theories about variation form. Whereas competing arguments can be put about the coherence of *Carnaval* or the *Dichterliebe* cycle and many scholars present powerful challenges to the analysts of unity in such cases, there has been little argument about the 'organic' status of variations. The techniques of variation are well understood and of general interest. That is, indeed, one of the least controversial areas of analytical study.[3] It is accepted that formal categories like sonata, rondo and arch-form are not often relevant to variations, so music theorists and composition teachers alike have said that there is a category called 'variation form'. What goes to make a variation structure, however, is hardly known.

3 For the fullest account in this field, see Robert U. Nelson *The Technique of Variation* (Berkeley 1948).

Schenkerians have not asked why Schenker could not or would not deal with this aspect of the history of tonal structure: neither have those who reject Schenker thought to point an accusing finger on this basis. A theory of Classical and Romantic musical structure which has no good explanation of variation structure should be treated with some caution, unless it is proposed that what are often called 'additive' forms like variation are not truly part of the history of tonal practice.

Although variations are discussed here only by analogy with the status of Brahms's collections, it is worth exposing the Schenkerian loophole more specifically from an appropriate source. Among Schenker's analytical essays is a study of the *Variations and Fugue on a Theme by Handel* Op. 24. The variations are analysed sequentially with little reference to an overall structure. In the 'Supplement', each variation has a separate graphic representation showing various forms of the fundamental structure of the Aria. There is great variety in these structures: those who know Schenker from *Free Composition* and the *Five Graphic Music Analyses* would be surprised to find that the model of a fundamental line descending from the dominant is varied by elaborate ascents and incomplete structures – for example $(\hat{1}\ \hat{2})\ \hat{3}\ (\hat{3}\ \hat{4})\ \hat{5}\ \hat{4}\ \hat{3}\ \hat{2}\ \hat{1}$ in Variation 5 and $\hat{3}\ \hat{5}\ \hat{4}\ \hat{3}$ in Variation 3. Variation 21 is the most promising place to look for some indication of whether Schenker thinks Op. 24 is generally goal-directed, since it involves the rare feature in variations of one number not in the home key:

This variation, quite detached from the previous one, opens a new group of variations which rely on a more or less static bass. Apart from that, it is the only one to abandon the tonic B flat; it is in G minor. But admittedly, the voice which presents the fundamental line behaves as it has before, that is as if it had stayed in B flat major. If one were to examine this on its own, it would not seem for a moment that the tonality of the theme had been abandoned . . . I assume that Brahms took as a model for this variation the sixth variation of Beethoven's *Eroica Variations* Op. 35, where the real tonality of the upper voice (E flat major) is contradicted by an artificial harmonization (C minor). One may well consider this artificiality to be out of place; on the other hand one can understand the temptation to reflect a familiar shape as it were simultaneously in two tonalities. It is not quite the case here, then, that the G minor tonality is altogether denied – this is and remains the tonality of this variation: it was simply the artist's job to introduce into this tonality an attractive, secret contradiction on account of its ancestry in a B flat major scale.[4]

4 Heinrich Schenker 'Variationen und Fugue . . .' *Der Tonwille* IV 2/3 3–46 and Supplement (Vienna 1924) 25–26 (my translation).

Any wider significance for this tonal oddity – for instance, in relation to the harmonic structure of the fugue – is ignored. Evidently Schenker is not thinking in terms of a fundamental structure for the whole work that is at all akin to the fundamental structures of other tonal forms. A passage near the end of his analysis bears this out:

For the images of variations do not somehow float by like pictures in a panorama . . . nor do they rely only on the connective effect of contrasts or of continuously increasing animation: formally the variations amount to a succession of generations, so that they join with the genealogies of the Old Testament in saying: And the first begat the second, the second the third, the third the fourth, and so on. There is nothing too small or too fleeting to be called up for further generation.[5]

This is not a particularly useful theory about variation structure, since it deals with the connection of musical ideas but not with the sum of such connections. From an important point of view such a theory cannot be considered adequately rich when it implies that, given the necessary generative connection between one variation and another, there may as well be two or a hundred variations making a piece. Nor can we rely entirely on the authority of the composer to say what makes a piece. There is many a case which underlines the difficulty of building structural theories on that authority alone – be it Beethoven's Op. 130 String Quartet or Berg's *Lulu*. If the only explanation for the overall number and disposition of the variations in Op. 24 is that Brahms decided it should be so, we must accept that the work is not amenable to analysis, certainly not in the sense that a Brahms symphony is. The lesson of variation form seems to be that a traditional view of unity has so diverted the attention of our scrutiny of nineteenth-century music that such issues have been considered unimportant. In view of the state of our understanding of variations, it is no surprise that there is no theory of genre to account for the

---

5 Ibid. 35. Two further sources provide a fuller picture of Schenker's account of variations. The first is 'Ein Gegenbeispiel: Max Reger Op. 81' in *Das Meisterwerk in der Musik* (Hildesheim 1974) II 171–92. Schenker's repeated point here is that a variation must relate to the 'organic' voice-leading structure of the Theme and it must in itself present an organic structure (which Reger conspicuously fails to carry out, he says, in the *Variations and Fugue on a Theme by J. S. Bach*). The second, also from *Das Meisterwerk*, is the analysis of the Finale in the essay 'Beethovens Dritte Symphonie zum ersten Mal in ihrem wahren Inhalt dargestellt' III 25–101. Here Schenker accounts for the movement in organic terms – with a $\hat{3}$ $\hat{2}$ $\hat{1}$ first level, and second- and third-level diminutions – and treats the variational articulations as formal, subsidiary aspects (74–84).

more obscure areas of what constitutes a multi-piece or a collection.

At another extreme, collections have been pressed into the service of the analysis of unity as if they were equivalent to pieces or to multi-movement pieces. The most decisive incursion into Brahms studies in this respect came from Réti. Although he did not deal extensively with Brahms's collections, he provided a model, with his analysis of the *Rhapsodien* Op. 79, for treating all Brahms's collections as pieces.[6] There appears to be no historical evidence for Réti's claim that Op. 79 makes a single piece. Moreover, we cannot disprove what Réti claims by reference to other collections which do not appear to cohere to the same extent: negative analytical 'proofs' of that kind are of little interest, since they hold true only until positive analytical results arise – a possibility that can never be discounted. Réti himself began just such a process. By demonstrating a unity in Op. 79, he effectively silenced those who may not have suspected it: one simply believes his analysis or not; and how could a counter-analysis hope to show that the diversity in Op. 79 is somehow more significant than the unity he describes? It should have seemed remarkable to Réti to discover such a composition in Brahms, the Brahms who was disinclined to write song-cycles despite all the precedents and who wrote a further rhapsody published with three intermezzos (Op. 119 No. 4). On the other hand, Réti was not in any case flying in the face of a mass of potential evidence in Brahms. In the instrumental music, the only roughly analogous material (pieces grouped into an opus) is Opp. 10, 76, 116, 117, 118, 119, 122, and perhaps also the Waltzes Op. 39 and the Hungarian Dances.

Various Brahms scholars have speculated about the unity of these collections, without Réti's tenacious commitment to a

---

6 Rudolph Réti *The Thematic Process in Music* (London 1951). The extent of Réti's commitment in these matters should not be underestimated. Consider his remarkable statement: 'Now it can in general be assumed that whenever a composer of structural consciousness includes two or more pieces under one opus number, this should, and frequently does, mean that these items constitute an artistic unit, that they represent a higher architectural whole formed from a common thematic material' (70). In his work on *Kinderszenen* he notes how the 'architectural design comes very close to a "Theme with variations"', and how the '*Etudes symphoniques* can hardly be regarded as much closer to the outspoken variation form', and mentions *Carnaval*, the *Davidsbündlertänze* and *Kreisleriana* as 'other examples'. The most significant comment of all in relation to my discussion is that, 'actually, all these works lie somewhere between mere suites on the one hand and genuine variations on the other' (32), revealing an authoritative awareness of the generic issue, if rather begging the question of what goes to make 'genuine variations'.

purely analytical case. A notable lead for such thinking is to be
found in the work of Kalbeck. He shifted from one diagnosis to
another rather than coming to any firm conclusion about the
formal status of the sets of piano music. Yet his willingness to
display an uncomfortable position in print is a sign that he recognized the importance of the matter. His points about Op.
116 provide ample illustration. Kalbeck suspects that there is
some degree of unity in this collection. The most revealing comment is one that seems to embrace all seven pieces: 'One piece
always seems to be contained as a kernel in another: or it
always has its shoot, which grows into some offspring (*Tochterpflanze*)'.[7] The most consistent idea to emerge from Kalbeck's
consideration of the four last piano collections, however, is
that all are interconnected, the division into four opus numbers having no special musical significance. It follows that
Kalbeck finds the history of Op. 116 unremarkable, although
he does mention how Brahms originally suggested to Simrock
that Op. 116 should be published in one volume of five numbers. This evidence means that two of the Op. 116 collection
were added by Brahms at a relatively late stage of the publication process. Since Kalbeck does not interpret Op. 116 as a
complete, logical structure in its final form, he assumes that
the added pieces were Nos. 6 and 7 but does not say why. In
general, it seems that the Brahms literature has gone little
beyond the kind of view outlined here in Kalbeck: it is thought
that the last piano pieces belong to a stylistic pool. One com-
mentator may notice motivic correspondences,[8] another the
possibility of a tonal cycle,[9] yet another the expressive coherence of works in one opus.[10] No violence will be done to the
suspicions of several generations of Brahms scholars if we
look more closely than before at the collection most obviously

7 Max Kalbeck *Johannes Brahms* IV (Berlin [2]1915) 286.
8 For an analysis of Op. 116 based mainly on motivic correspondence, but also
   referring to the tonal scheme, see Thomas Owen Mastroianni 'Elements of Unity in
   Fantasies, Op. 116 by Brahms' (Diss. U. of Indiana 1970), to which the credit should
   go for being what I believe was the first technical study of this aspect of Op. 116.
9 W. Siegmund-Schultze *Johannes Brahms* (Leipzig 1966) 112–18. Siegmund-
   Schultze hints at an overall function for Op. 116 No. 7. He also mentions the tonal
   plan of Op. 119: b–e–C–e♭ [E♭ ?], but not why it should be considered a meaning-
   ful tonal plan. It does rearrange a relationship found, for example, in Op. 116 No. 1
   (development: d–a–c♯–B♭), indicating harmonic constituents making some sense in
   Brahms's language as a roving progression; and the minor ending of Op. 119 No. 4
   brings it in line with the mode of the first piece. Nevertheless, such offhand critical
   diagnoses with no analytical explication are more likely to confuse than enlighten.
   No judgement is made here about Op. 119 beyond what is said below about the
   tonal schemes of all the late piano pieces.
10 Denis Matthews *Brahms Piano Music* (London 1978) 70 for example.

unified by the kinds of structural process found in multi-movement pieces or, indeed, in single pieces.

There is little by way of a norm for this kind of investigation. Since it confronts an admittedly problematic aesthetic issue, it is appropriate to approach more detailed analysis on the basis of simple questions that arise *prima facie* when a unity in Op. 116 is proposed. The first is whether Brahms's title supports or contradicts the notion of a multi-piece rather than a collection. In view of the history given by Kalbeck, we might assume *Fantasien* to be a generic rather than formal title. On the other hand, it is entirely possible that by the addition of two pieces Brahms saw a way to turn a collection into a slightly longer multi-piece, that is, that he recognized a latent quality in a collection he had already made. Nevertheless, it is hardly conceivable that it was because of this that he used the title *Fantasien*, or only if it had some meaning to him which he could expect no one else to know. The individual titles themselves varied: although finally the Op. 116 pieces were called either Capriccio or Intermezzo, No. 4 was originally Notturno before becoming Intermezzo. If Capriccio, Intermezzo and Notturno can all also be *Fantasien*, it is clear at least that the generic title allows sharp expressive contrast.

Further interpretation emerges from a comparison with other collections. The most neutral designation used by Brahms is *Klavierstücke*, used for Opp. 76, 118 and 119. Both Opp. 117 (*Drei Intermezzi*) and 79 (*Zwei Rhapsodien*) fall into a category similar to that of the *Klavierstücke*: since in these two collections the pieces are obviously in the same genres respectively, Brahms simply uses the generic name. An interesting comparison exists in these cases between Réti and Kalbeck. Just as Op. 79 makes a unified work for Réti, so Kalbeck observes that Op. 117 No 2 is connected thematically with Nos. 1 and 3 (Kalbeck 280). Although Kalbeck does not enlarge on why this should matter, clearly he did not think of Op. 117 as a strictly heterogeneous group of pieces in the same genre.

The case of generic title in Brahms apart from Op. 116 is the *Balladen* Op. 10. Here the relationship between generic and individual title must be important, since *Balladen* has an identifiable implication. Op. 10 No. 3 is called Intermezzo, and the fact that it is also a Ballade indicates that, like the other three pieces in the collection, it has a literary inspiration or reference. True, so does Op. 117 No. 1 with its poetic superscription; but *Balladen* is nevertheless the clearest case of a title with a reasonably comprehensible connotation. We have to ask, then, what *Fantasien* might indicate by analogy with *Balladen*. Certainly Op. 116 revives from Brahms's earlier life the Kreislerian world of the expressively bizarre. From a style-critical point of view it might suffice to accept that Brahms's title means a collection of pieces using rather singular musical ideas and treatment – the relatively dissonant and obsessively patterned No. 5 may be the best example. Further speculation could link Op. 116 with the Hanslickian world of *Phantasie* as the true aesthetic moment of music. Perhaps, then, Brahms meant to suggest that these are not sentimental pieces, that the title indicates a certain seriousness of compositional intention.

It is also possible that a *Fantasia* form is to be found in each piece. But *Fantasia* could cover many formal types from quasi-sonatas (Schubert Op. 15, Mendelssohn Op. 28, Schumann Op. 17) to so-called collections (Schumann's *Fantasie-Stücke* Op. 16 – the *Kreisleriana*), and in the field of the ubiquitous operatic fantasy it was bound up with the technique of variation and *pot-pourri* form. If the title *Fantasien* in Op. 116 does refer to form, the usage has little obvious generic reference. Nevertheless, a description of the forms and, ideally, of the form itself will be important evidence about the nature of this collection. It demonstrates not only a variety of traditional, 'closed' forms, but also an unusual closed overall pattern.

Nos. 1 and 7 are the most elaborate closed forms. The first piece is a symmetrical sonata form – symmetry in the disposition of material in an A–B–B–A pattern, sonata form in the harmonic relationship I–III–VI–I of this pattern and the tonal richness of the developmental middle section. No. 7 is broadly ternary, but also variational (in the sense well known from Op. 119 No. 2), and with a relatively long cadenza-style link to the reprise. Nos. 2 and 6 are ternary forms with equivalent modifications: both have an extensively varied reprise. Nos. 3 and 5 are the simplest forms, ternary and binary respectively, although the beginning of the second section in No. 5 introduces a new theme, suggesting ternary form despite the typical binary ending of the first section on the dominant (cf. Op. 119 No. 1 for an analogous case). No 4, the central piece, is not so easily classified in these traditional formal terms. It may be seen as a two-section form divided at bars 35–6. It is also an example of what Schoenberg termed 'developing variation'. Two ideas, antecedent and consequent at the beginning (bars 1–4/10–14), are varied independently, and each is transformed in extended cadential passages. By the end of the piece their

roles have been reversed. The antecedent which was originally part of a phrase leading to V (bar 9) now closes the penultimate phrase in the tonic (bars 56–61), the consequent providing a coda (bars 67–71). In summary, it seems that there is
formal variety when four different formal types are used in
seven pieces. On the other hand, the symmetrical arrangement
of these forms is hard to gainsay. No. 4 is the single type surrounded by pairs, Nos. 3 and 5 as relatively simple forms, Nos.
2 and 6 as modified forms, and Nos. 1 and 7 as relatively complex forms.

A different question to arise from speculating about the
unity of this collection is the nature of the unity of its elements,
that is, of the seven different pieces. It is one of the most remarkable facts about multi-movement structures, albeit one of
the least discussed, that the unity of each movement is thought
to be as thorough as the unity of the whole. Schenker hopes to
cater for this in principle with the idea of reduplication, the
transference of structural unities from one level to another. In
a case like the *Handel Variations* 'fundamental structures', if
such they are, can be arranged in sequence. But in Schenker's
explanations of multi-movement pieces the fundamental structures of the movements have to be embedded in the whole
reduplicatively. This means that, for example, an organically
sound, unified first movement can be embedded in an organically sound, unified sonata. Whereas the typical reservation
about Schenker's theory is to ask why all pieces should have
roughly the same fundamental structure, the tradition of multi-
movement pieces might lead us to ask why all movements
should in themselves display a closed structure at all. In the
case of collections, the focus is reversed. We expect that the
pieces will be complete. If they appear not to be complete, we
may justifiably look for their completion elsewhere, that is,
later in the collection: this may indeed be one of the best signs
we could hope to find of a multi-piece as opposed to a collection. It does raise difficulties. An exemplar is in Schumann's
Dichterliebe, where the first song ends (on V, or V of VI) in a
way that inevitably suggests completion in the opening of No. 2.
Yet there is little evidence that Schumann planned *Dichterliebe* as a structurally coherent cycle,[11] and even if he did it
would be an analytical problem to account for just one connection that is so close.

The fourth piece in Op. 116, already mentioned as the singu-

11 Rufus Hallmark *The Genesis of Schumann's Dichterliebe: A Source Study* (Ann
   Arbor 1980).

lar formal centre of the *Fantasien*, seems to offer an example of lack of wholeness or of excessive implication. Its opening is derived from No. 1. Here Kalbeck's notion of a *Tochterpflanze* is most appropriate, since it is an incidental moment from No. 1 (derived there from the chromatic lines of bars 21ff.) that becomes the main idea of No. 4 (see Example 1).

Ex. 1

In No. 1, this figure marks the first and strongest move in the piece to a remote harmonic region. In a sketch of the root progression for No. 1 as a whole, Example 2 shows how the C sharp harmony introduced by that figure may be interpreted as a progression in thirds between V of V (E major) and VI (B flat major), marked between bars 79 and 103. It is a moment of great expressive weight, but the larger coherence of the tonal structure is plain enough and not threatened by this local event (see Example 2).

Ex. 2

In No. 4, however, the development of this idea seems to question the degree to which tonal closure could be shown in the piece. Developments of the main idea in bars 32 and 50 can be understood schematically as a symmetrical filling-in of I–V and IV–I progressions (see Example 3).

Ex. 3

In the first case, there is no contextual problem either. Following the G sharp minor close at bar 36 there is a cadential passage returning in a reasonably orthodox manner to the tonic at bar 49. In the second main development of the opening idea, however, there is no similar continuity following the substituted C sharp major in bar 52. The harmony returns as quickly to the tonic in bars 53ff. as might be expected after a normal half-close. It is always possible – according to the kind of argument that arose in considering Réti – that some future analysis may show the harmonic and tonal continuity in this piece. Meanwhile, it is worth noting the casuistry this would involve and weighing it against the effect of connective characteristics in Op. 116. No discontinuity is suspected if this feature of No. 4 is understood as the elaboration of an implication in No. 1, fulfilled only later.

The unresolved, remote progression in No. 4 is taken up in No. 6, where C sharp major is again the substituted cadential goal (bars 7–8). This time, however, it is more integrated into the tonic region: the harmony moves in varied sequence to the subdominant (bar 12) and through chromatic supertonic chords and the dominant firmly back to the tonic (bars 22–3), at the end of the first section of the piece. Two larger-scale aspects of No. 6 support the idea that here the implications of earlier pieces are resolved. First, the first section with its C sharp substitution is followed by a middle section in G sharp minor, thus reversing the G sharp/C sharp process of No. 4. Second, the reprise in No. 6 avoids altogether a progression to the major submediant. No. 7 contains an appropriate sign of tonal closure. In No. 1, C sharp harmony progressed from the dominant of D, that is, from A. In the middle section of No. 7, C sharp harmony returns in a similar context. The sequence: A minor (bar 29) – B minor (bar 31) – C sharp minor (bar 33) leads back to A minor to close the middle section; and this A minor is of course the dominant of D minor in the overall tonality of No. 7. No. 5, with its simple harmony around the E minor tonal centre, does not interfere with the tonal relationship between Nos. 4 and 6, and the contiguity of Nos. 6 and 7 reinforces the final process. This final process is doubly appropriate in the sense that Nos. 1, from which it derives, and 7, in which it resolves, are in any case closely related.

The relationship between Nos. 1 and 7 is not only a matter of their shared key of D minor (an aspect of the structure to be discussed below). The closest detailed correspondence comes with the coda of No. 7, with its $\frac{3}{8}$ time-signature. This not only

transforms the material of No. 7 into the metre and typical
rhythmic patterns of No. 1, but the transformation begins with
the most characteristic sonority from No. 1, a (syncopated)
augmented chord. Example 4 shows this correspondence, and
other points in Op. 116 where the expressive role of the augmented chord is kept alive:

Ex. 4

The strong affinity between Nos. 1 and 7 can easily be gauged
by performing them consecutively. Comparing this case with
Op. 79, which according to one writer is 'performable as a
contrasted pair *despite occasional similarities*' (Matthews 56,
my emphasis), the relative kinship of the two Capriccios is
outstanding.

   The unifying elements examined so far have been prominent
rather than omnipresent. One should be cautious in exposing

consistent and continuous elements in a multi-piece, since from one point of view it is precisely lack of contrast which ought to characterize collections rather than multi-pieces. The simplest idea of a collection is that pieces of the same genre, for the same medium, are presented to the consumer because they are likely to be used in more or less similar ways. It may make a pleasing sequence to take such a collection all at once – for instance, with Brahms's Op. 39 Waltzes. On the other hand, there is a sharp limit to the effectiveness of such a formation, in the absence of a tension between contrast and unity to provide long-term musical 'logic': thus Brahms's Chorale Preludes Op. 122 are clearly not designed to be played as a group. In the tension between contrast and unity that marks genuine long-term logic, however, the elements of unity can appear as relatively intermittent although hierarchically deep features of the kind described so far in Op. 116; or they can be threaded into the continuity of the foreground. These latter may appear in genuine collections, as they do usually in variations, but not in combination with a deeper level of unity. In extended tonal structures it is the interaction of levels that is considered a sign of musical richness and coherence.

In Op. 116 there is a three-note motivic cell, present in all the main themes (see Example 5).

Ex. 5

It is characterized by note repetition, usually an initial surface feature of a piece. In Nos. 5 and 7 a structural level slightly below the foreground has to be brought into play, but this is a modest analytical step, a matter of the relationship between melodic ideas rather than adjacent notes. It is true, nevertheless, that such a motivic cell is not unique to these seven of Brahms's twenty late piano pieces. Example 6 shows only the most obvious cases where the cell arises elsewhere than in Op. 116 as an important surface feature. Even the chromatic progression of Example 1, said here to be a deeply effective source of overall unity in one collection, is a prominent figure in at least one other of the twenty pieces (cf. Example 1 and the Intermezzo Op. 119 No. 1, bars 17–18).

Ex. 6

Beyond the surface cells, however, there is a more thorough kind of thematic unity in Op. 116. Nearly all the thematic material is related to two figures in various transformations as demonstrated in Example 7 (x and y/Y).

Ex. 7

† and cf. b. 21–4 and No. 4 [Ex. 1]

The significance of this kind of unity lies not so much in the mere presence of thematic materials of a rather basic kind (a progression in thirds and a turn figure embedded in an arpeggiated six-four) but in the structure of themes as combinations of these materials. No. 2 is especially revealing. Its two-part theme combines x and y in one of the simplest counterpoints available with these shapes. The A major section from bar 51 provides a contrasting setting which, according to Kalbeck, 'betrays the real source of the melody, the upper-Austrian Ländler' (Kalbeck 284). It also betrays the contrapuntal basis of Brahms's thematic variation, for it is a straightforward inversion of the two-part setting from the opening (see * on Example 7). This is only the most explicit version of a process of combination to be found to some extent in all the pieces. Example 7 exposes only the highlights of this process. The music is saturated with these shapes in different combinations. It is only to be expected in Brahms's motivically taut compositional practice, well described in the Brahms literature, that the music should derive in readily explicable ways from the main idea of each piece. A more detailed version of Example 7 going through each piece would show only what is already a common wisdom - much to be valued - about the relationship in Brahms between idea and continuity. The essence of the analysis here is to show that the fundamental materials are related in something like the way to be found in conventional large forms, whether pieces, multi-movement pieces, variations or, as is possible, collections.

All the analysis so far leads towards the question of whether it is permissible to interpret Op. 116 as a large tonal form. Its elements of more and less hierarchically structured unity already distinguish it from what is expected of a collection, which may have one of these levels but not both. The arguments for why it is worth investigating the tonal character of Op. 116 have now been well aired. Yet it is not obvious how a tonal scheme should be expressed for a multi-piece. In single tonal forms, part of the work of analysis is to provide an articulation of the music. This expresses the relative importance of different sections, a question which has to do with the interaction of the various structural variables: in tonal music, these are traditionally named as thematic, rhythmic, harmonic, textural, dynamic and so on, even if there is little agreement in individual cases about how such categories actually apply to a piece. In Schenker, certain contrapuntal figures are supposed to be the fundamental bases of large and small forms, and this automatically accounts for various aspects of articulation. For example, because sonata form is always an interrupted form - to account for the recapitulation - it is necessarily a two-section form at the deepest level of articulation. Whether either of these points of view is pertinent for the form of a multi-piece is a matter of conjecture.

Should we take as the practical basis of articulation the division of a collection into pieces; or is it musically logical, given that a multi-piece is being analysed as if it were a single large form, to cross the boundaries between pieces where this seems appropriate? The idea that the articulation between one piece and another could be considered less pertinent than the articulation between tonal regions within one piece presents the most radical challenge to the conventional notion about how such pieces come to be published together.

Some degree of solution is available by incorporating the tradition of formal analysis. Example 8 shows a sketch of the tonal sequence of all seven pieces:

Ex. 8

No. 1 2 3   4 5 6   7

Its effectiveness as an analogy with conventional goal-directed tonal structures depends greatly on the relationship between Nos. 2 and 7. and 7. No. 2 is entirely in its own tonic, despite the fact that it represents in other respects a clearly articulated ternary form with a contrasting middle section following a tonic close. It therefore registers only one stage of the tonal plan. This means that it is entirely in a dominant relationship to No. 1. The first piece has a rich tonal structure of its own, as was demonstrated in Example 2, but it is also a through-composed rather than a sectional form, so that, again without misrepresenting the patent articulations of one piece ending and another beginning, No. 1 can register the single step of D minor in the sketch. No. 7, however, has its own I–V–I structure coinciding with the articulations of the sectional form. A piece at the end entirely in D minor would have suggested an overall tonal structure with no return to the 'tonic' D minor via the dominant. The V which makes up the middle section of No. 7 is clearly vital to any possibility of interpreting Example 8 as a goal-directed tonal pattern. Although Example 8 is neither in fact nor intention strictly conformant with Schenker's conception of tonal structure – and is in any case incomplete in that it fails to show contrapuntal voice-leading – it is worth noting also that the final dominant/tonic resolution in normal tonal forms nearly always does appear very near the end of a piece. The distinction between cadential and structurally resolving phases of tonal forms is one of the grey areas in voice-leading analysis. At least it can be said that the role ascribed here to the middle section of No. 7 is not, by analogy, unduly prominent.

This tonal interpretation of Op. 116 depends fundamentally on the relationship between the keys of the pieces. The more detailed relationships to emerge from Example 8 are a refinement rather than a contradiction of that basic evidence. Op. 116 in any case makes a relatively restricted choice of keys in comparison with other late collections (including Op. 76 from 1879):

Opus number	Number of pieces	Number of different keys not counting difference of mode
76	8	7
79	2	2
116	7	4
117	3	3
118	6	4
119	4	4

The choice is even more restricted in Op. 118, where the possibility of some tonal cohesion may be suggested by the patterning of keys in descending tones: a–A–g–f–F–e flat, and by the pairings a–A and f–F. The keys of the early Op. 10 collection also have the latter characteristic: d–D–b–B. However, the mere patterning of keys is not a structural function with which we would expect Brahms to have taken much trouble. The prolongation of a tonal centre, which appears in Op. 116 and, it seems, nowhere else in the collections, was his normal way of controlling a large time-span in unified works.

The final aspect of criticism is perhaps the most speculative, but it is appropriate to the view of Op. 116 as a multipiece. It would be ironic if the surprising discovery of a certain structural unity applied to a group of pieces where there were no signs of aesthetic balance. The idea of gestural coherence in Op. 116, though, appears to be quite fitting. This can be described by analogy with first-movement sonata form for which, despite the lack of a standard critical terminology, there is nevertheless the common notion of a gestural model. First-movement sonata form, the forms of multi-movement sonatas and of extended single movement pieces all exemplify aspects of this model. Thus, the outer sections of No. 3 represent a certain style in Brahms, relying more on manipulative skill than inventive variety: the tradition of Brahms criticism is replete with accounts of this 'constructivist' characteristic. Yet even for a tonal composer with the opposite tendency – be it melodic breadth or simply a more homophonic style – such constructivism is the normal and successful practice in developmental sections of extended forms. No. 7 also fits the sonata analogy. The function of a coda in extended forms is to resolve tonal processes, to collect and concentrate melodic and rhythmic figures from the work and – in Schoenberg's terminology – 'liquidate' them by reducing their characteristic features, and perhaps to provide a dynamic, and usually also a registral resolution. The last piece of Op. 116, somewhat fragmentary in its own right, surely fulfills these functions. Appropriately too No. 4 has a loose, rhapsodic construction – a type of developing variation as it was called earlier – in a phase of the structure that is the least likely to suffer from formal relaxation. No. 5, part of a 'slow' section of three pieces, can be interpreted as a succinct, trio-like prolongation between Nos. 4 and 6. And we may want to see No. 2 as a link between the weighty, sonata-form opening and the heavy, scherzo character of No. 3, which may well carry such a connotation even if, like the scherzo of the Fourth Symphony, it has a duple rather than triple metre.

This account, then, has both assumed and demonstrated that Op. 116 is as much a multi-piece (rather than a collection) as one could hope to find in the nineteenth century. This ought to affect our view about the kind of music Brahms was writing towards the end of his life, even if only to a small extent. The received critical view has it that Brahms was increasingly occupied with writing, or at least bringing to publication, small pieces.[12] While that is certainly the case, it does not necessarily follow that their assembly was haphazard, that Brahms gave no thought to the content of one or another opus, beyond the question of what makes a nice collection that will sell well. The nature of the unity of these collections need not be the same in each case, and it may be this proviso beyond any other that has been forgotten. For example, it is clear that whether

---

12 For a recent example of the unsupported critical assumption that Brahms was working with individual short pieces (by implication: wilfully collected) in the final publications excepting the clarinet works, see Siegfried Kross 'Brahms – der unromantische Romantiker' in *Brahms-Studien* I ed. Constantin Floros (Hamburg 1974) 42.

we insist on calling Op. 118 a multi-piece or not, it does have
paired items. The pairing between Nos. 4 and 5 is perhaps as
much a matter of key as of direct connection. But the pairing of
Nos. 1 and 2 operates on various levels. The tonal ambiguity of
Op. 118 No. 1 ensures that the closing A major will have strong
expressive significance.[13] This assumes a direct connective
significance in relation to No. 2, which begins with the melodic
C sharp which was the last note of No. 1, and moves to the first
downbeat D which prolongs the underlying melodic resolution
of No. 1 on E (bars 39ff. of No. 1). One sure statement to be
made about such a pairing is that it is remarkably like the pairings to be found in Brahms's variations. Yet to the extent that
these brief points about Op. 118 are relevant to its status as
collection or multi-piece, they do not throw up criteria which
can be applied to Op. 116. Similarly, both Opp. 116 and 118
make long musical shapes on the basis of contrast, yet this
does not apply to Op. 117 where major aspects of characterization, for instance the slow tempi, are sustained throughout.
There is indeed good reason to suppose that the heterogeneity
to be found in this repertoire is a sign that Brahms was experimenting. If we have just one good idea of what constitutes a
unified work, it will probably conflict with the evidence to be
found in Opp. 116–19: such an idea, as was described earlier,
simply diverts our attention from the evidence. If we have an
idea, however, simply that the fact of the division of these
twenty pieces into four groups should be an object of critical
scrutiny, then we may come to a conclusion about the forms
of connection which were of interest to Brahms beyond those
of the sonata and variation tradition. The historical significance of this goes beyond the nineteenth century. There is an
analogy to be made with the early music of the Second Viennese School; and it was just here that Brahms's compositional
techniques in general became a stimulus for development. On
the one hand, the tendency of Schoenberg and his pupils to
respond to a crisis in musical language by writing increasingly
short pieces (as well as by resorting more often to the use of a
programme or text) is incontestable: not only historians but
also the composers themselves have subscribed to that view.
On the other hand, Schoenberg, Berg and Webern certainly
had an idea of what a multi-piece could be. In many cases it is
plainly wrong to think that their collections of short pieces con-

13 A detailed study of tonality in Op. 118 No. 1 may be found in Edward T. Cone
    'Three ways of reading a detective story – or a Brahms Intermezzo' *The Georgia
    Review* 31/3 (Fall 1977) 554–74.

sist of – in the nineteenth-century sense – unconnected but generically similar items. For example, Schoenberg's Op. 19 and Berg's Op. 5 include an instruction to the player about timing the pauses between one piece and another – superficial evidence of a certain unity which in some cases has been and in many has yet to be examined thoroughly. If we acknowledge that such works, especially major works in the current repertoire like the Schoenberg Op. 16 Orchestral Pieces, are not collections but multi-pieces, there may be yet more to learn about Brahms's influence in the twentieth century.

ARNOLD WHITTALL

The *Vier ernste Gesänge* Op. 121: enrichment and uniformity

I

The seriousness of these songs stems from their sacred texts. But Brahms's late tetralogy is far from uniformly earnest and gloomy. After exploring the darkness, it progresses from darkness to light, from death to redemption, extinction to enlightenment. Its subject is not merely the scarcely cheering proposition that inescapable death is welcome to one who is old, weak, and has nothing to hope for, but that (for the believer) it is the gateway to a fullness of knowledge which will confirm that love is the most powerful of feelings and experiences. This textual contrast, most strongly evident between the first and last songs, calls for an equally strong contrast between concentrated minor-key music and expansive major-key music, and demands tonalities of palpably different colour as well as material of different contour: as Edward Laufer has put it with reference to Brahms's earlier song, 'Wie Melodien zieht es', 'the poetic idea, too, is composed. The words are not merely set: the poem, its structure, and the thought behind the discourse will become organically part of the composition.'[1]

The whole work must therefore progress: but the relationship of beginning and ending is no closer than it might be in an opera, or any series of miniatures grouped within a single scheme of some kind. Coherent transformation is more of the essence than a single, diversified unity. The songs are placed in an order which gives progressively greater emphasis to the triumph of light over dark – major over minor – and each song is linked to its predecessor in the very direct sense that there are notes in common between the first sounds of Nos. 2, 3 and 4 and the final chords of their predecessors. It is also not difficult to detect various motivic correspondences between the

1 Edward Laufer 'A Schenkerian approach' (Symposium IV: Brahms, Song Op. 105 No. 1) in *Readings in Schenker Analysis and other Approaches* ed. Maury Yeston (New Haven and London 1977) 255.

separate songs, but before any serious consideration can be given to the degree or nature of overall unity in the collection as a whole it is necessary to take account of the different ways in which each of the songs projects its tonic triad. In Song 1 that triad is minor, in Song 4 major, while Songs 2 and 3 demonstrate the process of transforming minor into major, so that the explicitness of the tonic note is balanced to some extent by doubt about the mode of the scale which stems from that tonic.

As 'the last great master of German tonal art'[2] Brahms did not need recourse to the lurid devices of those 'alternatives to monotonality' which so many nineteenth-century composers had employed in their desire for ever greater and more text-dependent expressiveness.[3] The *Ursatz* survives even in Songs 2 and 3, where monotonality is reinforced rather than undermined by the absence of monomodality, and its survival confirms Brahms's employment of the classic type of chromaticism described by Schenker in his *Harmonielehre*: 'Chromatic change is an element which does not destroy the diatonic system but which rather emphasizes and confirms it . . . The contrasts which chromatic change – apparently a purpose in itself – can conjure up illuminate the diatonic relationships all the more clearly.' And although this apparent licence to employ elaborate chromaticism of all kinds is qualified in a sobering footnote, Schenker still asserts that 'I may venture the principle then, that for the sake of the diatonic system itself we can never write too chromatically.'[4]

Later, in *Der freie Satz*, Schenker defined the structurally significant uses of chromaticism more in terms of limitations than of possibilities. Thus, in the Middleground, Mixture at the third 'is less form-indicating, less form-generating than division or interruption' (*Free Composition* 41), while in the Foreground it has 'even less potential for creating form than at the first level. It usually enters the composing-out process only to embellish and extend' (70). And although 'Chromatic Tones' are included under the heading of 'Specific Foreground Events', Schenker argues that 'in free composition direct chromatic successions are generally avoided (thus affording the possibility of more abundant prolongations)'(91).

2 Heinrich Schenker *Free Composition* tr. and ed. Ernst Oster (New York and London 1979) (hereafter *Free Composition*) 94.
3 See H. Krebs 'Alternatives to monotonality in early nineteenth-century music' *Journal of Music Theory* 25/1 (Spring 1981) 1–16.
4 Heinrich Schenker *Harmony* ed. and annotated Oswald Jonas, tr. Elisabeth Mann Borgese (Cambridge, Mass. and London 1954) (hereafter *Harmony*) 288–9.

The 'only' which precedes 'to embellish and extend' is a
revealing Schenkerian emphasis, consistent with his earlier
formulation that 'the musician must never sacrifice and destroy the primary element of his art, which is the diatonic
system, for the sake of a merely secondary element, that is
chromatic change' (*Harmony* 290). And there is some common
ground here with the Schoenbergian concept of extended
tonality, whereby 'remote transformations and successions of
harmonies were understood as remaining within the tonality.
Such progressions . . . function chiefly as enrichments of the
harmony and . . . their functional effect is, in many cases, only
passing, and temporary.'[5] In Brahms, the enrichment, or em-
bellishment, is indeed a secondary, temporary feature; and it
is expressed through what Schenker, without further explanation, describes as 'his own special mode of diminution' (*Free
Composition* 106). Carl Dahlhaus, from a more Schoenbergian
perspective, writes of Brahms as employing an '"expanded",
centripetal tonality. . . integrating remote degrees and regions
in one secure tonic'.[6] Schenker speaks of Brahms's 'masterful
capacity for synthesis' (*Free Composition* 106), while Dahlhaus
contends that 'the tonal centrality created by the enrichment
of the fundamental bass and regional connections in the music
of Brahms, the complementarity of differentiation and correspondence, express an ideal of form that strives for complete
and absolute integration – not the integration that comes as a
matter of course from following a plan prepared in advance,
but integration that must be won, often by force, from recalcitrant material' (Dahlhaus 69).

Brahms's purposeful pursuit of unity is therefore acknowledged by both Schenkerians and Schoenbergians; but their
views of the position of harmony in the methodological hierar-
chy is radically different. For Dahlhaus, 'the enrichment of the
fundamental bass is the correlative, both technically and
aesthetically, of developing variation' (63), an assertion developed from the Schoenbergian view that 'with Brahms the elaboration of a thematic idea is the primary formal principle' (50).
Such a strongly anti-Schenkerian position serves as a reminder
that the best-known technical discussion of the *Vier ernste
Gesänge* is Schoenberg's exposition in 'Brahms the Progres-

5 Arnold Schoenberg *Structural Functions of Harmony* (rev. edn.) ed. Leonard Stein
   (London 1969) 76–7.
6 Carl Dahlhaus *Between Romanticism and Modernism* tr. Mary Whittall (Berkeley
   and London 1980) 68–9.

sive' of the 'eminent motival logic' of the opening of No. 3.[7] In neither 'Brahms the Progressive' nor *Structural Functions of Harmony* does Schoenberg refer to these songs for examples of extended tonality, for the kind of 'deviation into remote regions' which he discovered in the C minor String Quartet, the G major Quintet, or an earlier song, 'Der Tod, das ist die kühle Nacht'. At least one such deviation – from D minor to C sharp minor – could certainly be instanced, in No. 1 of the *Vier ernste Gesänge*. But the tonality-extending devices which the music employs show that ample richness and subtlety could be obtained without the kind of spectacular excursions which Schoenberg saw as the result of extra-musical influences from drama and poetry.[8] And while these lower-level excursions or deviations are in no case destructive of the overriding discipline of the Fundamental Line and Bass Arpeggiation – they are diminutions, not disruptions – they do confirm that the need to win integration 'from recalcitrant material' could set up very fruitful tensions between the varied development of motives and the projection of the Fundamental Line. And it may ultimately appear that an 'eminent motival logic' has the power – perhaps even the function – to put linear continuity positively at risk.

II

For Schoenberg, the third song of Op. 121 was 'the most touching of the whole cycle – in spite of its perfection, if not *because* of it';[9] and the following discussion of the cycle, taking its cue from Schoenberg, and pursuing a technical rather than a chronological course, will begin with No. 3, and proceed in the sequence 2, 4, 1. The 'touching' quality of the music of No. 3 owes much to the fact that it uses one of tonality's most fundamental expressive devices, the transformation of minor into major. The transformation is not the kind of modification described by Schenker as Mixture, with the 3̂ of the Fundamental Line at Middleground level changed and corrected before completion as, for example, in Chopin's Mazurka Op. 17 No. 3.[10]

7 Arnold Schoenberg *Style and Idea. Selected Writings* ed. Leonard Stein, with translations by Leo Black (London [2]1975) 440.
8 Schoenberg *Structural Functions of Harmony* 76.
9 Schoenberg *Style and Idea* 439.
10 Schenker *Free Composition* Fig. 30a. It might be mentioned here that Schenker's reference in Paragraph 102 of *Free Composition* to Brahms's song 'Auf dem Kirchhofe' (Op. 105 No. 4) – which likewise moves from tonic minor to tonic major – is obscure in the context of Mixture as illustrated in Figs 28–30.

Instead, a form which moves from music in the tonic minor to a conclusion in the tonic major is unified by a descent from $\hat{5}$ in the Fundamental Line, with the $\hat{3}$ occurring during the final stages of the tonic major music. During the prolongation of $\hat{5}$, therefore, there is a sense in which the modality of the composition may be held to 'remain in doubt', and Brahms's often celebrated capacity for ambiguity[11] may seem to extend to using a descent from $\hat{5}$ (rather than $\hat{3}$) to delay the statement of the true tonic and tonality.

Both the principal parts of the third song are tripartite, with the third section repeating the first in the first part, and varying it in the second. The first, tonic minor part is based on three tonic–dominant progressions (bars 1–5, 6–12, 13–17), while the tonic major part has only one tonic–dominant progression, spanning its first two sections (bars 18–24 and 24–9). There is insufficient space here to consider and illustrate every aspect of enrichment achieved through voice-leading, but it should be noted at once that there is no fundamental shift from minor to major within the tonic triad, immediate and uninterrupted, as a foreground feature in this third song, comparable to that which occurs at bar 46 of Song 4. In No. 3 the first tonic major third (bar 18) is separated from the previous tonic minor third (bar 16) by a bar of dominant harmony; and this minor third is presented as a dissonance resolving ornamentally onto F sharp (bar 17). Such a progression is textually appropriate here, changing 'bitter' into 'sweet' with the minimum of shock. But there is an example in the first section of a shift from minor to major between two different chords which is more startling in its effect. This is heard in bar 2 (repeated in bar 14), as what has begun as a diatonic progression by descending thirds (I–VI–IV) rejects the possibility of a diatonic and therefore diminished supertonic triad on the second minim beat of bar 2. The progression in this bar is therefore from A minor to F sharp major, and while the piano makes the double chromatic shift required by semitones, the voice follows a more dramatic course. Instead of smoothing the ascent of the vocal line to the high E of bar 3 through, say, an F sharp on the third beat of bar 2, Brahms uses the C sharp just stated by the piano, an augmented octave above the singer's previous note. Instead of the vocal line completing an octave descent from the initial $\hat{5}$, the original register of that $\hat{5}$ is reas-

11 For recent studies, see: David Epstein *Beyond Orpheus* (Cambridge, Mass. and London 1979) 161–78; and Jonathan Dunsby *Structural Ambiguity in Brahms* (Ann Arbor and London 1981).

serted, and the lower B is not reached until the end of the second section of the song's first part, at bar 12.

Ex. 1   Song 3, bars 1-3

Example 1 interprets the song's opening as a process of elaborating the fundamental fifth, first by neighbour-note motion in the upper line, then by chromatic alteration and ornamental prolongation of that neighbour note. Since the upper line blends elements from both voice and piano, it reinforces the sense of Brahms using the special textural qualities of his chosen medium to balance the immediate, registrally restless motion of his principal motive with the obligatory register of his controlling harmonic concerns. But the enriching function of the C natural/C sharp transformation is itself a significant recurrent feature, even when registral displacement is not empolyed. The song's initial tonic–dominant progression, spanning the first section of the first part (bars 1-5) includes a second, more orthodox example of the same transformation in bars 4 and 5. Here it is part of the complex of ascending and descending steps of a kind familiar from much minor key music: that is, the sixth degree is major or minor depending on whether or not it descends to the dominant or ascends to the leading note. As Example 2 shows, this basic elaboration of the I–V progression (Ex. 2a) can be compared with that which Brahms employs in the second section of this first part (Ex. 2b).

Ex. 2   (a) Song 3, bars 1-5 (b) Song 3, bars 6-12

In bar 10 the chromatic C sharp appears for the first time in the bass, as part of the process of establishing the secondary dominant F sharp, and Brahms's sudden use of the low register for those C sharps seems designed to highlight their contradiction of the passing C natural in the inner parts on the previous quaver.

In the second, tonic major part of the song the most striking dissonance (bar 26) again involves a C sharp, though against a D rather than a C natural. This is a remarkable instance of motivic and harmonic 'logic' combining to produce a distinctly undisciplined effect: bar 26 is a variation by displacement and elaboration of bar 25. But it is also the first stage in the progress to a moment of particular tension, where, in bars 28 and 29, Brahms suggests that a return to E minor would be possible. Indeed, the enrichment of the subdominant chord from bar 25 involves a transformation from A major to A minor to prepare the E minor triad of bar 28. Yet this E minor is the last stage of the enrichment of IV on the way to V, and is structurally subordinate to them (Example 3).

Ex. 3   Song 3, bars 25–30

In the first section of this second part, C natural has been present as a passing note both descending (bar 23) and ascending (bar 24 – respelt as B sharp), in each case linking two diatonic tones. The relative minor tendency of that second instance is more fully worked out in the final section of Part Two. But the last hint of the song's salient chromatic device involves not C natural and C sharp but A sharp and A natural. In bars 36 and 37 the A sharp of the accompaniment is corrected in its proper register by the voice, although the A natural on the first beat of bar 37 (doubled an octave higher by the piano) is itself a dissonance resolving into the closing descent to the tonic.

As so often in Brahms, expressiveness here is a function of restriction, and for all its harmonic richness, this third song has little time for subsidiary tonicizations. Only G major (III) is touched on briefly by means of an independent perfect cadence during the second section of Part One (bars 7–8), but the diatonic dominant, whether major or minor, never achieves genuine independence of the tonic, even in bars 10–12. Both subdominant (bars 24 –7) and relative minor (bar 24, also bars 30 and 34–5) are touched on, but in ways which enrich the tonic, diatonic degrees. Nor are there any elements – the use of an outlined diminished seventh, for example – which place the identity of the tonic itself in doubt. This third song is as finely balanced in form as it is in process; and, far from being unnaturally constrained by considerations of structural harmony, motivic working seems to thrive under the clear registral guidelines of the Fundamental Line.

The second song is comparable to the third in its transformation of tonic minor into tonic major, its Fundamental Line descending from 5̂ within a concluding section which reveals the essential modality of the piece, and in its use of a motive arpeggiating the tonic triad. But in No. 2 the transformation itself – achieved fairly late, in bar 61 – is anticipated (bars 31–5) before the recapitulatory reference to the song's opening phrase (from bar 36). In No. 3 tonicization of III occurs briefly within the I–V progression of the first part's second section, and more than half of that song is in the tonic major. In No. 2, only 15 out of 75 bars employ the tonic major (or 20, if the five-bar anticipation is included); and the tonicization of VI, not III, begins in bar 15 after a full-close on I, and is transformed back towards I only after nine bars. Although the first parts of both songs move overall from I to V, their methods and materials are thus very different.

The second song is smoother, more flowing in style, and its first, 14-bar section is almost entirely diatonic, marking a preliminary descent from 5̂ to 1̂ in the Fundamental Line with none of the drama of the third song's second and third bars. In two places (bars 7 and 12) bass motion from the fourth to fifth degrees is enriched by insertion of the chromatic passing note C sharp, with corresponding change from E flat to E natural in the upper voice (Example 4a), an early indication that subdominant harmony has a more prominent role here than in No. 3. This chromatic, contrapuntal feature, embellishing the I–IV–V cadential progression, is given greater prominence in the developmental second section of the song's first part (bars 15–35), which combines cunningly decorated extensions of the descending third motive (now in the upper line) with three principal harmonic events. First, from bar 15 to bar 23, a toni-

Ex. 4

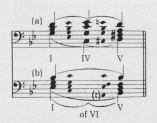

cized VI is projected through two variants of the I–IV–V model progression (Example 4b). With the second statement (bars 19–22) ornamental chromaticism is increased to the extent of introducing an accented F sharp in the upper piano line which is in false relation to the lower octave F natural immediately preceding it in both voice and piano (bars 21–2). The next eight bars (23–30) increase tension still further – 'with none to bear them comfort', as the text has it. The immediate goal is the V of I in bar 28, but the motivic parallel tenths, descending by thirds, now prepare an A in the bass to function *not* as an appoggiatura to the V of E flat (as in bars 17 and 21) but as a potential V of V with its own extending, chromatic neighbour-note motion (bars 24–6). The suddenness of the tonal shift here is demonstrated by the C natural/C sharp false relation (bars 23–4) at the moment when E flat also changes to E natural. And the reversal of this double transformation three bars later (bars 26–7) provides the song with its most powerful effect as both voice and piano employ sudden changes of register; the potential but unrealized V of V therefore moves to V of I (bar 28). The music from bars 1 to 28 can be summarized as a prolongation of the fundamental 5̂ over I in which a diatonic bass of descending thirds is coupled with a line a tenth above; and the diatonic motion of E flat down to C in that line is interrupted at bar 24 by a C sharp which is not prepared in the correct octave (Example 5). This second section of the song's first part ends with a further variant of its initial unit (bars 15–18) now transposed onto G and with its concluding dominant chord extended into a fifth bar (31–5).

Ex. 5   Song 2, bars 1–28

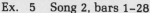

With the restoration of G minor at bar 36 the second part of the song begins, and this also divides into two sections, at bar 60. In the first section the basic I–IV–V progression is immediately enriched by the insertion of the chromatic F minor chord (bar 41). The alternation of A flat and A natural which this produces seems to strengthen the A natural, however. In the second phrase (bars 44–51), which varies the first, A returns initially as a root in bar 46, recalling its use as a potential V of V in the more disguised motivic manipulations of bars 24–6. There the A was prolonged by chromatic neighbour-note motion to G sharp. Here (bars 48–51) the thirds in the bass provide an opportunity for the combination of prolonging and motivic processes. Although the entire passage from bar 35 to bar 60 could be interpreted as the enrichment of a cycle-of-fifths progression from G minor through D major, A major and E minor to B major, the process is divided between the clear triadic character of the music from bar 36 to bar 52, and the sparser, less explicit texture thereafter, which reinforces the higher-level presence of a third-progression from G through A to B, providing the essential motivation for the tonic major music (Example 6). The change in bar 52 hinges on the trans-

Ex. 6   Song 2, bars 36–65

bars 36 39 43 51   52   54   57 60   61 65

formation of C sharp to C natural, and although the music at once becomes diatonic to the key of E minor, with A sharp the only chromatic note, that tonality is not securely tonicized. Instead, the root position of VI is absorbed into the final G major music of the second part's second section (from bar 61). So secure and inevitable is the pure tonic diatonicism of the music from bar 61 to bar 66 that the accented chromatic passing notes of the final cadence seem unnecessary, even blatant – a touch of *Tristan* both unexpected and inept, even though it reinforces the enrichment techniques which predominate in the song as a whole. The appropriateness of the major-key resolution may also be questioned in view of the nature of the text. But the purely musical inevitablity of the

movement away from the G minor after bar 47 makes any
thought of its reassertion at the end of the song entirely
academic.

Of the four songs it is No. 2 which has the least evidence of
surface contrast, with no changes of tempo or time signature.
No. 4 has an internal contrast which may seem all the more extreme for the plainness of the transition which prepares it
(bars 46–7), and the brevity of the later interpolated reminiscence of the initial material (bars 76–82). The use of the
chromatic shift of the third within the tonic triad is so obvious
in bar 46 that one might suspect Brahms of scepticism about
the value of the Art of Transition. He prefers to stress contrast
through the most artless demonstration of evolutionary continuity, the direct chromatic step in an inner part. And the de-
cisiveness of the full-close which concludes the song's first
part (bars 45–6) also suggests that the points of technical
interest in this section could have less to do with the extension
of diatonic harmony than with developing variation.

The second section of the first part (bars 13–29) is a notably
purposeful expansion of the first, made necessary by the additional clause of text – the double 'und hätte'. The last six bars
of the first two sections are all but identical, and are particularly well varied, and expanded, in the third section (bars
29–47). But there are also intriguing differences between the
opening stages of the first two sections. Those impatient with
Brahms's tendency to harmonic plainness – his unhealthy
devotion to the diatonic scale-steps – may well cite the ponder-
ous progression from IV to I at the start of this song in
evidence. Surely the only reason for starting on A flat is to
provide a link with the G sharps in the chord which ends No.
3? For although A flat returns in bar 5 and is briefly tonicized
in bars 7 and 8, there is unlikely to be much doubt about the
true identity of the tonic. And chromatic activity is concentrated on a 'flat side' enrichment of V (bars 10–12) which is
of far greater relevance to the main tonal shift of the song.

In fact, the beginning on IV has a quite specific dramatic
function, which can be gauged when the relatively small and
less stressed amount of tonic harmony in the first section is
noted. This section is not so much a model to be twice varied as
a preliminary sketch which is then presented in fully worked-
out form and subsequently developed. Because of the greater
number of words in the first clause of the second section,
Brahms shortens the lead-in so that bar 13 becomes, as it
were, a transposed conflation of bars 1 and 2 (Example 7).

Ex. 7   (a) Song 4, bars 1–2 (b) Transposition down a fourth (c) Song 4,
          bar 13

Since the first two sections of the song's first part both
prolong the fundamental 5̂ over I with descending octave
motions in the upper line and progression from V to I in the
lower, the second might be expected to intensify in its chromatic detail the diminutions of the first. The most important
chromatic shift in the first section is that from D natural to D
flat in bar 7, promoting the brief tonicization of IV. In the
second section the music equivalent to bar 6 is separated from
that equivalent to bar 7 by a five-bar interpolation (bars
19–23) which makes more dramatic and determined use of the
same D natural/D flat shift in a phrase which tonicizes the
minor dominant, and, as another new feature, brings out the D
flat in the voice's upper register (bar 19), altering bar 18's D
natural. With the D flat so well established, the first quaver
of bar 24 is also a D flat, not a D natural (cf. bar 7), and the
correction to D natural in bar 26 creates a still stronger sense
of a tonic held back. In fact, it will be held back until the final
cadence of the third section (bars 44–6).

The first two sections of the first part have both been constructed on the firm basis of progressions stressing tonic, subdominant and dominant scale-steps, with chromatic activity al-

most entirely confined to the upper parts. The third and final
section, half as long again as the first and one bar longer than
the second, startles at once by the tonicization of a supertonic
whose dominant is approached by way of a surprising chromatic progression (Example 8). As the manuscript of this song

Ex. 8   Song 4, bars 29–37

reveals, bars 30 and 31 were originally one tone higher, and a
dramatic anticipation at this point of the initial tonality of the
song's second part was not envisaged. After this phrase the
voice makes a smooth, diatonic transition from F minor to A
flat major (bars 37–40), but the accompaniment intensifies the
expressive difference between this presentation of the process
and its predecessors by a progression in which the D natural/
D flat transformation is preserved (bars 38–9).

Like Part One, Part Two of the song has three principal
sections: an initial antecedent–consequent structure (bars
48–61), prolonging B major without subsidiary tonicization, although some prominence is given to the chromatic passing note
linking the fourth and fifth degrees in the bass; a first variant
(bars 62–72) which progresses from V back to I (the fourth to
seventh bars virtually identical with the sixth to ninth bars of
the first section); and a second variant (bars 83 to the end),
which follows the interpolation of a transition and reference
to the 'con moto' material (bars 76 to 82). Variation of this lyric
material is less significant than with the 'con moto' material,
however. The interruption effecting the return to E flat is the
crucial structural event, and Brahms integrates this by en-
suring that the interpolation is essentially a prolongation of
the fundamental $\hat{5}$ over V, with resolution to $\hat{5}$ over I occurring
near the beginning of the Sostenuto, in bar 84. The emphasis
on V here contrasts strikingly with its exclusion from the
transition process in bars 46–7, a process which, if nothing
else, highlights the difference between the preparation of the
Adagio's B major and the earlier assertion of C flat major (bar
30). Put another way, the music from bar 46 to bar 83 does *not*

use the symmetrical progression I–V– ♭VI–V–I as scaffolding.
(If V has indeed been excluded after bar 46 it is clearly to
avoid tautology: it has been prominent between bar 41 and bar
45.) As for the chromatic inflections of the Sostenuto – mainly
the persistent A flat/A natural/B flat motion in the bass – these
are no more creative of ambiguity than those similar motions
in the Adagio. One feature is worth noting, however: the final,
contrary-motion arpeggiations in the accompaniment (bars
95–7), after the close of the Fundamental Structure, resemble
a diatonic version of the transitional (and modulatory) arpeggiations of bars 46–7 (Example 9).

Ex. 9   (a) Song 4, bars 46–7 (b) Song 4, bars 95–7

In the early stages of this essay a contrast was stressed
between the bi-modal character of the second and third songs
and the extended monomodality of Nos. 1 and 4. In No. 4 the
main contrast of tonic is reinforced by contrast of tempo and
time signature, which dominates the remainder of the song,
absorbing the re-establishment of the main tonic. In No. 1,
Andante and Allegro alternate: and not only is the first Allegro
also principally in the tonic, but its shortened, varied return at
the end of the song emphasizes those elements of the first
Allegro which confirmed that original tonic. Although the tonicization of C sharp minor as III of V within the main Allegro is
striking and powerful, the song owes its cumulative effect
more to the subtlety with which tonic and dominant chords are
enriched, in support of a Fundamental Line descending from 5̂
to close in bar 82.

The first part of the first song (bars 1–26) is concerned
essentially with prolonging 5̂ over extensions of tonic,
dominant and tonic, marking the tripartite sectional form
(bars 1–10, 11–17, 18–26). The spare chromaticism of the first
phrase strengthens focus on the powerful span of the vocal
line, its ascent from D through A to F recalled in the Allegro
triplet material; but one of the ways in which the second
section reveals its concern with A as V of I rather than as a
new, if temporary, tonic, is by the false relations of C sharp
and C natural, the former never appearing in the upper line.

The first section of the Allegro (bars 26–45) progresses from
I to V, as, on the largest scale, does the entire Allegro, up to
bar 75. But the tonic triad is already obscured in the first bar
by the chromatics which assert a cycle of diminished sevenths
and prepare possible tonicizations of IV and V, neither of
which is realized, although, as sketched in Example 10, V is
approached from two stages up the cycle of fifths (B and E).
Such devices enhance the purely triadic return of I at bar 46,
and make the rapid departure from V to its own III (C sharp
minor) the more exciting. The music from bar 46 to bar 76
offers an elaborate, symmetrical harmonic progression, some
aspects of which are summarized in Example 11. This progression achieves its greatest dramatic effect through the fact that
the central III is projected through its own I–V–I, involving a
wide registral span and the pregnant pause in bar 59.

Ex. 10   Song 1, bars 26–45

Ex. 11   Song 1, bars 50–76

The textual appropriateness of this shift to a relatively remote region – the contrast of 'aufwärts' and 'unterwärts' – like the general use of ascending and descending contours in all the songs, is too obvious to linger over. More striking is the fact that the motion to a chord of G sharp minor at bar 55 realizes the diatonic potential of a tone which occurs as a strongly chromatic feature earlier in the song (bars 6, 10, 21, 24). It is therefore also significant that the point at which G sharp begins to strengthen its structural relevance in the first part (bar 36) should be the point in the recapitulatory final part where the harmony changes to turn back decisively towards D minor (bar 90, beats 7–9). The other notable event in this final part is the overlaying of the conclusive V–I in the bass (bar 94) with the chromatic upper-line descent from D to A, a fuller version of that given in the bass between bar 89 and bar 91. In each of the second Andante and Allegro sections (from bar 76) the stronger hints of possible tonicization of IV (rather than V) suggest the conclusiveness of the all-but-complete tonal structure. And for the only time in the work there is no final, assuaging major resolution. D major appears in Song 1 only as the potential dominant of a IV which never materializes.

III

In the early stages of this essay I quoted Carl Dahlhaus's remarks to the effect that Brahms was concerned with an 'integration that must be won, often by force, from recalcitrant material'. Dahlhaus's bellicose imagery is unexpected, but salutary. After all, there is no recalcitrance more profound than an apparent reluctance to reveal whether a work is in the major or minor mode, and no tonal scheme more subtle than one which charts the gradual transformation of tonality from minor to major. It is in this respect that the final, published continuity of the *Vier ernste Gesänge* is more than a matter of the relevance of motives to texts. The explicit modal integrity of the first song provides a firm background for the regional excursion of the main Allegro section, but it proves an unsatisfactory model (too unrelievedly pessimistic?) for what follows. The tonicization of VI in Song 2 is the first evidence of the increasing importance attached to major harmony, and the first use in the work of the key in which it will end. And what in Song 2 seems like the precarious emergence of tonic major from tonic minor becomes, in Song 3, an equilibrium in which minor is decisively and irrevocably transformed into major. Fortunately it is not the case that Song 4 provides a mere mirror image of Song 1, having as little to do with minor as Song 1 does with major. But its exploitation of supertonic and dominant minor is probably less striking than its use of a non-diatonic region (flat submediant) for its main subsidiary tonicization. The 'dark glass' of modal ambiguity is now a thing of the past, and the turn to tonic minor in bar 46 is so simply stated as to make its transitional function entirely transparent.

It may indeed be that what Schenker saw as Brahms's 'special mode of diminution' stems most profoundly from the strength and subtlety of his use of chromaticism and dissonance, not merely to enrich diatonicism, but to question and challenge it in ways which ultimately reinforced those essentials of musical communication and organization which Brahms valued most. The sheer power of his impulse to exploit developing variation meant that the diatonic foundation could never be taken for granted. It must be constantly recreated; and in the specific foreground events of the Vier ernste Gesänge some of the techniques whereby a master at the height of his powers achieved this original and profound effect can be observed.

Index

18614385R00136

Made in the USA
San Bernardino, CA
21 January 2015